£4.99

4

HARDLY SURPRISING!

An apt description of the annual staff dance —
and their marriage, too, perhaps? It was time, she
decided, to do the unexpected!

By ELIZABETH ASHCROFT

CATHY tweezed out a stray eyebrow impatiently, and winced. She surveyed herself in the mirror, studying her light brown hair. She should've gone to the hairdresser's yesterday, she realised. But then, when could she have found the time, between Martin's appointment at the dentist and Paul's dinner suit to be picked up from the cleaners?

She sighed, picking up the tweezers again. She just wasn't in the mood for a dinner dance tonight. Especially not Paul's firm's dance, with the top table heavy with VIPs. She and Paul would be tacked on at the end, almost as an afterthought, she mused.

I should be glad, she thought, wishing, for the 50th time, that her eyebrows arched like Chrissie's. I should be glad Paul's got on so well, is in line for yet another promotion.

But oh, how she hated these formal office dinners, when she had to wear a permanent smile and be polite to people who really bored her.

The bathroom door slammed, and Cathy leapt to her feet and ran on to the landing, pink toes sinking into the new sheepskin rug. The hall air felt cold on her bare arms and she hugged herself in the thin cotton slip.

"Chrissie!" She thumped on the bathroom door, shouting above the hiss of the shower. When the door opened a crack, a cloud of steam eddied wetly on to the landing.

Cathy clutched at her hair anxiously. At the slightest hint of steam it became frizzy and unmanageable.

"Chris! I wanted the bathroom first! I did tell you!"

Chrissie, bare shoulders already splattered with drops of water, grimaced.

"Oh, Mum! I've got a date with Brian. You know, the one with the blond hair and little wispy moustache, from down the road.

"We're going to the new disco. Shan't be a minute, Mum. Do you mind — I'm wet already?"

Little wretch, Cathy thought crossly. "Well be quick, then," she said, as she retreated thankfully to the warmth of the bedroom, where she'd surreptitiously turned up the radiator.

Paul was on one of his periodical economy purges, but it was a cold evening.

Paul. Where *was* he? She glanced at the huge brass alarm clock at her side of the bed. It was already 6.15. He was late.

They had to leave at seven, so they could get there in time, and he would want to shower and change. She pulled back the curtains, peering outside.

It was raining, of course. It always seemed to rain when she went somewhere special. Now she'd have to wear a scarf, flatten her hair, wear sensible shoes and change when she got there.

Oh, darn it, she thought. I would like, just once, not to have to go. Not to have to wear a suitable frock like that new one, which makes me feel old.

In the department store, her inclination had been towards an exotic creation in brilliant blue and gold, but Paul, seeing her eye it, had frowned slightly.

"Cathy? It's the office, remember." So she'd gravitated to the dresses she'd always thought of as middle-aged. They had high necklines and longer sleeves; sensible dresses.

I wish, Cathy thought with sudden vehemence, *I* was going to a disco, like Chrissie. I wish I could wear something bold, outrageous. Just for once throw caution aside.

Or not go at all. I would just put my feet up, watch an old movie on TV, a wicked box of chocolates at my side, and probably drop off to sleep.

Involuntarily, she yawned. It had been a long day, would be an even longer evening. Five courses, long after-dinner speeches, followed by a sedate duty waltz with the managing director, and then the chairman. It was all so dull.

It's gone, she thought, startled. All the excitement of going out, meeting new people — it's just disappeared.

She must be growing old. Once, the mere prospect of an evening out with Paul had filled her with a tingling excitement, anticipation.

But, she thought, smoothing moisturising cream over her face, we've been married for 18 years. Going out together now is routine. Just a duty to be shared, because of office politics. What a terrible, dreary thought!

She rubbed her face harder, forgetting Chrissie's admonition to use the middle finger of her hand, and smooth gently round her eyes.

All I look fit for, she mused forlornly, is an early night; not an invigorating foxtrot with Paul's immediate boss, who would inevitably do a quickstep to it, as he did to everything.

When did I lose it, she wondered. When did I lose all the anticipation? Before we married, life was full of surprises and anticipation. Maybe, now, life is too safe, too settled.

I'd like to be Chrissie's age again. Just 17, with everything fresh and new, a different boyfriend every week and everything either an unmitigated disaster or heady triumph.

She held the new dress up in front of her, remembering Paul's nod of approval as she tried it on. It wasn't her style. She felt frumpish.

She no longer felt the Cathy Carter who had gone to art college, who'd worn the most outrageous clothes and once dyed her hair bright orange.

Does Paul feel the same, she wondered. The thought hit her with agonising clarity. Does he feel this sameness about everything, about our marriage? Do we know each other too well, perhaps?

Downstairs, the front door slammed. She realised she hadn't even heard the car turn into the drive, so shattered had she been with the realisation that something was missing from her marriage.

What happened to romance?

Don't be stupid, she told herself. That never lasts long in any marriage. It's taken over by mortgages and bills and children and measles.

The bathroom door banged again and she winced, the beginning of a headache behind her eyes.

Chrissie put her head round the door.

"All clear, Mum. I've left the bath water running and don't forget to put on a shower cap or your hair will go all frizzy."

Dear Chrissie — always so concerned about how she looked, a lively, sparkling 17-year-old who made her mother feel positively doddering.

Chrissie came bouncing into the room, housecoat floating behind her.

"Mum! You're not wearing *that?*"

Cathy nodded, seeing the dress through Chrissie's eyes. Too dark for spring, and the style was dated.

"Dad likes it," Cathy said shortly, and warm arms encircled her, hugging her.

"Mum! Give him a surprise. Wear your gorgeous white one. The floaty one that makes you look like a femme fatale."

A femme fatale. Me? Cathy stared at her daughter, flushing slightly.

She'd worn the dress to a neighbour's Christmas party last year, and hadn't enjoyed herself so much for years. She'd looked good, felt good, and it had shown.

"It's the office party, darling," she chided, and Chrissie laughed.

"Who cares? I'd never wear a dress like that at ninety, and I wouldn't have thought you would, either, Mum — even if Dad *does* like it."

"Maybe he wants livening up a bit? What do you think?"

With a cheeky grin she was gone, leaving behind a drifting fragrance of Cathy's own expensive bath oil and talc.

She looked at the red dress, remembering the soft, silky cling of the blue one.

I can't, she thought. The chairman would have a fit.

Mrs Catherine Carter, turning up in a white dress that's very low and slit up the side? Some impish devilment caught her. How she would love to wear it.

But there was Paul, Paul who appeared so staid now, the rising star in the firm. Paul would raise his eyebrows quizzically . . .

In fact just the way he was doing now, staring at her from the doorway, ripping off his tie, undoing shirt buttons.

"Cathy," he muttered. "Bathroom free? I'm late!"

"I know you are —" Her voice tailed off as he disappeared into the bathroom. When, she thought crossly, do I have *my* bath? It's getting so late.

The bedroom door was flung open then, and Martin, all legs and arms and a brown tow-headed shock of hair, grinned shyly at her.

"I'm off, Mum. Bill's dad is here. Have a good time."

Martin, her youngest, her cross, her love. He fell over things, stammered, embarrassed her and the whole family, and yet goodness and love shone out in everything he did.

"Right, love. See you tomorrow. Have a good time yourself and be careful."

He backed out, knocking into the landing table for the umpteenth time, just catching it before it fell.

"Mum! I'm going. Brian's just arrived!"

What a household, she reflected. Someone always either coming or going. It was like living on a railway station. She turned, still holding the red dress.

Chrissie stood in the doorway, golden hair brushed into a 40s topknot; a 40s dress she'd bought in a jumble sale, a vivid splash of electric blue in the bedroom of pale cool greens and yellows.

The dress had square, wide shoulders, a tight-fitting, flared skirt — Cathy vaguely remembered her mother wearing one like it — and scarlet stockings, blue boots. That was nothing at all like her mother.

"Like me?" Chrissie twirled, blew a kiss, and was gone.

Next door something clattered loudly, she heard Paul exclaim sharply and vehemently. He'd knocked the lid off the laundry basket again; he was always doing that!

And by now, she reflected dismally, there wouldn't be any hot bathwater at all. She'd have to have a lukewarm shower.

THIS was nothing like her first dance with Paul. Cathy sat hunched on the bed, suddenly hungry. She hadn't eaten since four o'clock, when she'd downed a quick cup of tea and toasted teacake. But at least the office dinners were good. Extravagant, almost gourmet meals.

No, this was not at all like that first dance. There Paul had fought his way to the buffet and grabbed a plate full of odd looking titbits on curled-up, limp toast.

They'd drunk heady punch, with shrivelled-up fruit floating across the top, bobbing wetly against her nose every time she tried to drink. It had been as sweet and smooth as nectar.

And then she'd had all the afternoon to get ready. She'd even taken a book in the bath with her, propping it on the bathrest. Imagine having time to read in the bath!

She'd poured in oil, topped it up with foam, and sat in a hazy cloud of fragrance and fright and anticipation.

It was the first time she'd been out with Paul and she'd known, somehow, that it would be important.

He'd appeared one day at her typewriter, brandishing tickets, informing her that if she bought one, he personally would make sure she got home safely.

"All the way to Wimbledon?" she'd asked, champagne bubbles of excitement popping off inside her. Paul was without doubt one of the nicest men in the office, and she'd only been working there just over a month.

"All the way to Scotland, if necessary," he'd replied with sudden, unnerving seriousness.

So, she'd bought a new dress she couldn't afford, all full twirling skirt and tight fitting bodice. She knew she looked her best when he came to collect her, to be introduced to her parents.

They had hovered suspiciously as she put on her mother's fake fur and her sister's glittery rhinestone scarf.

In the car, Paul had shyly presented her with a rose. A perfect, gorgeous, blood-red rose.

"For me?" she asked, taking it with suddenly shaking fingers.

He nodded. "I thought you might like to wear it," he muttered, pink with embarrassment. As if anything would stop her!

He's never done that again, Cathy thought suddenly. Paul padded into the bedroom barefoot, his thickening figure huddled in scarlet towelling robe. He glanced at her, surprised.

"Aren't you ready yet?" Irritation in his voice. "It's getting late, Cathy! We mustn't be late!"

"I know it's late!" she cried, brought back to the present with a stab of regret.

"*I* haven't been able to get into the bathroom! Chrissie left the bath running for *me*!" she pointed out crossly, and he looked momentarily taken aback.

"Oh, I'm sorry. I turned it off. I just had a shower. Run along then, quick, for goodness' sake."

As though she were a child, she thought with rising fury. She walked swiftly to the bathroom, surveyed the huddle of damp scattered towels, wet floor, powdery talc over everything. It was uninviting, like a school shower room after gym.

"What a mess!" Grimly, she stepped into the bath and ran the shower. She pulled still-damp, clammily cold shower curtains round her and shivered as they clung wetly.

I just don't feel like an evening out, she thought, realising too late she'd forgotten the shower cap. Her hair would be wild, frizzy.

Suddenly she didn't care. Weren't they wearing it frizzy this

9

year? Well, maybe for once she'd be in fashion.

She dressed in the bathroom, where the steam misted the mirror, and she needn't see herself properly in the red dress.

BACK in the bedroom, Paul was nearly ready. Grey trousers, dark jacket. He watched as she flew to the mirror, brushed frantically at her hair. Surprisingly, he was close behind her, hands on her shoulders.

"You do smell nice," he said.

"I do?" She wrinkled her nose at him. Chrissie had left just enough of her own talc for her to use. Their eyes met in the mirror. She thought briefly how nice he looked. Distinguished.

Surprisingly, her hair didn't look too bad.

He glanced surreptitiously at his watch.

"Oh, I know!" she exclaimed. "It's late, and I'm late! You go on down and wait for me. I'll be quicker on my own."

He hesitated and she pushed him towards the door, catching a whiff of his aftershave, seeing with a pang a new line under his eyes.

Dear Paul. He worried so — about the business, about her, about the children. Not like he used to be, with that devil-may-care grin which had turned her knees to jelly.

"Go on!" She smiled at him and heard him going down the stairs, stepping on the familiar creak.

She turned and caught sight of herself in the dressing-table mirror.

I won't! She thought rebelliously. *I won't wear it!* I won't dress like an elderly retired lady before I am one, whether Paul and his bosses like it or not!

I'm still me, Cathy Carter from the art college, who wore hand-knitted scarlet stockings before anyone else had even thought of them!

She went to the wardrobe, rifled through her dresses, pulled out the white one.

Dare I? It swung invitingly from the hanger, the colour showing up wickedly in the light from the dressing-table, and she thought of the managing director's wife with her disapproving frown, her thin tight lips.

It was rumoured that *she* ran the business, not her husband, and Cathy could quite believe it. But the managing director will like the dress, she thought with a gleeful chuckle.

She pulled it over her head before she could change her mind, wriggled it into place, stood looking at herself in the mirror, a slow delighted smile spreading across her face.

It was Cathy, the art student, looking back at her; hair ruffled from the shower, skin seemingly more tanned against the whiteness of the dress.

She whirled round triumphantly, the slit parting, showing a long slender leg. She felt so *different*, alive again!

Hastily she scrabbled in her jewel box, found a pair of gold earrings Chrissie had given her for her birthday and put them on.

She'd show them, she thought triumphantly. Already, amazingly, she was looking forward to the evening, filled with an exhilaration she hadn't known for years.

She stepped into high-heeled shoes, disregarding sense and the drizzling rain, threw a wrap round her shoulders, and went to the head of the stairs.

Paul was standing impatiently waiting, coat on, frowning at his watch.

She went downstairs slowly, wondering if he would even notice.

"I saw Chrissie on the way out with the new young man," he volunteered with a touch of amusement. "What a pair!"

He grinned, then frowned slightly. "Sometimes I envy the kids of today, they're so casual, so bright and free."

So were we, she thought with a pang — before all the responsibilities. Then she stared at him. Maybe he felt the same. Maybe he too disliked the formality of office dinners.

Paul, who used to live in jeans and T-shirt with "Choose Me For President" boldly emblazoned across his chest.

She stifled sudden laughter, and he glanced up quickly, his eyes serious.

"I was remembering the way we used to be," she offered. "All those years ago at our first dance."

He paused at the front door, looked back at her. "That," he uttered solemnly, "was the best dance I ever went to. The most nerve-racking, too! I didn't think you would come."

"You didn't?" Her capable, businesslike Paul, beset by doubts? She would never have dreamed it. He smiled at her, then his eyes travelled down, saw the white dress with the slit, the long leg provocatively exposed as she turned, and his mouth dropped.

"Cathy! You can't! You bought that other dress! The red one!"

"I know. And I felt old and unfashionable," she retorted. "Paul, I'm sorry, but I couldn't wear it. I felt so dreary!"

"You? Old? Don't be ridiculous!" His eyes met hers and there was a sudden spark in them. "You'll get me the sack, not promotion!"

But he was smiling, the old smile, and suddenly he looked years younger. She could almost see the young figure, the T-shirt, the dyed blond hair again. He didn't mind. He liked it, liked the way she looked. He didn't want a drab, sensible wife after all. What a relief!

To her utter astonishment, she felt his arms round her. Exuberantly he picked her up and swung her round in his arms. "You, Mrs Carter, look good enough to eat! Shall we stay home?"

"Can't, Mr Carter! Your job depends upon it!"

"Wait! Just a minute!" Abruptly he put her down and disappeared into the dining-room. He came back smiling broadly. "For you, Princess. For you."

He held out a rose. A dark red rose which he'd stolen from the vase on the dining table.

So he did remember! Dear Paul.

He hadn't really changed, after all, any more than she had. They'd just grown up, that was all. Suddenly, she was looking forward to the evening with all the old anticipation and delight.

He took her hand and squeezed it. Together they went out to the car, in the warm, soft rain. ■

NEIGHBOURS

A newcomer to Croft Douglas makes quite an impression and an older resident looks to him to save the day...

T must be winter because that's when a robin always calls to cheer me up with his company, when the weather is at its worst and the hills look like rows of rock cakes heavily sprinkled with caster sugar.

There's no doubt in my mind that this particular robin is another "Viking" who has just flown across the stormy North Sea to spend the winter with us, just as his ancestors did before him.

He is so friendly and knows no fear.

We meet every morning just before breakfast when he flits down to land on my hand or on top of the hens' mash tray, and I allow him some seconds to select the tastiest scraps.

Then I have time to study this bright-eyed bird at close range.

He is keeping the early morning frost at bay by blowing out his feathers to form a "thermal vest" of warm air next to his body.

I know he's a "visitor" by his distinctive dress, a smart coat of velvety brown and a large white vee which divides his red breast.

That's why I call him The Viking.

He's a much bigger and bolder bird than our garden robin and took over his territory just as soon as he arrived, driving the resident robin from the flower garden at the front of the house to a less exotic life amongst the leafless apple trees and the rows of snow-covered spring cabbages.

Strangely enough, the garden robin had submitted without even a flutter of protest.

This, I believe, is because he already owes his life to the courage of The Viking who, only the day after he arrived, had spotted the grey, menacing shadow of a sparrowhawk as it glided silently through the cover of some pine trees, hoping to strike down the garden robin.

The Viking frustrated the hawk with a fierce aerial attack so the garden robin was spared to live and sing his little skirling song again.

OUR house, with its surrounding shelter of firs and pines, is a haven for small birds in the winter, but the sparrowhawk knows this and makes regular visits.

The female of the species is, indeed, deadlier than the male, being far more formidable, about twice his size and not easily put off her stroke when she has made up her mind.

This morning the hawk had selected a tiny, plump blue tit for her breakfast but, as she was about to glide away with the shrieking victim in her claws, The Viking shot towards her like an avenging arrow and forced the hawk to release her hold on the little blue tit, which fluttered thankfully into the sheltering arms of a spruce.

THE VIKING pops up in all sorts of places. Tonight, when I am bringing a load of logs from the woods, he flits around my head and follows me all the way home.

I know he is trying to tell me that the darkness is coming down and he is still hungry. Fortunately, I always carry a crust of bread in my pocket for just such an occasion!

The Viking clasps my finger with his tiny claws before flying into the shelter of the beech hedge with his "supper piece" which, I hope, will help to fill his tummy and provide the fuel to warm him through this cold and frosty night.

What, I wonder, will he dream about — a sweetheart he has left behind in Stavanger, or one he hopes to meet here in the Scottish Highlands?

After all, there must be many a Highlander with the blood of the Vikings still in their veins! ∎

By Julie Dawn Newnham

THE NEW ARRIVAL

"Hello, little one." Even as she said the words, she was remembering another, sadder time when she'd said the same thing to another baby . . .

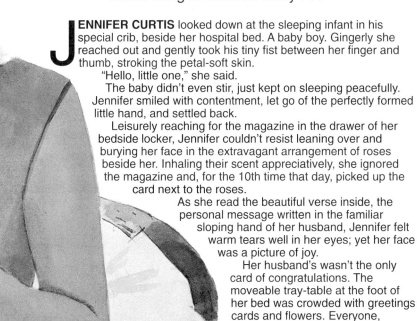

JENNIFER CURTIS looked down at the sleeping infant in his special crib, beside her hospital bed. A baby boy. Gingerly she reached out and gently took his tiny fist between her finger and thumb, stroking the petal-soft skin.

"Hello, little one," she said.

The baby didn't even stir, just kept on sleeping peacefully. Jennifer smiled with contentment, let go of the perfectly formed little hand, and settled back.

Leisurely reaching for the magazine in the drawer of her bedside locker, Jennifer couldn't resist leaning over and burying her face in the extravagant arrangement of roses beside her. Inhaling their scent appreciatively, she ignored the magazine and, for the 10th time that day, picked up the card next to the roses.

As she read the beautiful verse inside, the personal message written in the familiar sloping hand of her husband, Jennifer felt warm tears well in her eyes; yet her face was a picture of joy.

Her husband's wasn't the only card of congratulations. The moveable tray-table at the foot of her bed was crowded with greetings cards and flowers. Everyone, friends and family alike, had been delighted by the arrival of this baby boy.

For a moment, Jennifer's eyes clouded as she thought back to the other baby boy she'd given birth to years before. Paul, she'd called him. The name had always denoted strength to her — and if he was to make it in the world, he would need to be strong, she had decided.

Baby Paul's arrival hadn't been heralded with an abundance of cards and flowers. And yet she, Jennifer, had loved him every bit as much as this tiny infant lying beside her now.

Eight years ago, she'd looked down on that other baby boy. She'd gently held his hand with just as much wonder and love in her heart for the new life that she'd so haphazardly created.

But she hadn't had the dreams for little Paul that she had for this new baby boy. This baby was born into the security of a happy, loving marriage. She and her husband were free to dream dreams for his future, sure now that whether or not their dreams came true, their baby would always be safe in the world with two parents to protect him.

Jennifer hadn't dared to dream any dreams for Paul. What would become of him, she hadn't dared to think. Then, all alone and suddenly aware of the tremendous responsibility of another human life dependent solely upon her, Jennifer had lived for the minute — not willing, too afraid, to look to the future.

* * * *

"Oh, Jennifer! How could you?" her mother had wailed when her daughter had finally summoned up the courage to confide in her.

Jennifer had not replied. She stood stiffly in front of her mother, full of wretchedness, knowing the pain she had just inflicted with her confession.

"Why, you're hardly more than a child yourself," Mrs Ashcroft sighed.

Still Jennifer remained silent. Her mother spoke the truth; she was nearly 18, but as the youngest of four she'd remained immature in many ways.

"Oh, Jenny," Mrs Ashcroft whispered, the words catching in her throat.

Hearing her mother use the affectionate diminutive of her name, Jennifer looked up with red-rimmed eyes, her expression contrite.

"Come here, love," her mother said and, tears streaming down her face, she held her arms open and ready to comfort her daughter.

Gratefully, Jennifer had leaned her head against the warm, familiar shoulder and the two women had sobbed together — tears of fear, shame and despair.

For Jennifer, the relief of unburdening herself and sharing her guilty secret had been immense. She even managed a watery, courageous smile as she pulled away from her mother's embrace.

"What's going to happen now, Mum?" she ventured, uncertain she wanted to hear the reply.

Sitting down heavily at the dining-room table, her mother didn't hesitate for a second. She took Jenny's hand and patted it gently, her soft brown eyes full of compassion.

"I don't know what we'll do, Jenny. I haven't had time to think.

"I can't pretend I'm pleased about this, no mother wants this to happen to her daughter. But I can promise you that, whatever we decide, I'll always love you and be there for you."

OF course her father and the rest of the family had to be told. That hadn't been as easy as the confrontation with her mother.

Mr Ashcroft had been surprisingly protective of Jennifer, reserving all his anger for the baby's father. No-one had even asked Jennifer who the father was. There had been no doubt in anyone's mind.

Jennifer and Tom had been going steady for a year, and although Mr Ashcroft had liked the boy until then, he'd had to be restrained from leaving the house and going to "teach Tom a lesson he wouldn't forget."

"Violence won't solve anything, dear," Mrs Ashcroft told her husband calmly, her solid form blocking the doorway. "Now sit down and we'll discuss this quietly."

Then, noting Jennifer's face, taut and pale with strain, she inclined her head towards her daughter and murmured, "For Jenny's sake."

"All right. But when I think what that boy did to our Jenny, it makes my blood boil!"

Jenny had stood up then.

"Daddy, believe me, I'm truly sorry that this has happened. I never wanted to cause you this trouble."

She paused, not wanting to hurt her parents any more than she had already, but she couldn't let Tom shoulder all the blame.

"But . . . it takes two, you know," she blurted out. "I love Tom and I'm as much at fault as he is!"

"Jenny, don't talk like that!"

"I'm sorry, but it's true."

"In that case, the best thing would be for you and Tom to get married as soon as possible," her father suggested impatiently.

Sadly Jenny shook her head. "No. I won't marry anyone just because I'm pregnant." And with that she ran from the room.

When Tom found out, his solution was the same as Mr Ashcroft's had been.

"Don't worry, Jen, we'll get married," he offered straight-away, his gaze steady.

But Jennifer had been adamant. She wouldn't get married because she was pregnant.

"But we'd have got married sooner or later. You know I love you, Jen," Tom had persuaded. "Getting married now just means it'll be sooner instead of later."

"And how long d'you think it'll last?" she asked sharply. She felt she had to argue with Tom, yet she desperately wanted to accept his proposal and take the easy way out. "We're too young!"

Tom was three years older than she was, but still too young to take on the responsibility of a wife and baby, she was sure of that.

"You'd have to leave university and get a job. You'd soon regret it.

"And besides, you know how everyone would talk when six months after we got married I produced our baby. I won't have people saying that I married you because I was pregnant!"

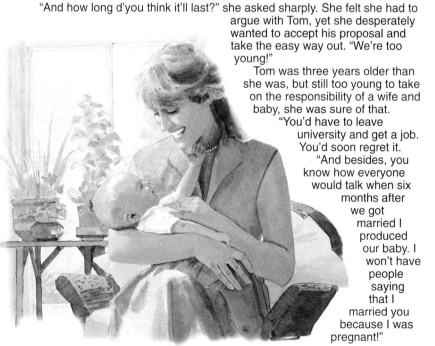

"Who cares what other people say!" Tom shouted. "I love you!"

"And I love you too — that's why I won't marry you," Jennifer stated forcefully.

Her mind was made up, and no amount of cajoling, reasoning, ranting and raving would change it.

And, six months later, Miss Jennifer Ashcroft had given birth to Paul, her baby son.

From the first moment she saw him, she'd loved him.

She'd gently taken the tiny curled fist in her fingers and gazed into the sleeping face.

"Hello, little one," she'd said. The baby stirred, opening his eyes, and she'd known she'd never let him go.

The sudden movement at the end of the quiet maternity ward as the first of the visitors began to file in brought Jennifer back to the present.

She smiled and waved excitedly as her husband strode down the ward to her bedside. It was three o'clock in the afternoon and she hadn't been expecting him till that evening.

"Hi, darling," he said, kissing her on the lips.

"This is a nice surprise, Tom," she said, her eyes bright with love.

And then, looking at the other two visitors Tom had brought with him she reached out and hugged them both.

"What are you two doing out of school?" she asked with teasing laughter in her voice.

"I thought they'd like to come and see their baby brother," Tom said, lifting four-year-old Katie up to see into the baby's crib.

"Well, what d'you think of your baby brother, Paul?" Jennifer asked her eight-year-old son, as he perched on the bed.

"I'm glad he's a boy. I didn't want another sister," he said with a cheeky grin.

Jennifer looked over his head at Tom and caught the wistful, faraway look in her husband's eyes as he glanced from Paul to the new baby. The baby looked just like Paul had as a new-born infant. She knew what Tom was thinking.

She was sure he was remembering the past, just as she had been earlier — remembering when he had come to visit his first-born son in this very hospital.

It was on that visit that he'd put his foot down. "I don't care why people think we're getting married. I only care about you, Jen," he'd told her.

"I love you more than anything, and I love our son. If that's not the right reason for getting married, I don't know what is! Please say yes, Jen?"

Somehow he'd made her see reason, and they married a few months later.

Those first few years hadn't always been easy. They had struggled in the beginning. But the struggle had been worth it, Jennifer thought as she sat proudly in her hospital bed, surveying her three beautiful, healthy children and their loving father.

Tom reached out for her hand and squeezed it tightly. "Did I ever tell you how much I love you?" he asked.

"Oh, yes," she said thickly, "and I'm so glad you did." ■

He's Been

Eyes gaze in awe at the wonderful sight,
The tree lit up on Christmas Eve night,
Wondering what secrets lie hidden within,
The beautiful paper, ribbon and string.

Bright fairy lights give a magical glow,
The children all wonder if tomorrow brings snow,
Reindeer and snowmen and Santa Claus, too,
Watch from the tree, which gift is for who?

Santa's milk and mince pie are placed by the tree,
They want to be sure that it's easy to see,
Then the children eagerly rush off to bed,
On legs which are normally heavy as lead.

With everyone tucked up and safely asleep,
The youngest creeps down for a curious peek,
The sacks they'd left empty the night before,
Are packed to bursting, with more on the floor.

With a smile on his face as big as the moon,
The little boy hurries back to his room,
He's been, he's been, on this wonderful night,
'Night, 'night, God bless, little one, sleep tight.

By Lisa Ashby

Sweet Dreams

by Gillian Souter

Our unusual sleep notice features Beatrix Potter's famous Peter Rabbit, in his classic pose, guarding the door of a sleeping child. As an option, you could replace "baby" with a name.

Materials: 30 x 25 cm of white Aida fabric with 11 thread groups per inch.
40 cm ribbon.
22 x 16 cm felt.
21 x 15 cm heavy white card.
DMC embroidery threads listed.
Stitch count: 50H x 80W.

Directions: Stitch the design, inserting a child's name if desired.
Carefully press the work. Cut a 21 x 15 cm piece of white card. Centre the embroidered work over the card, fold the edges over and glue them on to the back of the card, so that the work is taut. Cut a 40 cm length of ribbon and glue the ends at the back of the top right and left corners. Cut a 22 x 16 cm rectangle of felt and glue it to cover the back of the notice. The felt should extend evenly around all edges as a border.

KEY for Peter Rabbit			
	DMC	Colour	Stitches
✳	413	grey	2
⌐	437	dark tan	64
—	738	tan	64
○	739	light tan	48
✕	798	dark blue	535
∪	809	blue	71
+	3747	pale blue	54
•		white	18
＼	413	grey	backstitch

The Peter Rabbit Sleep Notice is extracted from STORYBOOK FAVOURITES IN CROSS-STITCH by Gillian Souter. Copyright © Off The Shelf Publishing, 1995, published by Little, Brown & Co., UK; Beatrix Potter™ Copyright © Frederick Warne & Co., 1995. Reproduced by kind permission of Frederick Warne & Co.

STORYBOOK FAVOURITES IN CROSS-STITCH and MORE STORYBOOK CROSS-STITCH by Gillian Souter are available by calling the credit card hotline on 01326 372 400.

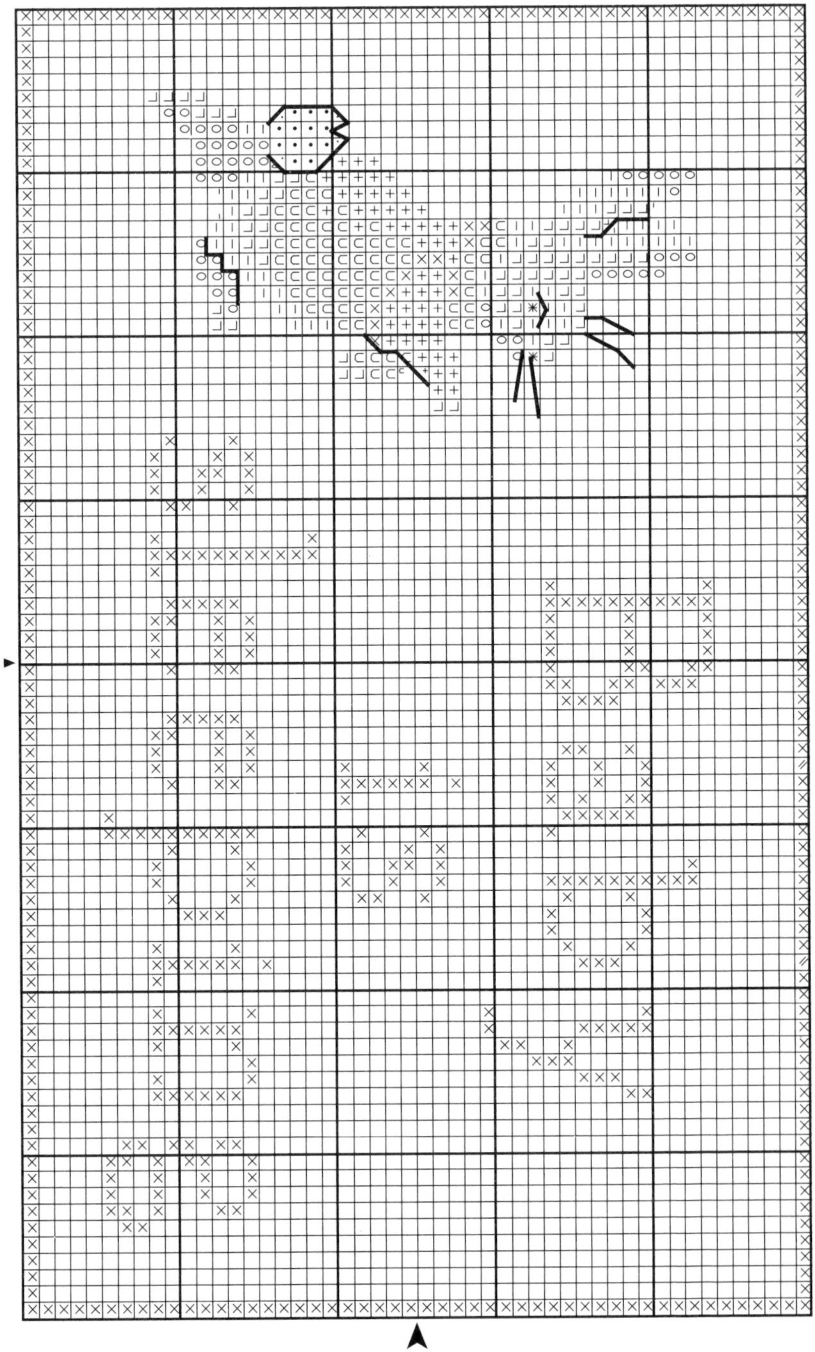

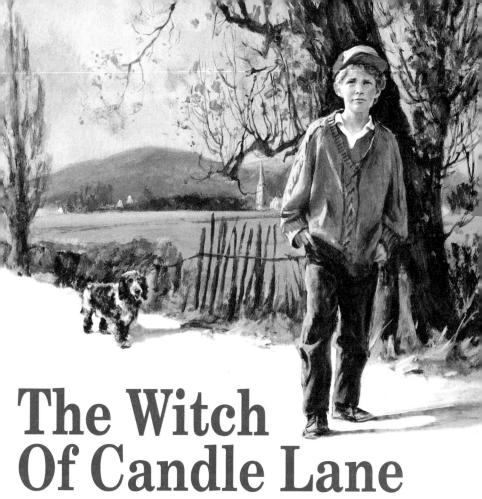

The Witch Of Candle Lane

That was how the boy thought of her, but when they met, he was the one who cast the spell.

By D.L. GARRARD

"**W**HAT are you doing in my garden?" Chloe Bayliss demanded.

The boy, scrambling for purchase halfway up the tree, gave a startled glance over his shoulder, lost his grip and came slithering down.

She saw his foot jar and turn as he hit the ground, then he twisted over to face her, crouching with his back to the trunk like a frightened animal at bay.

Chloe pushed the long hair back from her face. She had been walking round the edge of the grounds of the old house that had once been her grandfather's. Coming across the broken board in the fence and seeing the young trespasser, she had called out impulsively. Now, she found herself confronting a child with two scraped knees, and possibly a sprained ankle . . .

Tony Richards was just seven, with thin arms and legs sunburned from the summer now dying, and a stubborn chin.

His knees smarted and his ankle throbbed — but those pains were nothing compared to the wild thumping of his heart.

She had *appeared* — just like that! One minute the ground inside the fence was an empty jungle of thistles and brambles. The next — there she stood, all long dress, brown hair and dark wide eyes.

Perhaps there was something in what Steve and Colin Conway had told him, after all. Maybe the empty old house in Candle Lane was a witch's house.

He had been almost certain they were teasing. They were older and, though their mother kept an eye on him after school until his mum came home from work, they hadn't any time for Tony.

He had wanted to have a closer look at the house, but couldn't see it from the road. So he had wriggled through the fence and begun climbing the tree. He hadn't wanted to get too near, just in case.

"Have you hurt yourself?" Chloe couldn't help sounding abrupt. The very sight of a small, curly-haired boy twisted her heart . . . Alan — her Alan — had a son, and a wife.

He had assured her that his marriage had lost any meaning, especially now that he was away from home a good deal of the time, lecturing. And he had never loved anyone the way he loved Chloe, he'd declared.

But he couldn't take any action which might deny him access to his little son.

His wife could prove difficult, Alan had explained. They had waited a long time for parenthood; being only human, she might well choose that way of getting back at him.

"I do understand, Alan," Chloe had said — feeling miserable and in the wrong. All she wanted was to end the lies which made her mouth dry and her stomach knot with the awful deceit of it all.

"If you love me, give me time," Alan had asked.

She had never dared ask, how much time? Till the child grew up? But that was half a lifetime away!

After three years and one lonely weekend too many, Chloe had had a sudden, nightmare vision of Time as an endless tunnel, with no light at the end of it.

So, with the cathedral bells clamouring their morning summons across the city, she had thrown her belongings into suitcases and clattered downstairs to tell her landlady she was going back to the country to live.

Willard's Lodge had stood empty since her grandfather was taken to a nursing home. They had recalled many happy times there during his last few months and, when the house had become hers, Chloe hadn't wanted to sell it.

She had thought, at first, that it might have made a quiet retreat for herself and Alan. But he had shaken his head, smiling as if it was quite impractical.

"I want something much better for us than a tumbledown old house in the back of beyond, Chloe. Sell it and buy yourself the best flat you can afford. Property will always appreciate in value."

How much would it have 'appreciated' before she and Alan could be together? No. It had seemed like a step in the wrong direction and she couldn't take it . . .

THE boy was staring at her like a hypnotised rabbit. Blood had gathered into a bright drop on one knee and, as he huddled there, it began trickling down his leg.

She couldn't send him away like that. He was hurt and, besides, she didn't want some irate mother rampaging down the lane, accusing her of mistreating her child. But when Chloe moved towards him, he shrank back.

"I'm not going to tell you off," she assured him. "I just want to see that foot."

She eased off the scuffed blue sandal and peeled down his sock. The ankle wasn't too bad considering the fall he'd taken. The bones under her hand were as thin and light as a bird's and she felt a sense of awe.

This was the miracle of growing, of young life — she felt it through her fingertips, like a faint tingling.

Alan had joked that she had healing hands. How many times had she stroked his headaches into oblivion? She knew he really put it down to a release of tension — Alan was totally practical.

But with this child there was no scepticism.

Tony watched almost dreamily, the long supple fingers pale against his skin.

Chloe kneeled back with a twinge of reluctance. She had experienced a peculiar peace which she had not felt for a long time.

"It'll be all right now," she reassured him. "But I'd better bathe those knees."

As she stood up, stumbling over the hem of her skirt, she sensed his lulled suspicions come to life again.

"If you'd rather go straight home . . . ?" She shrugged and began to turn away.

The offer of freedom made Tony daring again. He would be one up on Steve and Colin if he actually went inside Willard's Lodge. And he'd see if they were telling the truth or not. A witch's house *must* be different to other people's.

"Well?" Chloe prompted. "Do you think you can walk OK?"

He wobbled his foot about, feeling only an ache where the throbbing had been.

"It's better," he said hesitantly. "But I'd better get washed. Auntie Conway will be mad at me if I go back dirty, and Mum will be mad at *her* for not looking after me properly."

Chloe found herself hiding a smile, wondering what was behind his elaborately-innocent gaze. Perhaps he was hoping for sweets or chocolate by way of consolation. If so, he'd be unlucky this time.

She had been satisfying what little appetite she had with food from her store-cupboards in town, tumbled in the bottom of her holdall. There had been a few usable tins and jars left in the house, too.

She'd not wanted to venture down to the shops, in case Alan should come while she was out.

Chloe led him through the field of long grass which had once been a lawn, to the long house of crumbling brick. A heat haze shimmered over it, distorting the tall, crooked chimneys even more. Tiny windows glinted at him in the sun.

In the kitchen, Chloe tipped water into a bowl from the warm black kettle, while Tony eyed the room furtively from his perch on the edge of a battered kitchen chair.

The stove was a mass of spidery black ironwork, rusted in places. The deep porcelain sink had a green stain under the dripping brass tap, and there were cobwebs in the corners. He saw a fat spider scuttle, and shivered.

"Sorry. Does it sting?" Chloe asked.

"No." He lifted his chin bravely. "Not really."

Tony thought of his mother's shining cooker, of the gay cereal packets on painted shelves, and the brightly-patterned vinyl on the floor. This floor was stone flagged and he couldn't see food anywhere.

A row of worn saucepans hung on hooks, and he spotted a pan with two handles which added to his doubts again. It vaguely resembled the picture of a witch's cauldron in one of his nearly-outgrown story books.

Chloe fetched a toilet-bag, cut a strip of adhesive plaster with nail scissors, and applied it to the worst knee.

"The other's only slightly grazed. It'll heal better if it's left uncovered."

She saw him on his way through the front gate and returned to the silent house, seeing it anew. His intrusion had jolted her out of her brooding, and she hadn't missed his transparent judgment of her surroundings.

Chloe hadn't been in a frame of mind to clean up its neglected appearance. She had merely taken yellowed linen from the chest of drawers, aired it in the sun, then made up a bed in her old room.

In spite of what she had said to her landlady, she hadn't expected to stay here for long. Deep down, she knew, she had hoped her flight would nudge Alan into positive action. He would come, they would talk things over and . . .

She stood, irresolute, in the dusty kitchen, her mind revolving round Alan like a moth round a candle flame.

He was a mineralogist based at the local college where, for a small fee, Chloe sometimes used the electric tumbler-polisher in the craft annexe.

In her spare time she worked with gemstones, minerals and even pretty pebbles. Fields, seashores, jumble sales, junk shops and sometimes mixed lots from auctions — all these yielded treasures from which she made simple, eye-catching jewellery.

She hung pendants on leather thongs, fashioned amulets, necklaces and bracelets. She gave some to friends, sold a few, and worked mainly for the

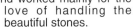

love of handling the beautiful stones.

Leaving the college one evening, Chloe had glanced at the notice board and seen that Alan Hurland needed a temporary secretary, while his own was on maternity leave.

Temping was Chloe's way of earning her bread and butter, so she'd promptly applied for the job. Pleased at the idea of combining her work with her hobby, she'd thought there would be much she could learn from an expert like him.

And so there was, though the notes she typed for his lectures held nothing of the folklore and ancient beliefs connected with the stones.

Alan always seemed faintly amused by the fascination these things held for her, and intrigued by her hobby. But something else had flashed between them at their first interview. She had never met anyone so knowledgeable — or so attractive.

When his calm, grey eyes began to show an unmistakable response to her presence, and when he finally invited her out to dinner, she was dizzy with excitement.

She didn't fool herself about her feelings, but she under-estimated her resistance to them. And so, though her job with him came to an end, their association grew.

Alan had become the most important thing in Chloe's life. Had she stopped to think about it, she could never have wrenched herself away . . .

I didn't find anything out, Tony thought to himself after his visit to the cottage. Mrs Conway hadn't even noticed the plaster, and his mother, hurrying to prepare the evening meal, merely ruffled his hair sympathetically.

He hadn't even been tempted to tell anyone his secret about the — the *person* in the 'empty' house. The grown-ups would scold him for going there, and Steve and Colin could go and look for themselves. And he didn't want anyone barging in on his adventure. He didn't feel it was finished yet.

By Thursday, Tony had plucked up the courage to go down Candle Lane again. The heatwave was about to break, and thunder growled in the distance like a bad-tempered dog. This time, after checking there was nobody about, he sidled in at the gate.

Tiptoeing along the path round the side of the house, he was disappointed to see washing hanging on the line, unmoving and limp in the breathless afternoon. Surely witches did everything by magic?

CHLOE sat at the big table in the kitchen, casting an occasional eye towards the window and the storm clouds beyond.

She had been working like a mad thing — dusting, scrubbing, washing, scouring. The mood had come upon her as suddenly as her urge to leave the city; a need to be busy. That way she didn't keep looking at the clock and remembering that Alan could have been here by now.

Too tired, at last, for more physical work, but still in need of something to occupy her, she had unpacked her linen bags of stones. The tools of her craft soon joined them on the table.

Tony paused by the open window to peep inside. The 'person' had her back half turned to him, and her head was bent over the table. What was she doing with that hook thing? What did she have in those bags?

Without any warning at all, lightning jabbed over the trees and a tremendous crash of thunder made him clap his hands over his ears. Then fat drops of rain splashed on his head.

He crouched low against the wall as the woman rushed out to the clothes-line, wrenching and hauling at the sheets while the rain increased to a hissing torrent.

Stumbling back to the kitchen with an armful of linen, Chloe saw him, too petrified by the commotion of the storm to make a run for it.

"Come in out of the rain!" she cried.

As another double crack of thunder sounded overhead, he obeyed, scuttling into the shelter of the kitchen. Once inside, he stared at her, shivering with fright.

"Just look at us!" Chloe forced a laugh, seeing him tremble and trying to make him more at ease. "We're like a couple of drowned rats."

She handed him a towel.

"Better dry off — we don't want a bad cold added to scraped knees and a sore ankle! Your mum would never forgive me."

He winced as another flash of lightning illuminated the room.

"To tell the truth, I'm not too keen on thunderstorms myself," Chloe confided.

"I think I'll put the kettle on to calm me down. Do you fancy tea and a chocolate biscuit, while we wait for the rain to stop?"

She proffered the packet. "Were you coming to see me?"

He nodded, comforted slightly because she didn't like storms either. Grown-ups always told him not to be scared, and that made it worse, because he couldn't help it.

"I . . . I came to tell you my knee's getting better." It was the only excuse he could think of.

"Well, that's good." She smiled. "What's your name?"

"Tony."

"I'm Chloe."

Klowy? That wasn't an ordinary name! But she looked nice — not like a witch at all, really.

"Let's put the light on till the storm passes," she was saying, her tone warm and reassuring.

Blinking in the brightness, he looked more closely at the things on the table.

"What are you doing?" he asked boldly.

"Making a necklace. Look, like this." She picked up a gold and brown stone and showed him how she twisted it into a delicate net of wire, next to a piece of sparkling quartz.

"This is called tiger's eye. Can you see why?"

He did, with a little thrill in his stomach. His eyes began to sparkle with interest as she took a handful of stones from a bag.

"This is coral," she told him. "It grows in tropical seas where the water is warm and all the fish have beautiful colours. This deep blue one is lapis lazuli. It's been around since prehistoric times."

"Like dinosaurs?" he whispered.

"Like dinosaurs," she agreed.

"This piece of amber is prehistoric, too. Sometimes insects got trapped inside it and you can still see them, looking just as they did when they were alive." She rubbed the yellow fossil resin vigorously with a soft cloth.

"It smells a bit like pine trees, even now. There — sniff."

He took it gingerly. But before he could find out if she was teasing, the kettle boiled over, starling him as the water made the gas jet splutter.

She gave him tea, sweetened with condensed milk from her grandfather's cupboard, and he told her he liked it better than the strong brew Mrs Conway made.

"She says you can stand a spoon up in hers," he said. "But I tried and it didn't."

They finished the chocolate biscuits and talked until the thunder died unnoticed into the distance. The rain fell quietly and steadily now, bringing out rich fresh scents from the wet grass and earth.

Beyond the front hedge, a bus swished up the wet road towards the village.

"Mum might be on that bus," Tony realised with a pang of anxiety. "What time is it?"

"Half past five. Does your mother fetch you from Auntie Conway's?"

"No, I go home by myself. It's only up the road," he explained.

"And she's not really my auntie," he went on, giving her a sideways glance that was half shy, half mischievous. "I like you better. You're more int'resting."

Chloe laughed, absurdly pleased.

"My grandad's old cape and sou'wester are in the cupboard. Shall I dress you up in those to keep you dry, then walk you home?"

"Like a lifeboatman." Tony's eyes grew wide, seeing the oilskins.

"We'll *need* a lifeboat, if this goes on," she remarked, pulling on her plastic mac.

T HEY met Tony's mother, a slim young woman with short fair hair, running down the garden path.

"Tony, I was just coming to . . . Goodness!" Suddenly noticing Chloe, she opened her eyes to their widest extent. Then, after the briefest of introductions and explanations, she ushered them both inside, out of the downpour.

"Thanks for bringing him home, Chloe," Dawn Richards said breathlessly over her shoulder, as she shook her umbrella in the porch.

"So, you were related to old Mr Bayliss?" she chattered on. "I should have guessed. You're the spitting image."

"Thanks!" Chloe laughed. "You knew my grandfather well, then?" she asked, surrendering her mac to drip in the kitchen.

"It was my father-in-law who knew him, really. He thought a lot of the old man. I didn't even know anyone was back at the house."

"And what were you doing there, Tony?" Dawn demanded, trying to look severe.

"He took shelter from the storm," Chloe put in. "We had — ah — met, earlier in the week."

"I'd hoped he might play with Steve and Colin Conway, but of course they're so much older." The worry in Dawn's eyes cleared a little as she went on. "At least all this rushing about will be over in a couple of months and I can spend more time with him . . .

"I'm getting married again," she confided, blushing prettily. Then the whole story of her husband's death and, later, her meeting with Bob, her fiancé, and their hopes and dreams for the future came tumbling out.

Some time later, she laughed apologetically.

"I'm sorry for going on like this — I'm the world's worst chatterbox. Tell me a bit more about you. How long have you been here?"

"I came down on Sunday evening," Chloe told her, smiling.

Dawn threw up her hands in mock amazement. "You've been here four days and nobody knew! And this village has the speediest grapevine on record!"

"I . . . never left the house, I expect that's why."

Perhaps Dawn read something in her tone, for she probed no deeper but looked at her sympathetically, which deepened Chloe's first instinctive liking for her.

"It's such a quaint old place," Dawn continued brightly. "It's sort of settled and permanent. I'd like somewhere with character, too, one day.

"Not that I haven't been happy here," she added softly. "The few years I had with Martin, Tony's father, were wonderful, and I'm glad Tony can remember him. We'll have good memories to take with us when we eventually leave."

Good memories. Chloe thought of Alan's wife and son. They wouldn't have many of those if . . . She realised now that though the facts had seemed plain enough, she hadn't considered all the feelings involved before.

Was that what Alan had been trying to tell her? Or perhaps he'd hidden the truth, even from himself . . . ? She was no longer sure about what to do — and maybe Alan wasn't, either. Perhaps that's why he hadn't come.

"Will you stay for tea, Chloe? There's plenty. I left a chilli con carne in the slow cooker."

"Thanks, I'd like to." And as the hours passed, Chloe knew she had found a friend.

"Are you going to be living in Willard's Lodge from now on?" Dawn asked as Chloe stood to go.

"It's . . . possible," she replied at last.

Relinquishing any certainty of a future with Alan was like letting slip a cloak which had kept her warm for so long. But there was other warmth — in the company of Dawn Richards, and a small boy who thought she was "int'resting."

"Oh, I do hope so." Dawn paused. "Tell you what — if you're interested in a clerical job, I'll put a word in with my boss . . ."

"Please, Klowy," Tony piped up sleepily, just as she was leaving. "What's that sort of cauldron thing for, in your kitchen?"

Chloe looked mystified for a minute.

"Oh, you mean my grandma's preserving pan! It's for making jam. When the blackberries are ripe, you could come and help me pick some from those bushes by the fence . . ." Her eyes twinkled at him, sharing their secret . . .

How they'd all laugh, if they knew he'd half believed Klowy was a witch! Tony thought as he climbed into bed. Witches didn't make jam, or come for tea, or go to work.

All the same, she knew some int'resting things.

And she could make hurt ankles better.

And there really was something a bit magic about her, specially when she smiled.

And she was his friend.

He fell asleep contentedly, thinking about it. ■

LOOK INTO MY EYES

by JAN SANDERS

If only he had looked — really looked — he might have seen the message hidden there . . .

CAN see the girl walking along the beach, almost at the water's edge. Although the sun is only a pale shadow of its summer self, the light is really quite strong, and today she's wearing a floppy hat and sun specs.

This is the fourth time I've seen her, and since that first morning she has haunted my thoughts. In fact, I decided to fish from this mound of rocks in the hope that she'd pass by.

The dog is with her as usual. He's a large, coal-black creature. Strangely, he doesn't dash madly along the sand, or plunge headlong into the spray, like most dogs running free. He simply trots beside her, watchfully.

"Hello there. Isn't it a lovely morning?" I call.

She pauses and I see, now, that the straw hat has a wreath of wild flowers around the crown.

"I'm fishing," I explain unnecessarily.

"I saw you yesterday. Had any luck?"

"Yes, now that you're talking to me." I grin, knowing it's a clumsy sort of compliment. But she smiles gently.

"It's quiet here, end of season. But in summer, you have any number of people to chat to." Her nose wrinkles in a mock grimace. "They swoop down with sunbeds and transistor radios."

"You live here?" I ask quickly, wanting to learn something about her before she vanishes. She seems so slight that a breath of sea wind could whisk her away at any moment.

She nods, waving vaguely in the direction of the clifftop.

"Mmm — and I must get back," she tells me. "I always forget the time when I start looking for shells."

She opens her hand to show me four shells, pink and pearly against her palm. I smile down at her. She smiles back, then turns to go. Already she's walking away, towards the cliff steps. She mustn't go — not yet. I only have a few more days here.

But when I make a movement towards her, the dog is there.

"It's all right, Benjie," she says, stroking his smooth head.

"Good luck with the fishing," she calls, moving away. "See you tomorrow, perhaps."

And every tomorrow, I hope, watching as she reaches the bottom of the cliff. Next minute, a shadow slants across the sun, and then she's disappeared.

I think of her face, partly hidden by those owl-like, dark glasses. It had the gentle appeal of a picture smiling out from an old-fashioned locket.

I remember we have just such a locket at home in the shop. I'd like to give it to her, as a token.

A token of what, I ask myself. Admiration?

Picking up a stone, I toss it out to sea. Suddenly I feel better than I've done since before I saw my brother off on that plane to Australia.

Ray has just started another life on the other side of the world, marrying a girl we'd both known at school. Her family went out there two years ago.

He left me his share in the shop, but it's not the same without him. I suppose it's just going to take time to adjust.

Ray was the one who polished the second-hand furniture and sold it to the young couples setting up home. He learned upholstery, too, and did marvellous things with bits of fringe and a box of tacks.

"But you're the brains of the business, Stevie-boy," he would sometimes say encouragingly. "You've a real talent for antique spotting."

It's true. I do have a feeling for what's genuine, and I've recognised quite a few treasures.

But Ray and I both know a lot about wood in its various guises. We learned it from Uncle Joe who brought us up. And in a way, it's due to him that I've leased the fishing hut.

Ray tossed a newspaper to me just a couple of weeks before he went abroad.

"Remember Uncle Joe always going on about working in a boat-builder's yard at Shellsea Bay?" he asked, and I nodded.

"When we were kids, he kept promising to take us there, but somehow he never got round to it."

"Well, they're advertising the old coastguard's cottage as a fishing hut. How do you fancy taking a break down there — my treat?

"Shellsea Bay's only eight-odd miles away. It'll be a change for you, after I'm gone. Phil can look after the shop."

I wasn't all that interested at the time. Although I've often tagged along on fishing trips with him, Ray has always been a lot keener on the sport than I am.

But when Phil came down offering his services, I decided to take him up on it. Since he retired, I know he likes to feel needed, and has helped us out before.

Our flat is over the shop, and Phil and his wife live over the radio shop nearby. It's all very convenient.

SO I came to Shellsea Bay and met this girl.
Today, as she comes towards me, the dog is with her again. She's wearing denims and trailing a huge spray of seaweed behind her. When she sees me, she holds it up in greeting, then waves it around her like a fan dancer.

She's unexpected, this girl, and fun, and I'd like to know more about her. I walk across the sand to meet her.

"Would you like some coffee? I've brought a flask," I tell her.

Laughing, she scrambles carefully over the rocks to sit on my old mac. Benjie joins her.

"I was afraid you wouldn't come," I confess, smiling.

"Why not?" She is looking at me over the rim of the cup and I can see her eyes without the sunspecs. They are a soft hazel colour.

Benjie's eyes are sharply golden-yellow and he never takes them off me.

"I don't even know your name," I point out.

"Emmie," she tells me. "And you?"

"Steve Lennox, dealer in antiques — at least, now and then I am. In between, I flog bits and pieces, all second-hand.

"My brother calls our shop 'Lennox's Leftovers'," I say, grinning. "He used to tell me that leftovers from one family can be a lifeline to another.

"He's just got married and settled in Australia," I add more quietly, and she's silent for a moment.

"You're lonely?" she asks softly, and I'm surprised at her insight.

"Not me," I say lightly. "I've met you, haven't I?"

She looks thoughtfully out to sea.

"Tell me about your shop, Steve," she prompts me.

I do, then, "Tell me about Emmie," I add.

She's getting to her feet, though, and so is Benjie.

"Not much to tell." She smiles. "We're a household of women — Mum, Gran and me.

"Mother makes pottery and one of the local shops sells it for her. The holidaymakers love it. It's called 'Cove Cottage Pottery', after the place where we live."

"You have a kiln then?"

"We part-share one with the school where Mum takes classes.

"That reminds me — I'm supposed to be helping her pack some stuff for an exhibition there this evening."

I want to offer to drive her to the exhibition, to fetch and carry. But she says "goodbye" quickly.

It's as if she suddenly remembers something which makes her want to escape from me.

"See you," she says, and begins to sprint over the empty sand towards the cliff steps.

"Tomorrow," I shout after her, and hope that wave of her hand means, "Yes, I'll be there."

It does. She's here again and the sun is with us. Once more she's a mysterious lady behind dark glasses.

I tell her how I drove into town last night, but that by the time I found the school, the shutters were being put up.

"Oh yes, we opened early," she explains. "People come from all sorts of little places along the coast, you see. And it's a bit dicey, driving round here in the dark."

"I came back and had dinner alone at the hotel," I tell her. "I suppose you wouldn't take pity on a lonely fisherman, and let me take you there tonight?"

She hesitates, then nods.

Impulsively, I gently touch her face. But she sits very still, as if she hasn't noticed, and quickly I draw my hand away.

However, later, I notice her the minute she steps tentatively through the door of the hotel. She's wearing a deep blue dress and carrying a little jacket over her arm. She looks simply fabulous.

Before, I've seen her dark hair only when it was wind-blown. Now, with it fastened back, I can see small jewels in her ears.

I'm still wondering why she didn't let me pick her up at home.

"Mum will be going to her evening class and she'll give me a lift. It's no trouble," she had insisted.

No matter. She's here with me now.

It's a quiet place, with only a few couples dining, and we sit at a table in the window, watching the moon shimmering on dark water.

We are in a world of our own and I'm half afraid that she may vanish into the sea, like a mermaid.

Yet she's still with me later when we stroll towards the beach and stop by the white rails at the top of the cliff stairway.

I turn her face up to mine and, for one magic moment, there's nobody in this moonlit place but Emmie and me.

But when I begin pouring out my growing feelings for her, she stops me with a finger on my lips.

"And I think I — like you, too.

"But don't rush me, Steve," she whispers. "And don't rush yourself. Give it time."

Then she's starting to say that she's left Gran alone in the cottage, obviously wanting to leave me. But she accepts a short lift in the car, stopping me before we reach her row of cottages.

"Thanks, Steve. I'll be fine from here. Our cottage is the nearest, at this end," she says.

I watch her moving through the shadows of her garden path, then she disappears . . .

I've been waiting here all morning on the beach, and still there's no sign of her.

Retrieving a stick thrown back in on the tide, I write *Steve loves Emmie* in huge letters on the sand. She will laugh at my artistic flourishes, if she comes.

She doesn't come, but the tide does . . .

And this morning I've had a letter from Phil, telling me that the auction we've been waiting for is fixed for tomorrow. Phil knows I've had my eye on several items at the stately home for ages.

Feeling as I now do about Emmie, I could have skipped the sale, but I sense a further worry in Phil's letter.

His wife has had an accident on the stairway leading up to their flat. Her injury's minor, but he's having to leave her while he attends to my shop. I can no longer expect him to cope alone.

But I can't leave Emmie without a word, so I'm heading for Cove Cottage before I return.

It seems to be deserted, although there are ominous, Benjie-type growls from within. I notice there's a glass outhouse with shelves displaying attractive, green-glazed pottery and a card saying, 'Lorna Ward, Cove Cottage Ware'.

But it isn't Lorna Ward I've come to see.

Sitting in the car, I write to Emmie on one of my headed shop bills, explaining why I'm called away. Then I'm off to tidy up the fishing hut and stack away my gear before I lock up and head for home.

My village is a pleasant place to live in, and as I drive up the High Street, I have a sudden vision of Emmie doing our shopping here.

Parking the car on the cobbles outside my shop, I wonder what she will think of it all.

THREE weeks later I am eagerly hoping she will like the antique box I bought for her at the auction. The wood is inset with pearl and, although the interior is pretty shabby, Phil is re-lining it for me with a snippet of yellow velvet.

I think I'll pop the antique locket inside it.

It seems a lifetime since I left Shellsea Bay but I'm returning at the weekend. Twice I've written to Emmie and she hasn't replied. But I must go back. Otherwise I'll know no peace.

Phil stared hard at me when he handed me the box.

"For someone special?" he asked, and I could only give him a wry grin.

Not that I have ever doubted that she's special. But after all, I know so little about her.

Soon I shall know more, though, because I'm steering along the familiar coast road. Without pausing to drop off my luggage at the hut, I have driven straight on to Emmie's place.

In the glass outhouse attached to Cove Cottage, a woman is busily rearranging the shelves of pottery and she looks up as I open the gate. She's gentle-faced like Emmie, but anxious looking.

Smilingly, I tell her that I'm a friend of Emmie; that I've written but there's been no answer.

"Could I see her, please?"

She hesitates.

"I'm afraid she's not here now."

"Well, I'm Steve Lennox — she's probably mentioned me. You must be Emmie's mother. Could you tell me where I can find her?"

"She's away," Mrs Ward tells me in a flat sort of voice.

"If you've already written, I'm sure she'll reply . . . If she wants to," she finishes.

A rough sea is booming behind me, as someone else appears beside Mrs Ward. She's an old lady who gazes steadily at me. Then, as if satisfied with what she sees, she speaks.

"You'd better tell the young man, Lorna. Ask him inside. That sea wind's like a knife today."

Inside Cove Cottage the first thing I notice is a large photograph of Emmie with the rounded face of childhood.

"Go on, Lorna. Give the lad a chance," the older woman urges.

Mrs Ward offers me a chair and clears her throat.

"I don't know if Emmie wants to see you, Steve."

The way she says my name convinces me Emmie has mentioned me, and my glow of hope deepens.

"She's far from well at the moment," Mrs Ward continues. "In fact, she's in hospital.

"It's her eyes," she explains.

Pieces of the puzzle click into place. The dark glasses, the sun hat; and Benjie — the guide dog.

"You mean she's . . . ?"

"No," she puts in quickly. "She's not blind, though there was a risk of that for a time.

"We were called to the hospital three weeks ago," she goes on. "Emmie had been waiting months to see a particular consultant and she was sent for suddenly."

Why didn't she tell me? I am thinking. Then, straightaway, *She was afraid . . .*

I'm staring at her mother and gran.

"I understand, Mrs Ward. I do really. But please — let me see her. I promise it'll be all right."

We've come up to the hospital in my old car. I'm waiting in a long corridor, after Emmie's mother and gran have vanished into a room at the end of it.

"You must let us warn her that you're here, Steve," Mrs Ward insisted. "It's only fair."

She's right, of course.

They have told me that Emmie's been having occasional disturbance of vision over the past two years. Now, after her treatment, she needs complete rest and quiet.

"Emmie's last boyfriend couldn't cope when they said she might go blind," her mother told me sadly.

"It broke her heart," Gran put in. "She's scared to get involved again."

"You see, Steve," Mrs Ward continued. "Emmie may always have some weakness. It could catch up with her again at any time. She can't afford to take chances."

I held her gaze steadily.

"Life's a chance, anyway, Mrs Ward," I said softly. "And sometimes it's worth the risk."

Emmie's gran suddenly looked as if I'd rekindled some fading light within her, and she beamed at me.

As she's beaming at me now.

"You can go in next," she says.

Mrs Ward is coming back down the corridor.

"Do be careful, Steve," she warns me. But she's smiling.

There are four beds in the ward. I make straight for Emmie. She is lying flat without pillows, by a window shaded with a dark green blind.

"Emmie?" I whisper.

"Hello, Steve. I — I'm glad you came."

I've brought along the antique box with the locket in it, and although Emmie can't see them too well, there is delight on her face as I describe them.

Then her voice drops low.

"I have to wear specs a lot, Steve," she's telling me.

"I'm looking at you through rose-coloured ones myself," I say, lovingly teasing.

She is silent for a moment, then her wide, warm smile lightens my heart, and she reaches out a hand to me.

"Yes," she murmurs. "I feel as if I'm in a rose-coloured world." ■

ANIMAL MAGIC

By DOROTHY L. GARRARD

No, this particular rabbit didn't come out of a hat — but it certainly made all her troubles vanish!

NORAH came downstairs at precisely her usual time, put the kettle and her egg water to boil on the gas stove and lit the grill.

While it heated for toast, she opened the back door to take a few deep breaths of morning air — and the rabbit hopped inside.

It was a brown-coloured rabbit with white bib and socks, and a splodge of black round its nose making it look as though it had been too inquisitive over a pot of paint.

"Here!" Norah exclaimed as it trod over her feet. "What do you want?"

It didn't actually answer her in words, but the way it gazed back spoke volumes. Then, head cocked, ears at attention, it sat up on its haunches and begged for breakfast like a dog.

"Now, look —" Norah said, amused. "You don't live here and my store cupboard isn't geared to rabbits. I buy my vegetables fresh every day and I don't have a lettuce in the place."

The rabbit must have understood for it abandoned its suppliant pose — which, in fact, seemed not so much suppliant as condescending, as if one had to perform thus for human beings in order to produce the appropriate reactions in them.

Instead, he lolloped into the lounge.

Norah's tiny cottage had once belonged to a neighbouring farm and since buying it some nine months ago she had spent a good deal of time and salary furnishing it to her satisfaction.

The rabbit gave the lounge the once-over, then settled its furry person in the centre of the luxurious circular rug, which had been an undeniable extravagance.

Norah often caught herself walking round that rug instead of over it, and the sight of the rabbit staking a claim dispersed her amusement. Besides, she was going to be late.

"Come along!" she said briskly. "Outside, if you please. Some of us have to go to work."

She extended a well-polished grey court shoe with the intention of nudging the rabbit in the right direction. It rose with outraged dignity, giving the distinct impression that it was moving from personal choice only, and walked into the hall.

Here it observed a delicate flower painting with the judicious air of an art critic, then with sudden agility, bounded upstairs.

"Come back!" Norah called indignantly, hurrying after it.

It ran round the landing several times, evading her clutches, then dived under her bed and played hide and seek between the suitcases she was obliged to store there through lack of space.

Finally it left her kneeling on the carpet, grasping at air, while it hopped over her legs and went to investigate the spare room.

It was so diverted by the sight of her sewing machine and the partially made-up dress on the dummy, that her fingers actually touched its fur before it spun round.

Kindly unhand me, madam, its expression clearly said. Its nose ceased to wobble and went stiff with offended dignity.

Norah started back instinctively, then put her hands on her hips.

"This is ridiculous!" she exclaimed, as much to herself as the rabbit.

"I've never been late for the office in my life, not even when I had to look after Mother. I'm not starting now, especially not on your account!

"Just take yourself out of my house or I'll — I'll fetch the yard broom and sweep you out!"

She pointed to the door. The rabbit gave itself a little shake to fluff up the fur her hand had flattened, and appeared to consider the alternatives.

Then, just slowly enough to preserve that air of choice, it sauntered downstairs, through the kitchen and out into the garden — whereupon she promptly closed the door and locked it.

The time was now eleven minutes past eight. Norah's bus left at precisely 8.22 from the war memorial in the centre of the village. The village itself was a brisk five minutes' walk away, up Oak Farm Lane . . .

The kitchen was now full of steam and the egg water had almost boiled away. Norah struck her bread under the red-hot grill and snatched it out scarcely brown, eating it while she hastily gave her pot plants their morning drink.

She restrained her compulsive urge to perform the whole of her morning routine, but she did swiftly clear the breakfast table, at which she'd had no time to sit.

It seemed too slovenly to leave the cloth on the table . . .

She slipped on her jacket, seized her handbag and departed at a trot. She would probably still have caught the 8.22 to Illsley if she hadn't realised at the last bend in the road that she hadn't turned off the grill.

T was a most unusual sensation to arrive at Sedgewick & Son to find everyone already hard at work.

Norah whisked through the general office with a breathless, "Good morning," slipping off her jacket as she went into her own room.

The voice of Alma Holland, the office junior, floated after her through the open door.

"Miss Purfitt isn't sick . . . she's *late*!"

Jean's awed whisper reached her, too, as the typewriter stopped its chattering. "And there's *fluff* on her skirt!"

Norah felt her cheeks flush, though she knew the remarks were made in genuine astonishment — unlike the deliberate sarcasm from an over-confident telephonist a couple of years ago. "You want Miss Perfect? Oh, sorry — Miss Purfitt!" *That* hadn't lasted long.

Barbara Fielding, the general clerk who had survived a good many office juniors, though not as many as Norah, appeared anxiously at the door.

"Is everything all right, Norah?"

"Yes — thank you. Missed the bus," Norah called back, scrabbling in the drawer for her clothes brush. That oatmeal carpet she'd laid upstairs was still shedding.

Mr Sedgewick appeared in the communicating doorway between his office and Norah's.

"I'm so sorry I'm late — but I just couldn't leave the rabbit in the house, it could have done all kinds of damage," she told him breathlessly.

"You have a pet rabbit?" He looked surprised.

"No — no — it just appeared on my doorstep."

"Well, when you're ready . . . Alma already made us coffee."

"Oh no!" The murmur of voices from the conference room jogged her memory. "The Molton representatives!"

Norah *never* forgot a meeting, and normally it wouldn't have mattered anyway, because she was always there in time to check the appointment book and prepare a coffee tray.

"Oh dear! I should have bought biscuits . . ."

"Of course not!" Mr Sedgewick smiled understandingly. "If they haven't eaten breakfast, that's too bad — it's only nine-twenty after all! Alma found your special director's sugar lumps and managed very nicely on the whole. I had the cup with the drips!"

Alma always managed to slosh coffee in the saucers. The twinkle in Mr Sedgewick's eyes flustered Norah even more.

"Don't panic, Norah," he told her. "We won't lose a contract just because my secretary had a contretemps with a rabbit!"

"But it's so . . . unprofessional!" She smoothed her neat, greying hair, feeling entirely unlike her usual calm, competent self.

That evening, Norah dismounted at the war memorial and set off down Oak Farm Lane. She still couldn't decide whether Oak Cottage, standing alone, had been a good choice.

After her mother had died last year, a move of some kind seemed imperative. While her friends and contemporaries had married and moved away, Norah had spent her life in a tall, narrow terraced house on the far side of Illsley in a district which was rapidly becoming run down.

Once the personality of the old lady had ceased to brighten the house with warmth and courage, it looked what it was — an old-fashioned, inconvenient place which got no real sunshine and cost a fortune to heat.

The sale of the property had brought her enough to buy somewhere smaller and cosier, a base from which to start a new life.

She didn't want to change her job. Mr Sedgewick had been a good boss in times of crisis and she wanted to make it up to him. Oak Cottage, at first sight, had seemed the answer to a prayer.

Once she had escaped her old environment, she thought, she would join things, mix and make new friends. She would try things she'd never had the opportunity to do.

It wasn't as easy as it sounded. Illsley Green wasn't the busy community it had once been. In fact, it had become quite a backwater and public transport there was quite inadequate.

In the winter, Norah joined evening classes in Illsley, but always had to leave early to catch the last bus home. So there wasn't really time to socialise, and most people had come in twos anyway.

She had joined more for the company than through an urgent interest in the subject, and became guiltily bored before the end of the course.

Going to the theatre or exhibitions alone was only partially satisfactory, and companionship was still largely confined to letters from distant friends. Sometimes, Norah despaired of ever finding the friendship, the companionship, she so desired . . .

When she arrived home, the rabbit was still there, looking larger than ever. That could have been due to the fact that it had most of her lawn inside it, she thought.

She shot an anxious glance at the rockery, where she had been experimenting inexpertly with plants from the garden centre, but everything there seemed intact.

"Lucky for you!" she observed sternly, and the rabbit gazed back from beneath disdainfully drooping lids. As if I would eat *those* things, it seemed to be saying with scornful dignity.

But pet rabbits didn't live on grass alone, she knew. Doubtless some child would be saying a prayer for its return and hoping somebody was feeding it. With more time to spare now, she felt guilty about her thoughtlessness that morning and took a carrot from the bag of vegetables she had bought at lunchtime.

"Feed a stray and it'll stay," her mother had chanted warningly in Norah's childhood.

"That's strictly for dessert," Norah told the rabbit. "Then, since you found your way here, you might start trying to remember the way home.

"Tomorrow I shall advertise your whereabouts in the newsagent's, so prepare to be repossessed."

The rabbit finished the carrot, then stretched one half of its body, then the other. It shook itself, then set off at a brisk trot down the garden. Norah watched as it gathered speed then soared magnificently over the fence into the fields beyond.

Goodbye, Rabbit.

NEXT morning, Norah opened the door and there it was again, looking somewhat dejected. Its ears had lost their jauntiness and there was a small clump of fur missing from its back.

Norah saw the caked blood and her nursing instincts took over.

"Here," she said, "let me see."

The animal was docile under her ministrations. She bathed the wound and debated about the use of disinfectant. Didn't animals lick their injuries? The taste might harm or deter it.

She was holding one end of a carrot while it nibbled the other, when she realised she was going to be late again.

"Miss Purfitt?" Jean regarded her hesitantly over the typewriter. "Is something the matter? I mean, this is the second — er . . ."

"It's this blessed rabbit!" Norah burst out, thankful that Mr Sedgewick was out that morning. "I can't get rid of it!"

Barbara laughed when she'd explained. "If nobody claims it you could always adopt it. It sounds quite lovable!"

"I think it's already adopted *me*!"

"Well, my place is a mini-zoo," Barbara said. "Jason's studying to be a vet. I could always look after it if you went on holiday . . . even take it off your hands, if it got too much."

Norah looked at her, feeling warmed by Barbara's friendliness.

"Thanks, I'll remember that . . . Somehow that rabbit seems too human to even consider calling in the RSPCA. It's had a close relationship with someone, somewhere.

"Meanwhile, would Jason know what to do about this injury? And what's a healthy diet for a rabbit?"

"Jason's away at college just now, but come home with me and we'll look at some of his books. It doesn't sound bad enough for a vet.

"Actually, I've been wanting to ask you round ever since — since you were free to come. But —" She looked a little embarrassed. "Well, my house always looks like a jumble sale!"

Norah flushed, embarrassed at this image everyone had of her.

"Barbara, my neat habits grew out of necessity. Mother didn't see too well before she took to her bed — everything had to be in its proper place for her sake. Being tidy just came to be second nature, eventually."

Now Alma was presenting her with a cup of coffee — in a swimming saucer as usual, but with a desire to please, and Jean was offering to bring in her mother's vegetable peelings for the rabbit.

The moment for refusing Barbara's invitation had gone, even though Norah was a bit shy of it. The thought of Barbara's energetic husband and four boys made her slightly nervous.

The boys were out on their various pursuits however, and her husband working late. Norah's shyness gave place to a rather wistful envy.

Sweaters behind the cushions, a jam jar on the TV full of screws and nails, the litter of newspapers and comics and an abandoned game of draughts on the coffee table made it far more homely, if less elegant, than Oak Cottage.

She borrowed Jason's rabbit book and a small bag of oats. Back home she emptied the stout wooden box of its kindling and found an old towel to crumple on the concrete for the time being.

The rabbit showed an interest, and settled half in, half out, as evening came.

"That's right, Rabbit. You stay away from the fields and the foxes, or whatever it was you tangled with. And if you're good, I'll get you some straw tomorrow."

She lugged home straw from the pet shop, and rabbit foot and extra vegetables. The rabbit was catching the last of the sun on the crazy paving by her fish pond.

He sprawled inelegantly on his back, legs limp, paws resting on his furry stomach. All he needed was a pair of sunglasses, and Norah laughed aloud. She must invite Barbara round for coffee and rabbit inspection.

AFTER a week it seemed as if Rabbit had been there forever, and there had been no response to her queries and advertisements. Mrs Jebbet at the newsagent's said she knew everybody in Illsley Green and nobody there had lost Rabbit.

Norah had got so used to him that when she opened her front door on Saturday morning to a strange man with a pleasant smile, she had a nasty sense of shock.

"Miss Purfitt? My name's Jim Dwyer —"

"And you've come for Rabbit," Norah blurted.

Why else would a stranger know her name unless he had read the card, and besides, that square capable hand resting on her porch lintel looked accustomed to bits of carpentry, like knocking rabbit hutches together.

He regarded her with friendly interest.

"If he's brown and white with a black nose and thinks he's a dog, then that's Houdini! He was brought up with Sunny, our golden Labrador."

"That explains a lot," Norah said lightly, suppressing a pang as she regarded Rabbit's owner.

"He'll be glad to see you. Please come through . . . how did you track him down?"

"Sheer inspiration — then seeing your card in the village shop, I thought, yes, that's Houdini all right! The great Escapist — he's always at it!"

If Norah had needed any proof it was there in the way Rabbit ceased munching like a child caught out, and regarded Jim Dwyer from the corners of his eyes.

"He looks quite . . . hang-dog!" Norah said, obliged to laugh.

"Another habit he picked up from Sunny!" Jim laughed back. He pushed a hand through his hair.

"We were moving house," he explained, "and I was taking the last of the stuff, including Houdini, down to Firfield in my van. Do you know Firfield?"

"I've been through it a few times," Norah told him. Firfield was a busy market town some nine miles farther on.

"Well, my van doors didn't close properly, so I tied the handles with twine, and when I got there and opened them Houdini's basket wasn't fastened.

"I hadn't secured the toggle properly and with the jolting and his manoeuvres — he hates that basket — it had worked loose.

"I took it for granted he'd wriggled out while I was unlocking the house and I've been hunting around locally — in between going to work and getting the house in some kind of order." He grinned ruefully.

"It took almost a week for it to dawn on me that he could have hopped it en route. And last night I remembered I'd stopped in Illsley Green to check my map . . ."

Without warning, Houdini took a flying leap into Jim's arms. He staggered under the sudden weight.

"Terry, my son, taught Houdini to do that when he was only a ball of fluff!" he puffed. "Unfortunately we can't unteach him! Thank goodness I found him before Terry joins me next week.

"Well." The man turned to go. "I mustn't keep you, thanks again. Will you allow me to reimburse you for anything he's cost you?"

"No, indeed, it's been a pleasure . . . Won't you have a cup of coffee before you leave?" Norah found herself asking.

She didn't know quite what had come over her, except that this man had given her an enviable glimpse of the family to which Rabbit belonged.

Jim deposited Houdini on the lawn again and smiled. "Thanks, I'd like that very much." He followed her indoors.

"This is a most attractive cottage, if you don't mind me saying so. I had to settle for something rather larger than I intended in the end. There are only two of us, you see. My wife died some years back.

"Still, I expect it'll soon be overflowing with Terry's friends! He's staying with his gran till term ends, to avoid disrupting his schooling. Sunny's with him."

"Will you tell him about Houdini's adventures?" Norah asked, handing him the coffee.

"Oh, yes." He gave her that ready grin. "Things tend to slip out otherwise. Anyway, we don't have many secrets.

"I think honesty is even more important when you only have each other — then there's no room for misunderstandings."

Norah nodded. "My mother and I had a very close relationship . . ."

The ease with which she could talk to him astonished her. He accepted a second cup of coffee and a piece of her home-made fruit cake. She was sorry when he eventually went through the front door, with Houdini dangling beneath his arm and trying to ignore the indignity of it.

"I must say Houdini had the sense to know a good billet when he saw one!" Jim said. "It's been very nice meeting you, Norah."

"And you, Jim."

At the front gate, he turned, shyly. "Em, if it's OK with you, I'd love to bring Terry along one day to say thanks himself?"

"I'd be delighted," Norah said.

"Oh, good. Be seeing you, then." With a relieved smile and a wave he strolled off.

Back indoors, Norah didn't have the slightest urge to plump up the cushions and wash the coffee cups.

Instead she stood looking through the window at Rabbit's abandoned box with a smile.

She had a wonderful feeling that her own great escape into a wider world of living was just about to begin . . . ■

The Magic In His Eyes

You can see the magic in his eyes,
So wonder-filled and bright,
Filled with such excitement,
On this very special night.

The room is warm, the light is soft,
The atmosphere is set,
Tomorrow will be Christmas Day,
What presents will he get?

Remember how it used to be?
Has the change been all that great?
It used to be so different,
To the Christmases of late.

When I was young, I'd never dream,
Of what Christmas means today,
Yet we were glad of what we had,
And shared our love a different way.

Though I see it all in his sweet face,
The love, peace and goodwill,
I know the spirit hasn't died,
Christmas is Christmas still.

By A. Johnson

IF anyone had asked Molly about Red, she would have said, almost truthfully, that she hadn't thought of him in years.

Yet, when he turned to close the door and began to walk, tall and straight, towards the reception desk, she felt the blush rise from her neck to her forehead. He'd had this effect on her before, all those years ago, when she was only 18.

" 'Evenin', ma'am." The soft, deep southern voice jolted her memory. "I'd like a room for a few nights."

Molly found herself wondering if he was still known as 'Red' Grierson, now that his once-thick, burnished hair had dulled to grey. Yet, the grey suited him. He was still a handsome man.

"Er, ma'am?"

Molly looked up and drew a long, deep breath to steady her nerves. He

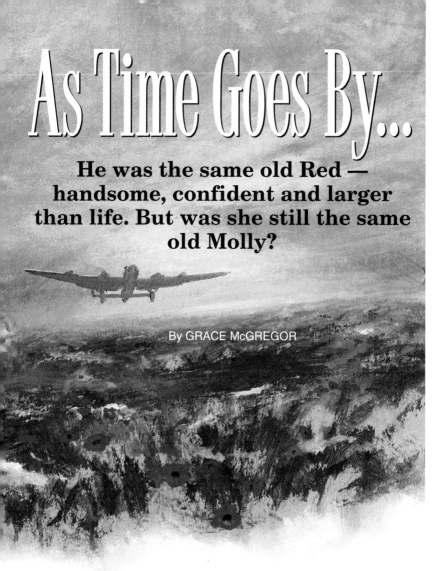

As Time Goes By...

He was the same old Red — handsome, confident and larger than life. But was she still the same old Molly?

By GRACE McGREGOR

didn't recognise her. Possibly, he didn't even remember her. Perhaps that was better considering she was plump now — cuddly, according to her granddaughter, Susan — and 58!

It was better that he should have forgotten how desperately she had loved him. Had she really been only 18, then?

"Yes, of course." Molly lifted a key from its hook. "Perhaps you would like to see the room, first? Will you want dinner?"

"I know the room will be fine," he said, giving her a warm smile and signing the register.

Later, Molly stood by the dining-room door, chatting to departing guests. She was so glad they'd enjoyed their meal and yes, her son-in-law was a marvellous chef. It was true, too, that her granddaughter, at catering college, was shaping up to be just as good.

Yes, lovely evening for a stroll. Yes, the hills *did* look their best at this time of day. Thank you. Good night. Good night.

At last, when everyone else had gone, she went over to where he sat. "May I get you something, Mr Grierson? More coffee, perhaps?"

He looked at her, thoughtfully. Then he looked down at his large, tanned hand, lying flat on the white tablecloth. Slowly, he lifted his hand. Beneath it, lay a ragged-edged studio portrait of an 18-year-old girl. He gazed up at its 58-year-old counterpart. Stunned, Molly gazed back, her mind filled with memories.

How young she had been — and how vulnerable. They had been so gloriously in love and Molly could still remember Red's parting words as she had given him her picture. "It'll be the closest thing to my heart," he'd vowed, "till you come to take its place.

"We'll marry the instant this war's over, honey. You know, you're gonna love the States."

"I'll miss my Scottish hills," she'd murmured into his drab olive jacket.

"Oh, we've got a couple of mountains back home!" He'd grinned in that boyish way that always caught at her heart — the way he was grinning now.

"Mr Grierson? You never used to be so formal, Molly," he said. She smiled back. "Hello, Red."

The house, later, was buzzing with excitement at this turn of events.

"Mum's old sweetheart turning up on the doorstep after forty years." Doreen, Molly's daughter, was incredulous. "I think that's so romantic. Jack, don't you think that's really romantic?"

"If you say so, pet. But surely, Ma, he didn't expect to find you still in the same hotel?"

"Well, no. But he did think it might be a good place to start making enquiries."

"And he hit the jackpot first go!"

"You see," Molly explained, "he retired last year and went to live in Florida. He's a widower . . ."

"Oh, yes!" Doreen said, knowingly, but Molly ploughed on regardless.

". . . and his two sons and daughter, Debra, with whom he seems to be close, are married. Now he lives alone in a condo-something or other."

"Condominium," Jack prompted, "which is American for a block of flats."

"And his is slap bang up against the ocean. Sunshine, golden sands, lots of other retired people and lots of clubs they all seem to belong to."

"Get on with the story, Mum," Doreen interrupted her impatiently.

"Well, with having a lot of time on his hands, he finally decided to come on a sort of pilgrimage to the places he'd been during the war. And, as this was his favourite place — he spent all his leaves here when your grandparents ran the hotel and I helped out — he . . ."

"Came back to find the girl he'd left behind," Doreen finished for her. "I could've been a little Yank. Only then I wouldn't have met you, Jack," Doreen hastily amended.

"You were just lucky," Jack assured her solemnly and winked at his mother-in-law. Molly giggled; she had an infectious laugh. "But I wonder you recognised him again, Mum. I don't suppose you've given him a thought in years!"

"Oh, you never forget your first love," she said lightly.

Nor the pain when you walked alone among bleak hills that had once smiled on you and your love. Nor the sick despair each day, when the postman shook his head sadly.

"Don't fret, lass," he would say. "Men are awful poor at letter-writing." But his words hadn't healed Molly's hurt.

She well remembered how their romance had begun all those years ago.

The soldiers had come on a 10-day-leave pass to her parents' small tourist hotel; three wise-cracking, quaintly courteous, handsome young men. They were as dazzlingly different from the lads she had grown up with as birds of paradise are from grey pigeons.

In no time at all her parents and their sprinkling of elderly guests were totally captivated, loving the young soldiers' attempts to talk 'Scatch,' and warmed by their sincere praise of the beautiful surrounding countryside.

In no time, Red had been rechristened 'Ginger' and had been assured that, with his colouring, he was *bound* to have a wee bit of Scots blood in him!

"I believe my gran'pa hailed from these parts, but I haven't any folk here that I know of. Leastways, not yet," he added, smiling at Molly. She'd turned away so that he shouldn't see the blush rise from her neck to her forehead.

And when Red told her, in his beautiful, drawling voice that he was a "southern boy," she'd known exactly what he meant.

Hadn't she taken a bus into town the year before, to see 'Gone With The Wind?' Hadn't she wept and yearned with Rhett, Scarlett and Ashley?

When Red showed her a picture of his 'mom' standing in a big, untidy garden that he called a yard, she knew that, just beyond the camera range, would be a magnolia tree, covered in white blossom, a white house with wedding cake columns and a long, white veranda.

Arms entwined, Molly and Red had strolled by peaty burns. With her leading the way, they'd clambered up hills to fall — laughing and breathless — on the summit. The heather had scratched her bare legs, the sun shone and the air was crisp and clean as an apple — and they had fallen in love.

Her parents and the sprinkling of elderly guests had envied them their youth — and their love.

By the time of Red's third pass, he was, as a prospective-member of the family, allowed to take the noisy old mower over the lawn, fetch a scuttleful of coal and help in the tiny bar.

"Such a thoughtful lad," her mother would say fondly, when he had presented her with a parcel of some rare goodies.

"Sensible young chap that," her father would declare after Red had listened respectfully to the old man's recipe for bringing the war to a speedy conclusion.

Molly hardly ever thought now about Alex, the quiet, dependable village boy with the gentle sense of fun, who had always been sweet on her, but who was now fighting in Italy with his regiment.

But then Red, too, was posted with his company to the war in Europe.

The oddly-marked envelopes that soon started arriving almost daily renewed his vows of love and his longing for her. But, as the weeks passed, the flood of letters gradually dried to a trickle and then finally stopped.

"There's a war on, Molly," her father had said. "Ginger's got more to do than sit scribbling letters!" Her mother had been brisk, too. "I always say what's for you, won't go by you. I just wish we knew whether he's alive or not."

When the war had finally ended, Alex, looking much older, came home in a greenish-grey demob suit. In spite of all that he had seen and done he had not lost his gentle sense of fun: and he was still sweet on Molly – a fact which her mother and father did not fail to notice.

"Alex's a fine lad: you could do worse," her father pointed out.

Her mother was more forceful. "What's past is over and done with. Do you want to end up an old maid?"

When they eventually married, the whole village came to their wedding.

But still, occasionally, when the dishwasher broke down, or a guest was particularly difficult, or the rain-drenched hills depressed her spirits, she would dream of a magnolia tree covered in white blossom and of a white house with wedding cake columns and a long, white veranda . . . .

HE'LL have asked you out?" Doreen's insistent voice brought Molly back to the present.

"I'm spending the day with him tomorrow, then dinner in town in the evening."

"Sounds good!"

"I can't imagine what we'll find to talk about for so long."

Next day, as Red drove along roads that had scarcely changed in 40 years, Molly sat in silence, feeling very ill-at-ease. She wished she could think of some clever, amusing things to say to this still handsome man who had come so far to see her.

"Hey!" The sudden exclamation made Molly jump. "Isn't that the little creek, no, whaddya call it, a burn, that you waded across one time? I had sense enough not to want to cross it till you called me a scaredy cat. Only then did I give in and wade across. It was freezing and I hadn't rolled up my pant legs far enough, either, and they got wet! You just laughed at me!"

"You always hated being laughed at," she teased.

After that, it was easy – there was so much to remember.

In fact, it was a whole, wonderful week to remember. They spent a day in Edinburgh, where she dug into her memory for scraps of half-digested history and Red bought a tartan bonnet in a Princes Street shop and – to her dismay – insisted on wearing it.

They toured the Highlands, inspected stately homes and sampled a Jacobean dinner, followed by what Red called 'a floor-show'.

And they spent a great deal of time just saying to each other, "Do you remember the time when we both . . .?"

"I think he still fancies you," Doreen declared abruptly one day while stacking a pile of dirty breakfast dishes. "Flowers every day, chocolates and other presents."

"Don't be silly, dear. Americans are like that."

"Why shouldn't he fancy you?" Jack broke his journey to the deep freeze to give her a warm hug. "You're still a very pretty lady and a very nice one – for a mother-in-law," he added, with a wicked twinkle in his eye.

"All I am," Molly explained carefully, "is part of what Red calls his 'skedule'. After all, why shouldn't he want to see this place again? The pair of you can stop looking at each other in that way. Red and I are nothing more than old friends."

But all too soon it was their very last evening together and they'd decided to dine out. The nice young waiter had been friendly and obliging. Now, the mirror in the powder room told her that her grey eyes were sparkling and alive, her dark brown hair shining with health.

"Not bad for fifty-eight," she told her reflection before returning to their table. But the smile she exchanged with Red was a little wistful. She would miss him.

"I was such a fool!" Red burst out suddenly.

Molly stared, unsure of how she should handle this.

"The biggest fool on earth when I walked out on you forty years ago!"

"We did wonder what had become of you. Mum and Dad would have liked to know you were safe. They were very fond of you."

"And you?"

"You knew how I felt," she said quietly.

He spread his hands almost helplessly. "Blame the war, Molly. Plus bad advice from a coupla guys who had married British girls, and it hadn't worked out. Scotland was a long way away. Beautiful, but not real. Just like you, Molly."

"Oh, I was real enough. And unhappy enough."

"I went back to college after I got home and then I got married. Lynn was a fine wife and by rights I shoulda forgotten about you.

"But I never did. I only had to close my eyes and I'd see you standing there listening so patiently while one of them little old lady residents groused about what the rations were doing to her bad stomach. And, so help me, I'd often wish that Lynn was you."

"Poor Lynn," Molly whispered, suddenly feeling sorry for this unknown woman.

"You didn't waste too much time grieving," Red added, almost accusingly. "You soon married somebody else. What was your husband like?"

"Oh, everybody loved Alex. When he died three years ago, the whole village mourned."

"Did you love him?"

"When I married Alex," she said, twisting the rings on her wedding finger, "I liked him better than anyone else, but I was still in love with you. Then . . ."

"Poor kid," Red murmured. "But, if you only knew the number of times I've sat in my office in Atlanta and wished myself back here. And, any hour of the day or night, all it took to make me think of you was this tune. Remember, honey?"

Before Molly could stop him, Red launched into song. "I'll be seeing you," he crooned, reaching across the table to take her hand, "In all the old, familiar places."

It was all too much for Molly. She hung her head so that Red shouldn't see the flush of embarrassment rise from her neck to her forehead.

When Molly finally dared to look up gain, she saw the same nice young waiter standing nearby, inclining his head to listen to the crooner.

She pressed her lips tightly together but it was no use. Laughter burst from both of them in paroxysms of gasps, gurgles and streaming eyes and soon became louder and more uncontrolled.

When it was all over, when the nice young waiter had rushed to proffer the glass of wine by her plate and urged her to try a sip, Molly was suddenly ashamed. "I've always been a giggler," she said apologetically.

"Nobody likes being laughed at," Red said stiffly.

"Oh, my dear, I wasn't laughing at you; I was laughing at the idea of anyone singing love songs to an old lass like me and laughing because I'm happy."

"That's what I want to talk to you about, honey. So let's get out of here, shall we?"

RED turned the steering wheel to the left and the car joggled for a hundred yards along the farm track before he switched off the engine. Molly wound down her window and surveyed the night faintly lit by a cloud-shaded moon.

"The final night of my very last pass was a night just like this," he murmured romantically, taking Molly in his arms.

Molly was deep in thought. What would we have found to talk about, she wondered suddenly, if there had been no memories?

"You said back there," Red went on, "that you'd never forget this week. What I've been thinking is, we could have a whole lot of weeks to remember . . . if you decided to come back to the States with me."

"Come back with you? You mean on holiday?"

"I mean for a long, long vacation that will last for the rest of our lives. I've thought it all out.

"We'd have a quiet wedding right here in the village. I'd wire Debra, my daughter, to fly over and watch her pa marry his old sweetheart. You'll like Debra. She's smart as paint. You'd find her very useful, Molly. She'd keep you right and help you adjust to our way of life."

Adjust, Molly thought, easing herself out of his arms. Did he mean learn to say drapes when she meant curtains? To call a lift an elevator? And to share the rest of her life with a man who was, she suspected, despite his recent lapse into song, just a little too careful of his dignity?

Forty years ago, she would've adjusted eagerly. But now?

"Dear Ginger," she said kindly, "you forget that I've spent all my life in my little village. My roots go very deep – I doubt if they'd transplant successfully. I don't fancy living in a condo-whatsit and I've never been much of a one for clubs.

"I'm not very used to hot weather, either. But, most important of all . . . I don't love you."

"Honey," he said, with a shadow of the grin that had once caught her heart, "all that sweet talk about love is for the kids.

"I'm lonely, Molly, and I'm very fond of you. You're part of a period in my life that, in spite of the war, was enjoyable.

"You weren't in love with your husband, but you seemed to make out all right." The look on Molly's face suddenly silenced Red.

"You didn't let me finish telling you about Alex, did you? I was such a silly girl when I married him, but a very lucky one, too. Because, within a few short weeks of our wedding, I found myself deeply and wonderfully in love with him.

"All of our years together were full of sun and laughter and of quiet happiness. I'm not sure that could happen a second time or that I would want it to.

"Be happy with your memories, my dear, and be happy that once we were in love . . ."

PUSHING aside the curtains of her bedroom window some time later, Molly stepped on to the little balcony. The moon had ridden out the clouds and now hung like a silver shilling over the black hills. The air was crisp and clean as an apple.

She drew a deep, contented breath.

She knew that, on days when the dishwasher broke down, or a guest was difficult, or the rain-drenched hills depressed her spirits, she might still dream of a magnolia tree covered in white blossom, and of a white house with wedding cake columns and a long veranda – and of a handsome young soldier.

But, most of all, she would remember the gentle humour and kindness of the man she'd loved above all others – Alex. ∎

It's Christmas

It's Christmas time, ring out the
bells,
Of joy, goodwill and cheer,
It's Christmas time, the year's
near done,
But first it's time for Christmas
fun!

It's Christmas time, light up the
lights,
Of hope, good health and peace,
It's Christmas time, the year's
near through,
But first we've got so much to do.

It's Christmas time, open up your
hearts,
To all those that you love,
It's Christmas time, the year's
complete,
And we are all with love replete.

By
Teresa Ashby

Home

The sun comes up to warm the
heather,
And the wind sweeps in from the
west,
But I don't mind about the
weather,
Because home is the place that I
love best.

I've seen this place in all its
splendour,
And I've seen it at its worst,
But the sight of it's enough to
render,
My full heart fit to burst.

It's always been my home, this
place,
Though I've travelled far and
near,
But I will always set my face,
To bring me right back here.

By
Teresa Ashby

Spring

On long winter nights when dark
closes in,
And the mornings are cold and
gloomy and dim,
I close my eyes and think of
spring,
When flowers bloom and the birds
all sing.

The colours in the garden so
bright,
The long, long evenings so warm
and light,
And the sky so clear, cloudless
and blue,
And every green in every hue.

When the little birds busily
gather food,
In order to feed their growing
brood,
And butterflies alight on colourful
flowers,
What better way to spend the
hours?

So when it's cold and the nights
are long,
And I long to hear a bird's happy
song,
I close my eyes and think of
spring.
When flowers bloom and the birds
all sing.

By
Teresa Ashby

SMALL BEGINNINGS

While some young hopefuls are about to make their maiden flight, Gideon remembers one unforeseen arrival at Croft Douglas, who taught him that good things do come in small parcels . . .

ON the high rocky hill behind our house, the ravens are now flying in playful family outings together.

Mum and Dad lead their four well-grown youngsters in formation, with a perfect take-off and glide into the western air space.

This is in mutual agreement with the peregrines who have also nested in the rocky crags of Creag Mhor, on a lower ledge to the east.

They are also more than busily engaged in giving their sturdy chicks flying lessons.

The youngsters still have silky spikes of baby down sticking out between their fast-growing feathers, and haven't yet learned the meaning of fear as they dance from one leg to the other in anticipation of their first flight into the great unknown.

The peregrines and ravens have come to another agreement, a defence pact if danger threatens either family.

The parent birds take off together to unitedly defend their territory if it is suddenly subjected to an aerial attack from determined predators.

These are mostly black hooded crows, who normally have nothing but evil revolving around in their minds, and gigantic black-backed gulls with a huge wingspan, that have come in from the sea for a change of scenery and food.

IN the peregrine family, the falcon is the female and her mate is called the tiercel.

She is the bigger, more dominant bird and, like a lionness, is the main provider for her mate and family.

The estimated speed of a plummeting peregrine, descending to destroy its prey, has been timed at a breathtaking 180 miles an hour!

Good gamekeepers maintain that a pair of peregrine falcons is essential to the well-being of a grouse moor, simply because the slow-flying or sickly bird is always the first to be selected and fall prey to the peregrine's strike, thus helping ensure that future families of red grouse will be healthy and disease-free.

MOST of our many visitors liken the Highland cattle calves to teddy-bears. Usually I don't agree because, in comparison with teddies, our calves are too long in the hair!

But we did have one very special one who was born prematurely and did, in fact, resemble a cuddly bear.

Highland cows and heifers, by living outside all the year round on a wholly natural diet, very rarely have any trouble when it comes to calving.

At seven years old, Stiallach, "The Striped One", knew what giving birth was all about and it had been a joyful experience for her up till now, but this time she was definitely in difficulty.

I took her, at a gentle pace, to a pen in the paddock and called the vet.

He wasn't long in coming and immediately gave his diagnosis, saying, "I'm afraid this cow is carrying a dead calf. She must have received a blow of some kind."

This was very bad news, and the vet went on with the business of retrieving a pathetic, limp little body.

Seeing my grave expression, he announced, "Cheer up! You've still got your cow and she's looking better already, although I'll just make one last check."

That's when the vet knitted his brows together thoughtfully.

Then, "There's something else in here," he gasped, "and it's still alive!"

He then proved it by producing the smallest Highland calf I had ever seen, with only little damp curls covering its tiny body.

"You'll have to knit a woolly jersey for this one," the vet said jokingly, then added more seriously, "Take care of that little calf. It could help to pay my bill and leave you a lot of change."

The vet was right. Teddy, as we called this tiny calf, grew like a mushroom on a warm moist morning and made his mark in life when selected as a stock bull by a prominent Perthshire breeder for his pedigree fold.

When he reached his new home, I had no time to wish Teddy "Good Luck" because he was suddenly surrounded by a circle of beautiful Highland heifers, all wanting to cuddle him. He looked so happy I stopped watching and tip-toed away. ■

WAITING FOR SANDRA

By ELIZABETH ASHCROFT

She had never felt so alone, pacing the house in the middle of the night. Then she realised she wasn't the only one . . .

JENNIFER shifted restlessly and pushed a leg out from under the duvet. Suddenly she was hot. On the bedside table the clock shone luminously, green figures ghostly in the dark. Ten minutes to twelve.

It was too bad, she fumed anxiously. Sandra should have been home by 11.30. She'd promised. And Cliff, lying heavily at her side, just a mound of flower-sprigged duvet, didn't seem to care. Yet she knew he wasn't asleep.

He'd climbed wearily upstairs to bed half an hour ago, eyes tight with strain after a long sales conference.

"Got to get some sleep," he'd muttered, pushing arms into his pyjama jacket and buttoning it up crookedly.

Sitting slumped on the edge of the bed, minus the horn-rimmed glasses and with his dark hair ruffled, he had looked, briefly, like the 25-year-old she had married. Not the 40-year-old, weighed down with business worries, an incipient ulcer, and a mortgage.

He's smiled blindly at her.

"Come to bed, Jen, love. Sandy's old enough to look after herself now."

She had left the window, pretending she hadn't been surreptitiously peering down the road, eerie in its darkness, and glared disbelievingly at him. How could he always be so unconcerned?

"It's snowing!" Surely even he must acknowledge that such freak weather conditions for the time of year were worrying.

Initially, she'd felt a childish elation. The world was always different when it snowed; a fresher, more innocent world, where strangers greeted one another and children lurked behind hedges armed with lethal snowballs.

"So?" His voice was ragged now and she'd felt a pang of dismay. Was she making a fuss about nothing? Had she grown into a fussing, nagging mum without realising it? But she *was* worried.

Cliff had fallen into bed, heaving the duvet clumsily over him. Irritation had touched her. He always stole it all, so she was left cold and goose-pimpled on her side of the bed before she dragged it back over herself.

"You've taken all the duvet," she'd said tightly.

"Come and cuddle up, then, love." He seemed suddenly to come awake, grinning at her, and she'd felt herself begin to tense again.

"Cliff, it's snowing! Sandra's out with that new boy. On a motorbike."

"I know." His grin had faded and he sighed heavily.

"He seemed a nice kid. Even brought her a helmet. And Sandy's a sensible girl, you know that. It's not even late, by her standards. Stop worrying, for goodness' sake! She's nearly seventeen!"

He *had* seemed a nice boy, Jennifer remembered now. Standing awkwardly in her neat suburban sitting-room, alien in black leather, like some strange insect in the shining helmet and goggles, till Sandra nudged him, giggling.

"Paul! Mum wants to see you, idiot! Take off the goggles at least!"

Flushing, he'd fumbled with them, and removed the helmet, showing himself to be dark eyed, and dark haired, rather long side-burns for a young man his age. Perhaps it was a new trend.

She'd felt a pang of something like nostalgia for times past, when she had been the daughter showing off a strange new boyfriend to cautious, almost suspicious parents.

"Hello, Paul." His hand had been firm, warm, his smile shy, self-conscious. "Take care of her, won't you?" She knew she'd made a mistake even as she spoke. Sandra flashed a scornful glance at her, and frowned slightly.

Cliff had spoken drowsily from the chair, where he'd waved causally to Paul. "He will. Don't fuss, love."

How does he know, she'd wondered indignantly, watching the two of them go laughing carelessly down the drive to the enormous, shining machine.

She'd watched them roar off up the road, heart in mouth, sighing with relief as Sandy's arms snaked round him to hold on firmly.

NOW she sat up on the edge of the bed. It was no use — she couldn't sleep. But she daren't tell Cliff that — he would be angry. He thought she worried unnecessarily. But didn't you have to worry these days, with daughters, she thought crossly — especially with pretty ones?

"I'm going to make myself some hot chocolate," she said carefully. "Would you like some?"

"No." His eyes widened, unguarded without the glasses. "You only want an excuse to go down and wait for her."

Trapped, she went silently downstairs in her woolly dressing-gown and slippers. She poured milk into the pan and stood at the kitchen table, waiting for it to simmer. Simon, the cat, walked daintily round her, making purring noises deep down in his throat.

Cliff just doesn't understand, Jennifer thought. He thinks all young men are the way he was and still is: decent — such an old-fashioned word for kind, honest. It had taken him weeks to even get up the courage to kiss her.

But that was a long time ago, in another age, she thought, spooning the rich brown powder on top of simmering milk. Suddenly hungry, she took a biscuit from the tin and went back upstairs, to find Cliff had turned out the light, and was snoring gently.

So now, she thought indignantly, I have to crawl into bed and drink my chocolate in the dark. Cliff, who used to play tennis all weekend, dig the garden, paint the house, now began yawning the minute they finished supper. But then, she consoled herself, touching his back briefly, he's working harder, has more responsibility, and he's older.

We're both of us getting older, that's all. What a terrifying thought, when inside she still felt young, unsure of herself, as she had done at 16.

She sat in the darkened bedroom sipping chocolate.

Outside there was an odd silence. A winter snow silence, into which there came the slow, muffled sound of a car engine, the scrunch of tyres in deepening snow.

It must be coming down heavily, she thought, sliding down on the pillow, tugging at the duvet. Somehow Cliff had wrapped it round himself, and in the tugging he half woke, growled in protest. She huddled down, still wide awake.

If only she would come home . . .

Always there was an excuse. A car had broken down, she'd missed a bus, they'd got lost, or lost track of time.

Last time, she'd even admitted it.

"I'm sorry, Mum. I just forgot the time. We were talking."

Flushed, scarf thrown casually twice round her neck and dangling to her knees, she looked starry-eyed. Jennifer, with a nagging, tense headache, had exploded.

"Then next time, miss, you just remember the time! While you live under this roof you'll keep to the rules and come home when we say you will come home!"

"When *you* say!" Mutinously she glowered at Jennifer. "Dad doesn't make such a fuss! He doesn't go on and on about me being a bit late! If you're not careful, I won't stay under your roof, so there!"

Childishly she'd run upstairs, leaving Jennifer trembling, staring at Cliff who had appeared in the hall, eyes aghast.

"Jen, she's *ten* minutes late!"

"She has a watch," she'd said tightly. "She can use it. She's still at school, Cliff."

It was odd, she thought, that Cliff just didn't seem to worry about his only daughter the way she did.

"She's a sensible kid," he said before the first date not so long ago. "She can look after herself."

"That's not what worries me," she'd replied. "It's the boys. They're so different, so casual, nowadays."

Now the phone rang two or three times a week; strange, immature but masculine voices asked for her. She bought odd, colourful clothes, sweaters down to her knees in vivid colours. Football socks, brightly-striped.

Bizarre, Jennifer thought she looked, but Cliff laughed.

"Didn't you go through that phase, at her age?"

But she never had. She watched dismayed as Sandra appeared with silky brown hair pulled sharply back from her forehead and cheeks, tied with huge, colourful ribbons.

Cliff liked it all; delighted in taking out the new, sparkly Sandra.

But Jennifer distrusted it. She felt her sensible daughter sliding away from her, even envied her in a melancholy way.

JUST 17, she mused in the dark, listening to Cliff breathing next to her, what a wonderful age; you're immortal, none of the aches and pains of the passing years, no straggly grey hairs or deepening wrinkles . . . Not like me. She knew she was feeling sorry for herself.

"Sandra Mary Wilson," she whispered into the darkness, "you should be home."

The green figures on the clock shouted at her, 12.15.

She turned to Cliff, stretched out a hand, then pulled it back.

He was tired, had to be up early. She would go downstairs again and wait a little.

Here, with him, she was restless, would wake him. Downstairs she could roam through the house, make another drink, even talk to the cat. Anything to make time pass till Sandra came home.

She stumbled downstairs, turned up the central heating and felt a welcome blast of warm air round her feet.

In the sitting-room the cat greeted her with mild disbelief then muted joy, kneading her shoulder as she picked him up and went to the window.

Whiteness met her eyes, thick snow whirling across the garden, clinging to hedge, shrubs, and the lone fir tree. No sign of traffic, no living thing.

They're held up somewhere, she tried to comfort herself, noting, distractedly, that she'd put slippers on odd feet.

In the mirror by the door she looked haunted; dark-eyed, tousle-haired, a witch with her familiar cat on her shoulder.

Down the road came a light. Two lights. A car, slithering on loose snow as yet untouched. Her breath went out in a sigh; rage suddenly burned.

It was now 12.30. Sandra had no right to do this to her. It was the latest she'd ever been.

Hadn't she heard of the telephone, couldn't she have phoned, if they'd been delayed? She realised she was trembling with anger and foreboding.

Why didn't Cliff care enough to stay awake, to help her, comfort her? He'd know whether to phone the police or not — her hand stretched out to the phone, hesitated.

"An hour late?" they'd ask, disbelief in their voice. She heard a sound at the door, turned.

Cliff stood there, rumpled, peering short-sightedly at her. For once he'd forgotten his glasses. He blinked in the light, rubbing stubbly beginnings of a bearded chin.

"Not in yet?" Anxiety sharp in his voice. He glanced at the clock, frowning in annoyance. "I can't see — what's the time?"

"Nearly one o'clock." She faltered. "Cliff, do you think we should phone the police? The snow — it's very bad."

"Snow or not, she could have phoned." Uncharacteristically his voice was harsh. She stared, surprised. "She must know we'd be worried by now."

"You? Worried?" Startled, she met his eyes. He nodded, frowning, angry.

"Of course I worry, Jen. I've been awake ever since you came downstairs, worrying. But I try not to show it. *You're* bad enough." He grinned slightly, suddenly strode to her side, staring out at the driving snow.

"Good grief! I had no idea it was so bad. Jen, where did they go, have you any idea?"

"Some disco or other," she said vaguely. "A new one, out on the by-pass."

Suddenly she was overwhelmingly glad that he'd come downstairs, so grateful for his company, even if his concern increased her own.

"I know the one." He was businesslike, the office Cliff, not the home Cliff she knew.

"The kids in the office go there, Jen. I'm going to see if I can find them. Maybe they've broken down."

"But, Cliff!" She followed him to the hall, watched him struggle into a duffle coat with disbelief. "Cliff, you can't! You might even get stuck yourself! Cliff —"

He was impatient, hopping on one foot, pulling on waterproof trousers over his pyjamas.

"Look, Jen, it's not too far — they're probably just marooned at the disco. I'll just fetch them home, OK?" He struggled into his woollen coat.

"You haven't got your glasses!" she wailed ridiculously.

He crammed an old fur hat on his head and fumbled in his coat pocket for car keys.

"Fetch them for me, will you? While I'm getting out the car you can phone the disco —"

She ran upstairs, near tears, grabbed the glasses, ran to the telephone directory. "What's it called? What's the disco called?"

He frowned, hooking the glasses round his ears, becoming familiar once more. "Can't think, Jen, don't bother. And don't worry. She'll be all right, I promise."

"Then why?" she demanded, "are you careering off in the middle of the night in your pyjamas in a snowstorm?" This was Cliff, her husband who didn't worry.

"Be back soon." He cut her short, kissed her nose and disappeared through the front door. She saw him bend low against the wind, struggling to open the garage doors. Heard the car engine whine reluctantly, grind to a halt, whine again then begin churning busily.

The car backed slowly down the drive slipping sideways on reaching the road. Jennifer leaned forward, peering into the snow. Two figures were stumbling down the road. One tall, bulky, with an arm round the smaller.

"Cliff!" she screamed through the open door, wind whipping at her words and snowflakes billowing into the warmth of the hall, melting at her feet, on her dressing-gown. "Cliff, I think that's Sandy!"

But he'd seen them. Already he was getting out of the car, staggering towards them. Then the three figures met and headed towards the house.

She swallowed hard, suddenly realising that Cliff did indeed care for his daughter, very much. He just didn't show it the same way she did.

Cliff's caring came in a different way, in the care with which he chose birthday presents, Christmas presents, drove Sandy to school on a rainy day, mended her bike when she had a puncture or the brakes were slow.

Suddenly she remembered when Sandy caught measles and how he'd stayed up with her all night. Jennifer had found him next morning asleep in the wicker chair, hunched uncomfortably, clutching a teddy bear to his middle, glasses slipping down his nose.

He might say Sandy's a sensible girl, she thought wryly. He might tell me not to worry, but deep down Cliff worries just as much as I do.

AND now she was home. Jennifer held the door wide, caught Sandy's arm as she staggered wearily into the hall, covered in snow.

Paul stopped a little behind her, looking awkward, unhappy. For a second Jennifer was so relieved she could find no words. Then suddenly Sandy broke the silence.

"Dad? What were you *doing*?" The girl stared wide-eyed at her father.

He grinned shame-facedly. "Uh, coming to see if I could find you, love. Your mother —" He flushed slightly. "Your mother was worried."

Liar, she thought, smiling to herself. She looked at him, crumpled, bearded, not caring how he looked so long as Sandy was safe.

"Dad was worried too, Sandy," she said calmly. "We do worry when you're late. But I don't suppose you could help it, on a night like this."

Paul rubbed a hand across pale cheeks. "The bike broke down, Mrs Wilson. And we couldn't phone because the lines are down. I'm sorry — very sorry."

For a moment he seemed incredibly young and ingenuous, and she knew suddenly that she could trust Sandy with Paul anywhere, any time.

"Sandy insisted on walking home," he went on softly. "She said you'd worry." Jennifer touched Sandy's cheek, silently begging forgiveness, then spoke briskly.

"Hot drinks all round. And then Cliff will run you home, Paul, it's the least we can do."

Cliff shot her a resigned glance, smiled agreement at Paul and followed her out to the kitchen.

She poured more milk into the pot, brought out four mugs, and spooned chocolate into them.

Cliff watched her, smile broadening.

"Told you she was a sensible girl," he said smugly, and she smiled back at him.

She'd known that all the time, really. But a mother couldn't help worrying, now could she?

And at least she and Cliff could worry together — now she'd found him out at last . . . ■

THE LADY REGRETS...

Her penfriend's letters meant everything to her — until the day he wrote to say he was coming to meet her ...

By Phyllis Demaine

JESSICA put the letter aside and turned her chair round to look at the photograph on the shelf.

It showed a girl whose long, brown hair tumbled about the shoulders of her crimson blouse.

She was smiling, her eyes bright, her red lips parted over even, white teeth, one hand raised to tug nervously at her left ear. It was a habit Jessica had never been able to cure, and the day the photo was taken she'd been particularly nervous.

She remembered how the photographer had teased her.

"What's a pretty girl like you to be nervous about? You should see some of the subjects I've to deal with.

"The camera never lies, they say. Huh! Well, that's a lie for a start. You can make a bad-tempered old harridan look pleasant, if you know how.

"Now, you just relax, be yourself," he had told her. "In your case the camera doesn't need to lie."

But it had lied, Jessica thought, reaching once more for the letter. Or rather it hadn't told the whole truth.

It hadn't, for instance, shown the narrow arm of the chair where her elbow rested as her fingers reached for her ear.

It hadn't shown the straight back of that chair, and certainly not the wheels which made it possible for it, and her, to move about.

But was that lying? Was it lying to hide the truth as she had?

But there was never an opportunity to tell Tim, she argued, not once she'd posted that first letter. How could she have told him?

Perhaps she should have added it to the list of interests she'd written on the application form to the pen-pal club when she'd begun it all.

Reading, sketching, writing letters, riding around in a wheelchair.

Or perhaps she should have mentioned it when Tim first wrote and asked what she looked like.

Brown hair, hazel eyes, five foot three . . . when I stand up, only I can't stand up any more. At least not without support.

Perhaps, as their letters continued to fly backwards and forwards, she could have dropped it casually into their talk of favourite foods.

Steak, of course. Yes, rare. And fresh strawberries. No, no cream, because I don't get enough exercise.

There might have been an opportunity when Tim wrote of the cycling holiday he'd enjoyed in Holland.

Sounds fun, maybe I'll come along next time. I have my own two-wheeled transport.

Jessica sighed. She could never have written any of these things, if only because they would have sounded bitter. And she wasn't bitter, not really . . .

The accident could have been worse, much worse. She could have been completely paralysed, or disfigured, or brain damaged.

You could have been dead, she told herself, and smiled wryly, remembering the anecdote someone had told her in an effort to keep her sane during those first, dark days. The one about the elderly man who, when asked if he disliked growing old, had replied, "Well, it beats the alternative."

But there should have been a way to tell Tim.

I should have told him in that first letter, honestly and without self-pity . . .

Yet, would there have been any more letters? And she had needed those letters, then more than now . . . or did she still need them?

But Tim would have written anyway, at least for a spell. He was kind, she'd discovered that over the months of correspondence.

But, I'd always have suspected his motives, examined every word, in case he was pitying me.

And I never expected this.

Her fingers flipped the pages of Tim's latest letter, and she lifted the companion photograph from the shelf and stared at the dark-haired young man who laughed out at her, his blue eyes seeming to mock her belligerence now.

"**W**HY couldn't you have stayed up in Scotland?" she questioned out loud. "Why did you take it into your head to come all this way to Cornwall?
"OK! I know! You said."
She picked up the letter, scanning its pages.

Legend has it that there's a place where the coastline is almost as rugged and beautiful as ours, he wrote. *And I know for a fact that some of the girls are just as bonnie!*

Jessica loved it when he occasionally introduced a Scottish word or phrase, knowing that he did it to make her smile.

Will he really be so Scottish, she thought, and tore her mind from the possibility of hearing him speak.

So I thought I'd come and see for myself, he had written. *And whilst I'm down that way I thought I might as well take tea with a young lady I know. You have been warned!*

Saturday the twenty-third, at three o'clock. Have the kettle on, and if you can provide some of those Cornish pasties I've heard so much about, I might see my way to eating one or two.

But remember, you'll be expected to eat our haggis when you come up, he'd joked.

When! Jessica's heart beat faster. Tim had written *when*, not *if*. What did that signify?

But what did the whole episode signify? The trip down here, his plans to come to Wheatley Manor? His wish that they should meet at last?

Oh, Tim, Tim! Why did you have to spoil everything? We were happy as we were, weren't we?

Well, I was . . . she considered. Yes, I was, she admonished her heart, which would insist on missing beats whenever she thought of meeting Tim and actually hearing him speaking the nonsense he wrote.

Of course I was happy, I never expected anything other than friendship from our letters.

Wasn't that what the advert had promised? A friend? Someone to write to, to exchange ideas with, to learn something of another person's life. To be lonely no longer.

That's all I wanted. A chance to gain a glimpse into someone else's world. Just to escape from my own a little — just to take me out of myself . . .

I wasn't looking for more. Not love, no, nothing like that. I know that can never be. I've come to terms with that.

I've directed my energies into my work, my creative instincts into my sketching and painting. I've done everything my doctors and psychologists suggested.

Isn't that enough? Must I be tormented now? Don't I deserve some peace?

It's not fair. It's not kind of you, Tim, to disturb me this way. I don't want to see you. I don't want to look at you, to touch your hand or to have you here, sitting across this table from me. Because then, when you know the truth and have gone away, I'll remember how it was to have you here.

And that would be too painful. But most of all, I don't want to see pity in your eyes.

Tears rolled slowly down Jessica's cheeks and she shook her head angrily, so that they scattered over the photos and made little grey splodges on Tim's letter. She *never* wept, now. Never!

"I won't see you," she cried out loud. "I'll be out. That's what I'll do. I'll go out for the whole day."

"He'll know you're avoiding meeting him, Jessica," Mrs Wardle, the sheltered accommodation superintendent, said quietly, when Jessica told her of Tim's impending visit, some days later.

"And surely when he sees this is part of the hospital he's going to ask questions?"

"He knows I work in the labs here. I told him that."

"He sounds a nice young fellow from what you've told me. I'm sure —" Mary Wardle began, but Jessica turned her chair savagely, wheeling herself across the room to stare out at the lawns and flowerbeds.

"Oh, he is!" The bitterness she'd worked so hard at coming to terms with almost seemed evident in her voice once more. "He's very nice. And very polite. Very well brought up altogether."

"Well then?"

"I don't want his politeness, or his kindness. I don't want to see him," she declared fiercely. And then more quietly, more controlled, "If you say I'm out he'll have to believe you. He'll go away.

"I'll write later and tell him I was called away, unavoidably. Isn't that the phrase people use? I could say I had to go to my mother, who was suddenly taken ill."

She turned back to face the superintendent, her eyes hopeful. "You could say that, tell him I'd been called away to . . . No, of course not. I told him my mother is dead.

"Something else. There must be something," she said desperately. But she'd told Tim too many details about her life for there to be any room for lies.

"I told him everything, everything but the one thing that matters," she said wryly, smiling crookedly up at Mrs Wardle.

Noting the return of something closer to Jessica's normal spirits, Mrs Wardle smiled.

"No matter what excuse you fabricate, my dear. I suspect he'll come back the next day, or he'll telephone. After coming all this way to see you," she said matter-of-factly, "I doubt if he'll return home before he has."

"He would," Jessica began, but knew it was a lie. Tim was coming to see *her*, whatever he said about the beauties of Cornwall.

"Then, then . . ." Jessica bit her bottom lip. "Please, will you tell him? About the accident and . . . this," she added, thumping the arm of her chair.

"That way he could simply go away, couldn't he? He wouldn't *need* to see me. He could go back home.

"And, well — maybe he'd still write to me. He could even pretend he never came here. And it would be just like it was before." She looked into Mary's kindly face with desperate eyes.

"It could, couldn't it?"

Mary watched the expressions flit across Jessica's face, read the fear and hope, and walked round her desk, to stand beside the young woman.

"All right, my dear," she said at last. "If that's the way you want it. I'll let your Tim into the secret."

"He isn't my Tim . . . at least I . . . No, of course he's not. We've never even met . . ."

She laid her cheek against the hand Mary had put on her shoulder. "Thanks, Mary. I'm sure that will be best."

Her hand went to the controls on her chair and she ran it swiftly to the door. There, with her back still to the superintendent, she spoke.

"And if he should — only if he asks where I am — I'll be in the garden," she told her hesitantly. "Maybe he'd like to say hello, you know. Maybe he would."

"I'll tell him, if he asks, and I'm sure . . ."

Jessica hadn't waited to hear what Mary was so sure about and as she sat in the gardens of Wheatley Manor the following Saturday, she was glad she hadn't lingered.

She knew she had been right to do it this way.

She'd given Tim the choice. And if he did want to say hello, well then, that would be fine with her.

But it was better this way, and she was glad she wouldn't be there when Tim learned about her stupid legs, and the wheelchair, and the pulleys over the bath, and all the other paraphernalia being a paraplegic necessitated.

She was glad she wouldn't see the look in Tim's eyes, that hastily-veiled look which not even the kindest person could suppress.

And Tim was kind.

Involuntarily her eyes went to her watch. Almost three!

Tim would be walking up the drive now, his long legs covering the distance easily. He'd be looking about him, interested in everything, because that was the way he was and also because this was her background.

He'd be remembering the things she'd written about Wheatley. Old George who swept the paths and berated the very birds for dropping their feathers.

Jessica had described how the old man would stand, shaking his fist up at the sky where the birds circled derisively.

Four minutes past three!

He wouldn't be late, not Tim. He had a thing about promptness.

One of the auxiliaries would be leading him towards Mary's room now. Jessica hoped it would be Susan. Susan was very pretty and very young, with a trim waist and long legs. She knew Tim would smile at her, winning her approval.

When Susan stood aside to let him pass into the office she wouldn't be at all surprised if Tim didn't wink, making Susan giggle behind her hand.

Jessica brought her own hand to her mouth, the knuckles gleaming white as she pressed them against her trembling lips.

She wouldn't think of what Mary must be saying. Wouldn't let herself imagine the look on Tim's face. She wouldn't think of it. She wouldn't!

Jessica closed her eyes tightly, squeezing them shut like a child does, so that the blackness was peppered with tiny points of light.

If you concentrated you could make the dots move, making patterns. Jessica concentrated very hard.

Then, somewhere, gravel grated under someone's feet and Jessica's eyes shot open, colour flooding her face at the thought that old George might come across her sitting there like an idiot with her eyes shut.

Dazzled by the bright sunlight, Jessica peered about her, but there was no sign of George's barrow, no elderly, limping man.

There was just a tall figure in faded blue jeans and a denim shirt. A young man whose hair seemed to have trapped the sun so that it shone about his head. A man whose legs were long, his body straight and supple. A man who played squash and went cycling in Holland.

Jessica drew a long, slow breath and swivelled her chair to face him. There must be a mistake.

Tim raised his hands above his head, waving them excitedly. And he was grinning — a huge, wide, happy grin.

Then, all at once, he quickened his pace until he was running towards her, calling her name. ■

WHAT'S NEW PUSSYCAT?

She was a beautiful vet. He was a sober-suited city type who claimed to know all about animals — even pigs with sore paws!

Complete Story
By Elizabeth Ashcroft

RUSSEL parked his car and stared morosely at the wrought-iron sign swinging gently in the breeze.

Mrs Smith's Cattery. He sighed.

Duty visits to his Aunt Sylvie were all very well; he loved her dearly. But he did *not* love her cats.

The sign creaked as he walked up the drive, and he felt his skin begin to prickle warningly. He'd disliked cats since one had scratched him at the tender age of four when he was playing with it. He still had the scar on his arm.

And it had, he recalled, been one of Aunt Sylvie's cats.

For as long as he could remember she'd been besotted by them. After Uncle Harold died, she'd devoted her life to their well-being, moving to the country and opening the cattery. Overnight it became a big success, as it was the only one for miles around.

Russel turned up the collar of his raincoat and surveyed the grey sky suspiciously.

67

Usually the only time he ventured into the country was when he took a girlfriend for a drive, or a meal in a country pub.

He was a city man. Theatres, nightclubs, the noise and bustle of busy streets and the continual feverish toing and froing of crowds, were music to his soul.

He squelched up the drive in his shining leather shoes and surveyed streaks of mud on them with resignation as he stood on the doorstep, finger on the bell. Still, at least Aunt Sylvie would have the kettle on. Her home-baking was delicious!

But no-one answered his persistent ring. Drat it! He'd have to go round to the cattery, see if he could find her there. He hurried through the side gate, bolting it behind him and making his way down the narrow passage to the new wooden buildings his aunt had put up. They smelled of cedarwood, and looked, he conceded grudgingly, rather handsome.

"Russel! Russel, dear! How lovely to see you."

Aunt Sylvie, in disgracefully muddy brogues, tweed skirt and hairy sweater, squelched through the mud left by the recent rain. Her sweater, he thought grimly, looked as though she'd knitted it herself, from cats' hair.

Russel was not surprised to see her followed by an equally sensibly dressed female. Cat lovers were forever hanging about his aunt. This female wore enormous green wellingtons, liberally adorned with mud.

But there the similarity with his aunt ended. Russel's mouth fell slightly open. This girl was utterly, gorgeously, delectable.

Where Aunt Sylvie's sweater sagged, hers fitted snugly and was daffodil yellow and fluffy.

He fought back an urge to touch its fluffiness.

Control yourself, Russel Dean, he told himself firmly. *You are a city-bred, 25-year-old accountant, and you socialise with sophisticated personal assistants and models. Not cat lovers in wellies!*

But this cat lover had large blue eyes, and he felt something in his stomach go weak as she looked up at him over the head of an enormous white cat.

"Hello, Aunt Sylvie," he said heartily, the sight of the pretty girl resurrecting some of his city manners. He hugged his aunt. The scent of cats from her clothes made him back away. He sneezed explosively.

The girl took a step backwards, and the large Persian cat in her arms stared furiously at him. It began struggling to get away, claws extended and tail swishing like a windmill.

"Sorry," he muttered. "Ah, an allergy."

"Not to cats, I hope," the girl said. She had a low, musical voice.

Aunt Sylvie laughed. "No, he loves cats, don't you, Russel?"

Somehow, on his infrequent visits to his aunt, Russel had managed to keep his mild phobia to himself. It was the only reason he didn't visit her as often as he should.

Now, he looked pointedly at the girl and Aunt Sylvie took the hint.

"Lorraine Anderson, Russel Dean, my nephew. It's my birthday next week and he's probably brought me a potted plant, as usual. Right, dear?"

Russel, to his shame, flushed.

He had indeed brought a potted plant, being convinced that it was the ideal present for an aunt. He was glad he'd left it in the car.

It hadn't, till now, crossed his mind that she might prefer something else, a luxurious box of chocolates, for instance. Right then he made up his mind to ditch the plant or give it to his mother and send Aunt Sylvie something else. She was a pet, really.

"Well, hello there," he said, in his telephone voice which always impressed.

He held out a hand. Lorraine took his hand, lifting up the spitting cat in her arms. It was all fluffy white hair and slitted venomous green eyes. Inwardly, Russel flinched at its proximity, but made a careful effort not to let his sophisticated image slip.

He put out a careless hand to touch the cat's head, and Lorraine moved away hastily.

"Careful, she's just had a pill. It's made her a bit touchy. She might scratch."

Russel snatched his hand away, momentarily losing his cool. "Pill? What's wrong with it — or her — then?"

"Nothing much. I'll put her in her cage now."

She walked to the nearest shed and disappeared, curly hair swinging jauntily behind her in a pony-tail. Russel turned to his aunt.

"Have you taken on an assistant, then?"

She shook her head. "Goodness me, no! She's our vet. Very good one, too. Took over from old Mr Thompson in the spring."

A vet! He didn't believe it! She looked too fragile, too delicate, to do all those ghastly things vets usually did.

He peered into the depths of the cattery. She was settling the enormous Persian, talking gently to it.

She had very long legs, he noticed, clad in grubby but well-cut jeans . . .

A vision of Lindy, his latest girlfriend, came into his mind.

She wouldn't be seen dead in wellingtons. Or a cattery, come to that.

Nightclubs were more her scene. And, he remembered with a jolt, he had a date with her tonight.

But suddenly, Lindy, and the city, seemed a long way away.

Over tea in Aunt Sylvie's kitchen, drinking from odd mugs and with Lorraine sitting opposite him in the old rocking chair, Lindy seemed a being from a different world.

"You really are a qualified vet then?" he asked bemused, watching as she took a huge bite out of Aunt Sylvie's famed chocolate fudge cake. Lindy, and her perennial diets, flashed before his eyes. Aunt Sylvie smiled.

"Or course. Lorraine is a qualified vet — and a very good one, too. She's living in the old cottage by the green. You wouldn't recognise it now."

Russel nodded. He felt, for the first time in years, positively tongue-tied. "You — uh — like living in the village then?"

The large blue eyes gazed serenely back at him. There was a smudge of chocolate on her chin and he had a ridiculous urge to lean forward and wipe it off.

"I love it. And what do you do, Russel?"

"I'm — uh — an accountant."

Suddenly it seemed a very dull profession. He saw himself through her eyes. Dressed formally in a city suit, with a city coat and muddy city shoes. And a city pallor to boot.

She was slightly tanned, bursting with health. He felt like the "before" part of an advertisement for muscle building.

I bet, he thought gloomily, her friends are great hulking farmers who heave bales of straw about with total ease.

For the first time in years, Russel's confidence in his attraction to members of the opposite sex started to waver.

Aunt Sylvie began to talk learnedly of cat ailments, and Lorraine spoke enthusiastically, eyes lighting up, absent-mindedly taking another piece of cake.

"Cows suffer terribly from it," she said matter of factly, and Russel, who'd been feeling, unusual for him, rather left out of the conversation, looked at her in horror.

"Cows?" he uttered. She looked at him as though he were an idiot.

"Mastitis," she said loudly, as though he were a foreigner who couldn't speak English.

"Oh, yes. Yes, of course." He nodded enthusiastically.

Cows, cats . . . He'd never really thought about them, or had much time for them. Now, he dredged up odd bits of knowledge he'd picked up somewhere, and surprised himself.

Aunt Sylvie smiled and went out to feed her boarders, leaving Russel and Lorraine to themselves in the untidy, cosy kitchen.

R USSEL realised that evening, at the theatre with Lindy, that he'd completely forgotten to give Aunt Sylvie her birthday present — the much maligned potted plant.

Beside him, Lindy moved, sending out wafts of exotic perfume. He thought fleetingly of Lorraine's hair, which had smelled of fresh herbs.

Lindy had refused a box of chocolates on their way into the theatre, patting her slim figure complacently.

"No, Russel, thanks. I've got a photo call tomorrow. Chocolates put *pounds* on me."

And Lorraine had eaten half a chocolate cake that afternoon; Lorraine with chocolate smudged on her chin. He shut his eyes for a moment, blotting out the vivid stage before him.

Just what was the matter with him? Here he was with Lindy Lane, one of the city's leading models, and he was too busy thinking about a country vet with mud on her wellies to pay her proper attention.

He couldn't get Lorraine out of his mind all week. She stood beside him, laughing, holding the white Persian, while he added figures; she strode, in her daffodil sweater, at his side, as he went to lunch in a restaurant.

Her imaginary presence brightened his drab office till he knew, with chagrined resignation and a joyful leap of the heart, that he had to see her again.

He decided to buy Aunt Sylvie the largest, most expensive box of chocolates he could find, and take them out to

her, pretending he hadn't come to see Lorraine.

One thing he would *not* do, he thought, turning out of the entrance to his spick and span bachelor flat, was tell her how he'd spent a couple of mind-boggling hours with his encyclopaedia, mugging up on vet's jargon and animals in general.

Well, he thought, overtaking a coach full of holidaymakers and heading for the clean, country air, I have to impress her somehow. Mind you, you don't usually talk about mites in a dog's ears, or a cat's sore feet, in normal conversation.

He could now discourse learnedly upon cat flu, the habits of tortoises in winter, and what to do if hens started pecking each other.

No, he thought, some of his confidence returning. There was no way she could possibly resist him now.

Aunt Sylvie greeted him joyfully.

"Russel! Lorraine's here, too. Go and find her in the cattery while I put the kettle on." Her eyes lit on the beribboned box of chocolates.

"Oh, you wicked boy! Lovely!" She had the lid off and was munching away before she reached the kitchen door. Russel went to find Lorraine.

She didn't seem at all surprised to see him. Just stood there with a black bag — like a doctor, he thought irreverently — and smiled at him.

Her hair was loose today, fluffy round her cheeks. But she still wore a yellow sweater and jeans, and the green wellingtons.

He realised with surprise that he'd not even bothered to dress up today. Just pulled on an old pair of jeans and a sweater.

She looked him up and down, approval in her eyes. "You look different."

"I feel different," he said. And realised he meant it. The confident city man slowly ebbed away again. Going to her side, he looked down at the white Persian. She sat serenely in her blue-lined basket, her eyes blinking sleepily.

He reached out a finger to stroke her head, and with one movement, she flattened her ears and spat. Russel leapt back.

"She doesn't — uh — seem to like me."

Lorraine stroked the cat, and immediately a noise like a car engine began to vibrate through the cattery.

"There," Lorraine said. "Hear her purr? She's a darling, really, aren't you, Queenie?"

"Queenie!" He didn't believe it. Lorraine bit her lip, trying not to smile, and suddenly they were both laughing.

"What's wrong with her?" he asked learnedly, remembering his thick seldom-read encyclopaedia. "Sore feet? Or has she perhaps swallowed some of her fur?"

"What?" Lorraine looked at him blankly for a moment, then, eyes sparkling, she nodded. "As a matter of fact, that's just what she has done. She misses her home when she's here and gets bored.

"How did you guess? I didn't think you knew much about animals."

He nodded smugly. "Oh, you'd be surprised. I love animals. And the country," he elaborated, walking out into the bright clear air and taking a deep breath.

He realised with surprise that the air actually did smell different out here. He could smell flowers, leaves, a — a green sort of smell, he thought. Not diesel fumes and smog.

She smiled at him. "It smells better than the city, I'll bet."

"It does."

"And you really know something about cats?"

"Of course." He lied without compunction, feeling her arm brush against his as she leaned over to fasten Queenie's cage. She smelled today of flowers. Roses?

"Then maybe you'd like to help me," she said diffidently.

"Anything. Of course," he said grandly. She'd fallen for him all right, he thought.

A moment later he wished he'd never laid eyes on this pretty vet. He, Russel Dean, help judge at a *cat show?*

"*Me?*" he echoed hollowly. "But I've never — I mean — I've never done anything like that! I'm not a — a cat judge!"

"That doesn't matter," she said coolly. "It's only the village fête next Sunday. My usual helper had to cancel at the last minute. I thought — well, you seem very knowledgeable about cats, and animals in general."

You've really done it now, he said to himself. Unless he did quite a bit of studying she would realise he knew nothing whatsoever about the blasted animals.

"It's held in the village, then?" he asked weakly. She nodded, smiling widely.

"You'll do it, then, Russel? Oh, that's wonderful! It's at two-thirty on the village green, and we have a record entry this year. It should be great fun."

Great fun, he thought. Time to consult the encyclopaedia again — or catch something contagious.

T HE next Saturday, however, saw him at the village fête, scrutinising hordes of cats. Grey cats, black cats, fat cats, thin cats. Slitted green eyes stared disdainfully and hooded blue eyes blinked sleepily.

Proud owners brushed and combed and pulled out tufts of hair and hid it, and even puffed talcum powder on white cats. Queenie, inevitably, was there with her owner. She looked magnificent, purring like an engine as he approached.

Lorraine was by his side, a vision in a floaty, blue and white summer dress.

"Hello, there, Queenie," he said diffidently. Queenie drew back her lips and showed him her perfect teeth in a ladylike snarl then turned to rub affectionately at Lorraine's hand as she tickled her ears.

"What do you think, Russel?" she enquired earnestly. "First prize for Queenie? She really is a beauty."

I'd rather give her the booby prize, he thought dourly. But he nodded agreement. Queenie was indeed the finest cat in her class.

And Lorraine was the loveliest girl he'd ever seen.

Suddenly he felt an astonishing surge of something very like affection for the assorted moggies who allowed him, shakily at first, to pick them up and examine them with affected knowledge and aplomb. And he'd only been scratched once.

Maybe, he thought, surveying the dark red blood streaking his knuckles, he should have tackled his fear, dislike, whatever, of cats long ago.

Maybe with Lorraine at his side he could even grow to like the ferocious Queenie, now gazing down her aristocratic nose at the other cats, wearing a "Best of Show" red ribbon round her beautiful neck.

They went back to Aunt Sylvie's after the show, collapsing round the kitchen table with a huge hotpot she'd left in the oven all the afternoon.

The smell made Russel's nose twitch. He was hungrier than he'd been for years. Afterwards, they drank tea in the garden, accompanied by the inevitable bevy of cats. Lorraine talked about the show.

"And Russel was really quite an expert," she told Aunt Sylvie. She smiled across at him and he felt an absurd pang of pleasure. He shrugged.

"Not really. You did most of the actual judging," he said truthfully and she was suddenly serious.

"Did you really enjoy it?"

"I loved it." But most of all I loved being with you, he wanted to add.

"Would you like to come on my rounds with me next week to some of the local farms? We could make it Saturday, if you like."

Russel felt his heart sink to his boots. This was it. She'd know now he was a fraud, despite all the information he'd memorised about ticks and hepatitis.

But still, it meant he'd have a whole day with her . . . And anyway he'd never pretended, he comforted himself, to be a vet. Just an interested layman.

He remembered, too late, he had a date with Lindy, remembered her immaculate presence at his side, and consigned her to the past tense with scarcely a pang.

It had been nothing serious anyway.

"I'd like that," he said now. "Very much."

After all, that gave him a week. In seven days he could read every James Herriot in print.

THE next Saturday, it rained.

He arrived at Lorraine's cottage early, and was astonished at the changes in the old place.

A neat, businesslike surgery had been built at the side, and the cottage was painted apricot, with old-fashioned roses climbing round the doors, and white frilly curtains at every window.

Lorraine was waiting for him. She pulled a face when she saw him: city suit, city coat, city shoes. He'd wanted, foolishly, to impress her with his sophistication. It had been a mistake.

"You can't go round muddy farms dressed like that!" she exclaimed.

She disappeared and came back with a voluminous green coat. "This belonged to Mr Thompson," she said as he turned up his nose. "It will at least keep you dry. When it rains on the downs, it really rains. And you'd better put on his boots, too."

Wellingtons. Enormous black wellingtons plastered with the mud of years in huge dried chunks.

Gritting his teeth, he shoved his feet into them. They clumped out behind her delectable back, clad in a serviceable anorak. He felt a complete idiot in the ridiculous outfit. And Lorraine's smile of amusement hadn't helped.

Her sensible estate car smelled of dogs, cats, horses and medicine. She suddenly seemed a stranger to him. Someone who held the power of life and death in her slender hands. For a fleeting moment, he felt useless, able to contribute nothing.

He belonged to the city, not to these wet, sodden downs, the bleak farmhouses shrouded in drizzling mists. He was, he thought bleakly, a fool. This wasn't his sort of day at all.

But the farmers made Russel feel at home. He helped Lorraine give an injection to a coughing horse, inspected a litter of collie pups, and watched her examine a donkey, marvelling at her expertise. Trying to remember what he'd read, he put in a few knowledgeable comments. Lorraine smiled and nodded.

They sat in the car, and drank hot chocolate from a flask and ate cheese sandwiches.

"I have to eat when I can," she said between bites. "I rarely get time for a proper meal on a day like this."

"Are all your days like this?" He hadn't thought it would be such hard work. It was dirty and, at times, backbreaking. He marvelled that her slight form could take it.

"Not always. Surgery is most mornings, of course. I catch up on rounds in the afternoons. Sometimes it's so beautiful. Driving through the country in the frost, or on a spring day. Very different to today."

She grinned at him, and he put out a hand and brushed back a stray curl from her forehead, listening to the rain beat heavily down on the roof of the car.

Suddenly businesslike, she turned away.

"Now we're off to Solly's Farm," she stated. "That's the last visit, unless there's a message there for me."

Solly's Farm was different to the others. Not so well kept, not so freshly painted, the fences not so neat and orderly. But it was, Lorraine informed him, a good little farm.

New people had taken it over, determined to make a go of it. They had asked her to come over to check a cow.

That sounds simple enough, Russel thought. We'll soon be finished. All things considered, once he'd got used to the wellingtons, it had been a rather good day . . .

Ten minutes later, Russel was wishing he'd never come. Had never left the city.

They were crouching in the straw of a draughty barn, both cold and wet.

Lorraine knelt beside a cow in labour, her voice gentle, eyes compassionate. The farmer hovered, wordlessly offering help, till she told him to go and get boiling water.

She glanced at Russel, a slight smile in her eyes.

"They always want to help," she told him gently. "And I always tell them to go and get plenty of hot water, just like a doctor helping at a birth.

"But this one —" she glanced at the cow, moaning slightly, her head twisting and turning on the straw, "— this one is going to be difficult."

Russel's stomach turned over. He knew how to change a wheel on a car, he could ski, he was one of the best accountants

74

in his firm; but he had never before in his life felt quite so useless as he did now.

Lorraine, on her knees, looked up at him, her eyes bright with unshed tears.

"We might lose her," she muttered.

He was seeing a new side to her now. The compassionate surgeon, not the laughing judge at a cat show. This was, truly, life or death.

"We want a little brute strength, Russ." She gasped. Her hands were busy, blood drenching the slender fingers. He swallowed hard. He'd never realised things would turn out like this. He should never have come.

"Can I help?" He heard his voice as from a long way off. He swallowed again, felt the nausea rise as the cow gave a tremendous heave and something — surely not a small leg — appeared in Lorraine's hands. She gave a gasp.

"Yes, quickly. Come over here!"

Then he was on his knees, beside her. She told him what to do, and automatically he did it and suddenly, his revulsion was gone. He was caught up wholly in the little drama, pulling when Lorraine told him to, comforting when she told him to.

The cow's eyes, huge dark pools of fear and incomprehension, seemed to watch him, somehow trusting him.

Then, astonishingly, there was the calf.

A tiny, tottery little black and white calf. The cow licked it fondly. Lorraine looked up at him and smiled.

This must be what it's like to have a child, he thought. This tremendous, utter relief, that everything is over, that the child has all its toes, its fingers. The calf was perfect, nuzzling its mother, the fur curly and wet. He touched its forehead gently.

"I never saw one so young," he said softly.

"You never saw one born before, did you?"

He shook his head, suddenly unable to meet her eyes. "Lorraine, I'm a fraud. I don't really know a thing about animals. I just mugged it all up in my encyclopaedia. I just — wanted to impress you, I suppose."

"I know," she said solemnly. Then she laughed. "Some of your earlier remarks were so funny, I could hardly keep a straight face!"

Russel stood up in his muddy wellingtons, listening to the farmer go shouting to the farmhouse with his news.

"You knew?"

"Of course." She smiled. "Russel, horses don't eat meat. And pigs have trotters, not paws! I — sort of strung you along, Russel. I wanted to see you again, too, even if you didn't know a thing about animals. But I was — glad that you wanted to impress me."

"I did. But I didn't know — I was going to fall in love with you."

The words were out before he realised it. But he knew he meant them.

He'd never met anyone like Lorraine before. She'd opened a whole new world to him. A world of open skies, and animals, and birth, and cats called Queenie.

And he wanted to share it. He could move, he thought. Get a job locally. And he could learn more about the country and the ways of animals.

And about Lorraine . . .

The cow, placidly licking her new-born calf, looked on with soft eyes as the two figures merged into one; the tall, not-so-immaculate man in an old green coat, and the small curly-haired girl who had just saved her calf.

She mooed, very gently. ∎

SOMETHING OLD... SOMETHING NEW...

By GYLL MULLINS

Take an old marriage . . . two people feeling blue . . . add some borrowed time . . . Could they find something new to remind them of the love they once had?

THERE were 12 white tables in the hotel tea garden. Louise Duke counted them from the window as she waited for Benedict to organise his newspapers at Reception.

They looked rather brave, fixed to the wet, deserted concrete, quite undaunted by the swirling mist which dropped off the bare trees or the heavy sky, threatening more snow. Their pristine newness was in direct contrast to the general age which seeped through the hotel.

Benedict disliked this place already. She'd sensed it as they'd signed the register. But even when they were making plans for this weekend she'd known he wouldn't like the hotel, however nice it was. And then she was irritated with herself for knowing — because there was no *discovery* left any more.

Benedict wasn't very adaptable. He liked to be settled and he approached any sort of change with caution.

"Do we have to?" he'd asked, gazing at her hopefully.

But Louise had wanted this weekend alone with him. She wanted to be away from everything and everyone, even the children.

They'd booked a weekend in Chartwell — advertised as a romantic retreat in the country — arranged a babysitter for their nine-year-old twins and left after an early lunch on Friday.

"We'll arrive late on Friday afternoon and that'll give us two full days," she'd said. Two full days together in the bright cold of the wintry countryside. It had seemed such a short time together when they'd first booked it. Now the two days seemed to stretch ahead of them interminably.

It would've been different if they'd established the mood they'd hoped for. Instead, she was conscious of the start of a headache and the stirring of the discontent she'd hoped to leave behind.

Benedict was coming towards her and she forced a more cheerful expression on to her face. It was a trick she'd learned as a child and had used almost unconsciously all her life. By pretending to be happy when you weren't, you could fool almost anybody.

She linked her arm companionably through his. But he was disappointingly unresponsive as they were shown to a small chalet, one of a cluster surrounding the main building of the hotel.

It had a chocolate-brown carpet, ball and claw furniture and two single beds covered in washed-out pink candlewick.

Someone, somewhere, was playing "If You Were The Only Girl In The World" on an old piano. And someone somewhere owned a dog which had attached itself to them and followed them into the room.

After leaving mud all over the carpet it settled down next to the luggage with a deep sigh.

Louise looked around doubtfully. "It's very comfortable," she said, "but I imagined it quite different — quaintly romantic and rustic somehow."

"It's rustic enough." Benedict was prowling around the room like a wary cat, lost in strange surroundings.

Louise resisted an impulse to snap at him and instead took a painkiller. Her headache was slight but it was still there. Like the niggling dissatisfaction which had spurred her on to arrange this weekend in the first place.

She had seen it as a sort of second honeymoon for Benedict and herself. Both of them would find again that fragile quality they'd once had — a quality they'd lost somewhere along the years. It was a freshness, an eagerness, an effervescence she missed in their relationship.

It had been diminished by familiarity, she thought, by 15 years of daily experience. She loved Benedict, she always would. There was nothing deeply wrong with their relationship — just a certain curling at the edges, a sense of boredom and dullness within her.

Benedict completed his inspection and reported that the bed was much too short and the heater not connected.

"I don't suppose they realise it's midwinter and everyone's got frostbite," he said.

"The bath water's hot, though." Louise's arms were full of clothes. "Look, I'm putting these shirts here, right up top to the right, hankies next to them and the rest in the drawers over there."

"Oh, you're unpacking for me," Benedict said, and smiled briefly in that special way he had, giving his rather roundish face a sweetness and innocence, making him look rather cute.

Normally it was a smile that could secretly delight her. But today it failed.

"Yes, I'm unpacking for you," she said dully. "Where shall I put your camera?"

"Anywhere," he answered, gingerly testing the bed. "Silly to have brought it. What's there to take pictures of?"

"Well, *me*," Louise said. What she'd meant as a joke didn't work because her voice was too sharp. Still trying, she went on. "On our honeymoon you photographed me from one end of Italy to the other."

But it didn't make it better, only worse. She sounded petulant and childish.

"Oh, our honeymoon." Benedict was pulling off his shoes. "That was different. Good grief, this bed's lumpy!"

He was teasing her. She looked across at him.

He was trying to make himself comfortable on the bed and she could predict exactly what he would do next: take off his watch, put it next to his cigarettes and matches, feel for an ashtray, pinch one of her pillows and put it under his knees . . .

SHE knew this as surely as she knew the sounds of his showering every morning; every step of his technique for curing hiccups; how to choose his library books and how much sugar to put in his tea.

She wanted to tell him then and there how she was feeling, to ask him to understand.

She sat down on the bed next to him. He was idly scanning a hotel brochure and he'd put on his glasses.

"Benedict." She prodded him to get his attention. "Benedict!" He turned inquiringly, but it was clear he was trying to settle down and regarded this as an unwelcome interruption.

She jumped up.

"Oh, never mind!"

Muttering that she was going to arrange for some tea, she put on her coat and, slamming the door behind her, left him wrapped in the pink candlewick with his feet over the edge of the bed which was too short for him.

In the cold little reception room she asked if there was any tea. The girl was busy and brusque and told Louise tea was now over. A tray would have to be specially ordered. And no, there was no room service in the afternoons, so could she wait while it was prepared?

Louise said "Yes," although she didn't want to wait; she didn't want to sit in the cold reception room; she didn't even want to concede that tea after hours probably *was* inconvenient for such a small hotel.

She thought about going to phone the children, then remembered that they'd been invited to an afternoon party. So she sat down, tapping her feet impatiently and taking a fierce pleasure in disliking a young couple who'd just arrived.

Their very new luggage was spotted with tell-tale drifts of confetti, and the boy, in trying to assume a nonchalance and confidence he lacked, was a little paternal.

The girl looked happy — they both looked happy; too happy, Louise thought, as she contemplated the sort of bridal suite that awaited them.

Her headache was still there, in spite of the pills. The girl laughed suddenly, throwing back her head. The noise jarred Louise's nerves.

It was then she recognised that her irritation was due to envy — envy of their newness and excitement which transcended their immaturity. She wanted that — that same headiness she could suddenly recall so vividly, that same magic energy.

She sighed and peered up to see if her tea had arrived. It had. It was there on the desk, growing cold.

Louise stood up, annoyed, and reached over. Beside her the girl finished signing the register and stepped back — right into the loaded tray in Louise's arms.

Louise tried to steady the tray. It wobbled, tilted, remained suspended for a second, then sent teapot, milk, sugar and cups crashing to the floor.

Her temper flared.

"For goodness' sake," she cried — and then stopped, conscious of the tension in the room.

A slow, deep flush was staining the girl's face. She wasn't looking at Louise but was watching her husband, waiting for his reaction.

He'd lost his expansive air and mumbled with an embarrassed ineptitude. "These things happen, Trish. Don't worry. It was an accident."

Louise began to feel contrite as she stood there surrounded by sugar, broken crockery and the clucking receptionist who was busily commiserating and ringing bells.

The whole incident was really so trivial, she thought guiltily. She had over-reacted about nothing at all.

The girl was fighting tears.

Clumsily, her young husband patted her shoulder. "Trish, please don't cry. Please." He felt around for his handkerchief, couldn't locate it and swore quietly. "Blast it."

Louise could bear it no longer. She became very brisk and proffered a tissue. "No, don't cry. Your husband's right. It was just an accident."

"I'm most awfully sorry. Really, so sorry." The girl looked quite miserable.

"Stop apologising, Trish."

Louise repeated that it really didn't matter, well aware that the apology was not directed at her, that the girl was actually meaning the apology for her new husband.

She was apologising for embarrassing him, for pricking the enchanted bubble of happiness, for still being so young and so unsure.

Knocking over a tea-tray, Louise realised, was just a minor mishap. But when you're still strangers, still trying to impress each other, it assumes great importance.

It brings into sharp focus how untried and unsure you are — it shows up how long you still have to go before you've forged a relationship which offers the deeply satisfying and comfortable security of ready and instinctive understanding.

Sometimes, though, Louise thought with sudden clarity, you can mistake that ease for staleness, that sureness of touch for boredom.

And suddenly she wanted Benedict. She wanted to see him, to hear his voice, to reach out and touch him — her dear familiar husband, the man she knew so well.

With relief she noticed the maid carrying a mop and bucket. "Look, here's someone to help clean up. We'll do it together, shall we? It won't take a moment."

She wanted to add, "And then you can get on with your honeymoon," but decided against it. They'd have to repair this on their own.

The girl was already giving tentative, watery smiles. If they had any sense, Louise thought, mopping at her coat and shaking sugar off her shoes, they'd order a bottle of champagne as soon as they reached their room.

O N the way back to Benedict, carrying a fresh tray, she walked as fast as she could.

The mist had lifted and the unseasonable white tables looked almost jaunty in the late afternoon light.

Someone was playing the piano again and Louise, her heart lifting, wanted to sing.

She covered the last few steps in a rush, pushed through the chalet door and stopped.

Benedict was *singing*.

Standing in the doorway with the pale light softening the interior of the room, she listened to his voice floating from the bathroom, then joined in for a few bars before going to sit on the edge of the bath.

She watched as he towelled himself.

"Do you realise we didn't read the brochures properly?" he said to her, beaming. "This place is steeped in history. There's an old cemetery nearby with early settlers' graves, a museum in the hotel and various descendants peppering the district. Should be quite interesting to have a look round."

"And compensation enough for the lack of rustic charm." Louise reached out and rubbed his back lightly.

He met her eyes in the mirror. "Headache better?" he asked.

She nodded. "Lifting." She was quiet for a moment before she went on. "You usually know, don't you? Even if I don't tell you." She was conscious of the fact that they were both talking about more than the headache.

He was still watching her. His tone was deceptively light as he spoke. "I'm somewhat well acquainted with you by now, Mrs Duke."

She smiled then and he smiled back, his brief sweet smile.

"Let's go outside with the camera and catch the last of this light," he said then.

"I thought there was nothing to photograph."

"There's always the dog," he teased. "Or those white tables, or maybe we'll find an old cemetery or two . . ." And then he relented and held out his hand.

"Come on, sweetheart," he said. "I want to take your picture." ■

By SARAH BURKHILL

MRS DO-AS-YOU WOULD-BE DONE-BY!

What do you do with those persistent do-gooders? Well, if you can't beat them, join them!

THE trouble with society today, Lena Wagstaff thought sourly, was that people didn't have enough to do with their time. If they had, then they might stop poking their noses into other people's business.

She cast a malevolent eye over the girl who had brazened her way into the living-room, introducing herself as Myrtle Hogg and commandeering Lena's chair.

Not so much a girl really, she was more a woman, Lena supposed.

81

Myrtle must be about thirtyish, and she was wearing one of those jovial, well-scrubbed smiles that do-gooders usually wore.

Lena would soon get rid of that. Myrtle Hogg would not be the first interfering social worker to be ejected with a flea in her ear.

"But I'm not from the social services department," she explained hurriedly. The smile grew broader and, if anything, even more jovial.

"No, this is a neighbourhood group we've started up. We're just a bunch of ordinary people who give some of our time each week to provide practical help or companionship to the elderly people in the area . . ."

Elderly? Lena's brows lowered. Elderly, indeed! She was only 67.

Her mother had been 97 when she died two years ago, and her mother had had a bad heart, mind you. Lena's heart was sound as a bell.

". . . So if there's any way we can be of assistance —"

"There isn't," Lena snapped.

"Gardening, for instance." Myrtle Hogg was the persevering type. "We have some young people who could come round and give you a hand with —"

She tailed off as Lena beckoned her from the chair and directed her to the window.

"D'you see that garden?" Lena demanded. "Look at it, now!"

The back garden was about a fifth of an acre in size, and was laid out in three neat sections of lawn, flower beds and vegetable plot. It resembled something that might be found in a horticultural magazine under the heading: 'How To Make Best Use Of The Town Garden.'

"Do it myself," Lena said smugly. "Every inch of it. Digging an' all."

"Can you find me somebody who could do it better?"

"Er — perhaps not." Myrtle's smile wavered only fractionally. "No, it's really beautiful, Miss Wagstaff. You've done a wonderful job."

The smile came back in full force. "But perhaps there's something else that you find too much of a chore? Shopping, perhaps? It's quite a distance to the shops. We could —"

"I walk a minimum of three miles a day," Lena interrupted. "Got to keep yourself fit, haven't you?

"That's the trouble with young people today." She peered out of the front window at Myrtle's little red motor car. "They drive about on wheels all the time and don't know how to use their feet. A ten-minute walk to the shops and their legs would drop off."

"Um — quite." But Myrtle was not discouraged. "Painting and decorating?"

"Do that myself, too," Lena pointed out. "It's the only way to make sure it's done properly. You get a firm in to do it and as much paint ends up on the carpet as on the walls."

"Yes, yes, I see. What about cleaning, then . . .?"

"*No!*"

"No." Myrtle hastened on, looking around Lena's spotless room. "No, perhaps not."

Then her eyes brightened and she wagged a conspiratorial finger.

"*I* know! How would it be if somebody popped in each week just for a cup of tea and a natter — give you a bit of company?"

Lena didn't want company, thank you very much. In truth, she didn't care much for people. They were a nosy, interfering, busybodying lot, and she wouldn't give them the time of day if she could help it.

Anyway, she had far too much to do. There was more than enough work to keep her occupied during the day, and then at night there was the TV.

Not that TV was all that good, she admitted. Diabolical, the kind of things they put on it nowadays. And they had the cheek to ask for a licence fee!

"So there's nothing at all we can do for you?" Myrtle Hogg looked sad.

"No, nothing at all. Manage fine myself," she said. "Thank you for calling. Goodbye."

She made for the door, but Myrtle remained seated in the armchair.

"*Marvellous*!" she enthused suddenly. "Then you're *just* the kind of person I'm looking for!"

"What?" Lena said.

"You see we're always on the look-out for volunteer helpers," Myrtle rushed on.

"You're so active and capable — make such good use of your time and skills — you'd be ideal. Now I'll just give you —"

"Hang on," Lena began, but this unexpected development had wrenched control of the situation from her hands.

"— give you a list of some people you might care to call on," Myrtle continued heedlessly. "Just give it what time you can spare. An hour, two hours a week. More if you like."

"But —"

"The volunteers meet at my house every Thursday night, to discuss what needs doing and where. Six-thirty to seven-thirty.

"We'll see you then. Cheerio, now. Must get on."

Bemused for the first time in 67 years, Lena stared out of the window as the little red car tootled off.

The cheek of the woman, she thought later. Well, she wouldn't go on Thursday. She hadn't said she would go, and she wouldn't!

On the other hand . . . She flicked through her television guides to see what would be on the box between six-thirty and seven-thirty: a Western on one channel, documentaries on two of the others, and a thing about avant-garde films on the final one.

Lena screwed up her face. Maybe she would go, after all. If nothing better turned up. The woman would probably be expecting her. She might even have laid on tea.

LENA'S first case was a Mrs Ina Briggs in Crescent Road.
Housebound. Walks with a zimmer, the brief notes on her said. *Needs shopping brought in.*

"Housebound, are you?" Lena said, eyeing her up.

"That's right, dear." Ina Briggs returned slowly to the chair after letting Lena in, and abandoned her zimmer.

"Haven't been over that door in four years," she added. *Proudly.*

Lena sniffed.

"Well, it's about time you were. OK, I know you can't go traipsing about a supermarket with that thing, but you could be sitting out in the yard on a nice day like this, getting some fresh air."

Ina regarded her with horror.

"But it's cold!" she squealed. "I'd get a chill!"

"Put a coat on, then," Lena countered the objection. "You'll not come to any harm in a coat.

"Come on, I'll help you out. Do you the world of good."

She bundled the protesting invalid into a black wool coat and half carried her to the back yard.

"There, that's better," she said. "You just stay put till I get your shopping, then I'll take you back in again . . . If you're good," she added warningly, when Ina opened her mouth.

The list clutched in her hand, Lena went off, unconcerned about the black looks that were directed at her from above the black coat.

The shopping took almost half an hour.

"I've changed your brand of soup, by the way," she informed Ina on her return. "The kind I always get's much nicer, and it's a penny cheaper, too, so I got that instead.

"Did you have a nice sit?"

The invalid glowered at her.

"You've no business getting things I didn't ask for," she said huffily. "Or leaving me out here in the cold. You're a bully, that's what you are. I'm going to complain to Mrs Hogg about you!"

"Complain away," Lena said, trundling her back indoors. "See if I care!"

No complaint could have been made, however, because at next Thursday's meeting Myrtle was as nice as pie.

So, indeed, was Ina Briggs when Lena went back the following Tuesday. There was a cup of tea ready on her arrival, and the black coat was laid over the back of the settee, in readiness for her removal to the yard.

"Just take your time," she said when Lena went off with the shopping list. "It's really quite pleasant out today. Puts roses in your cheeks, a little air. Doesn't it?"

Lena glanced at the list, pleased to see it headed by two tins of her favourite soup.

The second of Lena's 'old people,' as she thought of them, were a retired couple, Mr and Mrs Hartley. Apparently they could no longer manage their painting and decorating and hadn't the means to employ someone to do it.

Myrtle had not been too keen on Lena taking on that task. There were plenty of younger helpers — teenage boys — who could oblige.

"Yes, and a right mess they'd make of it, I'll bet," Lena had said. "They're not careful, young people. They'll get paint over things."

She was adamant. She would do it herself. The room requiring redecoration had a low ceiling, and it was one of those papers that just had to be emulsioned over. There would be no problem.

No problem, that is, except for the Hartley's choice of colour.

"Mushroom?" Lena made a face. "Oh, no. You don't want mushroom. Not in a room like this that doesn't get any sun."

She
looked
around
thoughtfully.

"White, I
think, for the walls
— one of those
shades that's got a
touch of green about it,
if you look the right way.
That'll go nice with your suite.

"And a kind of pinky-tan for
the doors and windows," she
told them. "Now don't look like that! It'll
be lovely. Just you wait and see."

It was lovely.

"You should have been an interior
decorator, Miss Wagstaff," Mrs Hartley said
admiringly. "I'd never have thought of those
colours looking so good together!"

Lena was well pleased.

She was well pleased with everything these days, except possibly the
state of her own home. It was not the spotless, well-kept little palace it had
once been.

Occasionally, had visitors called midweek, they would have noticed a
speck of dust on the mantelpiece, or some stray hairs or bits of fluff marring
the perfection of Lena's carpet.

The same visitors might have raised a surprised eyebrow at a single
dandelion poking up in the vegetable patch, or a couple of roses that
needed dead-heading.

Lena wasn't too concerned about it, though. Some people made a fetish
of tidiness just to fill in their time . . .

And besides, Lena didn't have visitors calling midweek. Which was just as well for the visitors, for, had they done so, they would have found a locked door.

Lena would have been out, busy with her old people, whether it was with gardening, shopping for them, painting and decorating, or just having a friendly chat.

"I think the scheme should be extended," she said to Myrtle Hogg one day. "You know, widen the boundaries. We could move into Brumley Wood and Lowminster.

"I could spare an extra few hours in the week, and I'm sure the others could, too, if they were asked in the right way."

Having been asked in the right way by Lena, the others had no option but to agree. The neighbourhood group extended into two new neighbourhoods.

Lena's role extended, too. She took to going round like Myrtle had done, asking people if they wanted help with anything.

Lena liked that bit. She enjoyed telling people what they needed.

Like this old codger here, for instance, she thought, eyeing the man who had grudgingly admitted her — after a struggle on the doorstep.

"It's a volunteer neighbourhood group," she explained. "We provide practical assistance or company for elderly people who are —"

"Who's elderly?" he asked belligerently. "You're no chicken yourself!

"I'm fed up with goody-goodies coming round here and insulting me. I'm seventy-six and I'm as fit as a flea!"

"Really?" Lena sniffed. "You look a bit liverish to me. It's probably your diet. If you'd like me to get your shopping for you I could pick out the sort of things that —"

"I wouldn't! I've been getting my own shopping for fifteen years, since my wife died. And I'll go on getting it, thank you."

"Keep your hair on," Lena reproved. "Well, what about walking the dog? Or housework? We could do that."

"Do you see anything wrong with my house?" he demanded. "Go on. You run your finger over that furniture, and if you can find any dust I'll give you my next week's pension!

"Now go away. Me and Patches manage fine."

"Hmmm."

Company, Lena thought. That's what he needs. Anyone who could keep a house like this obviously had too much time on their hands — dog or no dog.

86

"Who's that in the photo?" she asked him.

"My son and his family. They live in Canada," he retorted. "Not that it's anything to do with you."

Lena smiled gleefully. She was right! His family was a long way off and he was lonely.

"Right then!" she announced. "I could come round every Friday morning for a little chat and a cup of tea. We could —"

"Not on your nelly! If you think I'm keeping you supplied with tea, you've got another think coming.

"Go on, hop it!" He ordered her out. "I don't need anyone having little chats with me. I'm perfectly all right. Push off!"

MYRTLE HOGG clucked sympathetically into the phone.

"And he's not all right," Lena continued. "It's quite obvious that he's not. He's a poor, lonely old man — which is hardly surprising, really, as he is such an objectionable, cantankerous old fool!

"But objectionable or not, we should be doing something about him, don't you agree, Miss Hogg?"

"He's probably too proud to admit he could do with some company," Myrtle agreed, tactfully saying nothing about Lena's character assessment.

"There're a lot of people like that," she went on. "Do you know the best way of dealing with them — the ones who are fit and healthy, anyway?"

"What?" Lena said.

"Ask them to take part as a helper instead of as one of the helped. It always works, and it's doubly advantageous in that we get an extra volunteer to call on, and the old person meets new friends and finds an interest in life."

"Is that right?" Lena said slowly.

"Look, I'll have to go now," Myrtle put in. "The kids will be home from school and I've to get the dinner started."

Lena glared into the purring receiver.

Give them an interest in life, indeed! She had been conned! As if she had *needed* an interest in life, she whose days were full to overflowing!

Why, anyone would think she had been one of these lonely old dears with nothing better to do!

Well, they'd see about that. She'd give it up — immediately, without a moment's notice! That would teach Myrtle Hogg.

Lena replaced the receiver and marched back into her living-room with a determined air.

On the other hand, though, she thought after tea, all these poor old folk were depending on her. It would hardly be fair, letting them down, just to spite Mrs Myrtle High-and-Mighty Hogg.

Old Mrs Harrison on a Thursday, for instance. She'd want to tell Lena how her grand-daughter in Birmingham had got on with her exams.

And there was Ina Briggs. Who'd take her out to the yard if Lena packed it in? And what about Miss Inglis' shopping?

No, she decided. Conned or not, she would have to keep it up. People depended on her. She was needed.

Lena put on her hat and coat and walked briskly round to Beech Lane.

"Ah, Mr Struthers! It's me again!" she said with a jovial, well-scrubbed smile. "After our little chat this afternoon it suddenly occurred to me that you're just the kind of person we're looking for . . ." ■

DOWN ON THE FARM

by Kath Dalmeny

Our cute little pigs and piglets, taken from the book, Kath Dalmeny's World of Knitted Toys, are so easy to make. The four different designs of pig you can choose from are all based on the markings and colours of traditional breeds.

Approximate sizes: – Adults 20 cm *(8 in)*; **Piglets 12.5 cm** *(5 in)*
Needles: 3¼ mm *(size 10)*
Scraps of DK yarn in dark brown
Pair 10 mm *(⅜ in)* toy safety eyes
Tapestry needle
Washable toy stuffing
Yarn for pigs: Large White Pig: 40g DK in pale brown; Saddleback pig: 40g DK in black; 20g DK in pink; Gloucester Old Spot pig: 40g DK in pink; scraps of DK in brown; Tamworth pig: 40g DK in ginger
Yarn for piglets: Large White piglet: 20g DK in pale brown; Saddleback piglet: 20g DK in black; 10g DK in pink; Gloucester Old Spot piglet: 20g DK in pink; scraps of DK in brown; Tamworth piglet: 20g DK in ginger
Note: One 50g ball of DK is enough to make a pig and piglet
Abbreviations – cm – centimetre(s); **DK** – double knit; **foll.** – follow or following; **g** – gram(s); **inc.** – increase or increasing; **K** – knit; **mm** – millimetre(s); **P** – purl; **rem.** – remain or remaining; **rep.** – repeat; **st.-st.** – stocking stitch; **st.** – stitch; **sts.** – stitches; **tog.** – together

How easy is it to make?

Easy! The pigs and piglets that are made in a single colour are simple to knit. The Saddleback pigs are only slightly more complex, with a change of colour on their bodies. The Gloucester Old Spot pigs and piglets may prove a bit more challenging with their embroidered spots.

Tension

Over st.-st., using 3¼ mm *(size 10)* needles, 26 sts. and 34 rows to 10 cm *(4 in)*.

Also ...

Figures in [square brackets] give the total number of stitches or rows you should have at that stage.

ADULT PIG

The following instructions are for an adult pig of the Large White breed. Colour variations for other pig breeds are included at the end.

Body and Head

Make one, using pale brown
Cast on 24 sts. Working in st.-st. throughout and beg. with a K row,
work 2 rows.

Next K row — inc. one st. into first 2 sts., K8, inc. one st. into next 4 sts., K8, inc. one st. into last 2 sts.; [32 sts.].

Next K row — inc. one st. into first st., K(14), inc. one st. into next 2 sts., K to last st., inc. one st. into last st.

Next row — P. Rep. last 2 rows, with number of sts. in brackets 2 more each time, until you have 44 sts. total. Work 39 rows; [48 rows total].

Next row — (K2 tog., K18, K2 tog.) twice; [40 sts.].

Next K row — (K2 tog., K16, K2 tog.) twice; [36 sts.].

Next K row — (K2 tog., K14, K2 tog.) twice; [32 sts.].

Next K row — (K2 tog., K2 tog., K1, K2 tog., K2, K2 tog., K1, K2 tog., K2 tog.) twice; [20 sts.].

Next row — (P2 tog., P6, P2 tog.) twice; [16 sts.]. Work 8 rows; [64 rows total]. Cast off. This is the snout end.

With smooth sides outwards, fold body and head piece in half and join long side seam. Position and fit toy safety eyes. Fill with stuffing and sew back end closed, leaving snout end open.

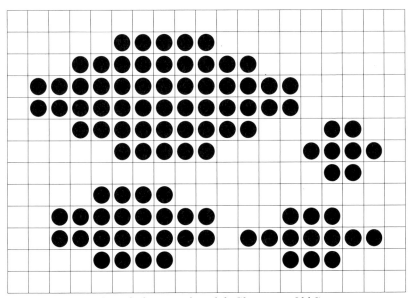

Swiss darning stitch guide for spots for adult Gloucester Old Spot pig

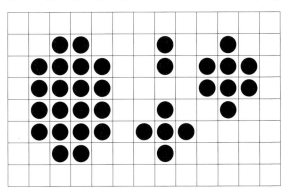

Swiss darning stitch guide for spots for Gloucester Old Spot piglet

Snout

Make one, using pale brown
Cast on 8 sts. P1 row.

Next row — inc. one st. into first st., K6, inc. one st. into last st.; [10 sts.]. Work 3 rows; [5 rows total].

Next row — K2 tog., K6, K2 tog.; [8 sts.].

Next row — P. Cast off.

Cover snout hole in head with snout piece and sew in position.

Front Legs

Make two, using pale brown
Cast on 12 sts. Work in st.-st. throughout and beg. with a K row, work 8 rows.

Next row — inc. one st. into first st., K4, inc. one st. into next 2 sts., K4, inc. one st. into last st.; [16 sts.]. Work 3 rows; [12 rows total].

Next row — inc. one st. into first st, K6, inc. one st. into next 2 sts., K6, inc.

one st. into last st.; [20 sts.]*. Work 5 rows; [18 rows total].

#Next row — (K2 tog., K6, K2 tog.) twice; [16 sts.].

Next K row — (K2 tog., K4, K2 tog.) twice: [12 sts.].

Next row — P. Cast off.

With smooth sides outwards, fold leg piece in half. Join narrow end and side seam, fill with stuffing and sew closed. Sew a 2.5 cm *(1 in.)* line of stitches up centre of foot, at right angles to base of foot, forming trotter. Ladderstitch leg to body.

Back Legs

Make two, using pale brown

Work as for front leg to *. Work 7 rows; [20 rows total]. Work as for front leg from # to end.

Make up back leg as for front leg (above) and ladderstitch to body.

Ears

Make two, using pale brown

Cast on 8 sts. Work in st.-st. throughout and beg. with a K row, work 10 rows.

K2 tog. at both ends of next and every foll. K row until 2 sts. rem.

Next row — P.

Next row — K2 tog. Break off yarn, slip end through rem. st. and pull tight. Hide end of yarn by sewing it back through knitting.

Sew straight edge of ear to head.

PIGLET

The following instructions are for a piglet of the Large White breed. Colour variations for other piglet breeds are included at the end.

Body and Head

Make one, using pale brown

Cast on 16 sts. Working in st.-st. throughout and beg. with a K row, work 2 rows.

Next row — inc. one st. into first 2 sts., K4, inc. one st. into next 4 sts., K4, inc. one st. into last 2 sts.; [24 sts.].

Next K row — inc. one st. into first st., K10, inc. one st. into next 2 sts., K10, inc. one st. into last st.; [28 sts.]. Work 25 rows; [30 rows total].

Next row — (K2 tog., K10, K2 tog.)

twice; [24 sts.].

Next K row — (K2 tog., K3, K2 tog., K3, K2 tog.) twice; [18 sts.].

Next row — (P2 tog., P5, P2 tog.) twice; [14 sts.]. Work 6 rows; [40 rows total]. Cast off. This is the snout end.

Make up as for adult pig body and head.

Snout

Make one, using pale brown

Cast on 5 sts. P1 row. Working in st.-st. throughout, next row: inc. one st. into first st., K3, inc. one st. into last st.; [7 sts.].

Work 3 rows; [5 rows total].

Next row — K2 tog., K3, K2 tog.; [5 sts.].

Next row — P. Cast off. Attach snout as for adult pig.

Front Legs

Make two, using pale brown

Cast on 8 sts. Work in st.-st. throughout and beg. with a K row, work 6 rows.

Next row — inc. one st. into first st., K2, inc. one st. into next 2 sts., K2, inc. one st. into last st.; [12 sts.].* Work 5 rows; [12 rows total].

Next row — (K2 tog., K2, K2 tog.) twice; [8 sts.].

Next row — P. Cast off.

Make up as for adult pig leg and ladderstitch to body.

Back Legs

Make two, using pale brown

Work as for front leg to *. Work 3 rows; [10 rows total].

Next row — inc. one st. into first st, K4, inc. one st. into next 2 sts., K4, inc. one st. into last st.; [16 sts.]. Work 5 rows; [16 rows total].

Next row — (K2 tog., K4, K2 tog.) twice; [12 sts.].

Next row — (P2 tog., P2, P2 tog.) twice; [8 sts.]. Cast off.

Make up as for adult pig leg and ladderstitch to body.

Ears

Make two, using pale brown

Cast on 6 sts. Work in st.-st. throughout and beg. with a K row, work 6 rows.

Next row — K2 tog., K2, K2 tog.;
[4 sts.].

Next row — P.

Next row — K2 tog., K2 tog.;
[2 sts.].

Next row — P2 tog. Break off yarn,
slip end through rem. st. and pull tight.
Hide end of yarn by sewing it back
through knitting.

Sew straight edge of ear to head.

Finishing pig and piglet

Tail

For an adult pig, make a 7.5 cm *(3 in)*
length of single chain in pale brown
yarn. For a piglet, make a 5 cm *(2 in)*
chain. At one end of chain, hide end of
yarn by sewing it back along chain, and
make a stitch to hold chain in
characteristic curly loop. Sew other end
of chain in position on pig's back.

Nostrils and Mouth

With dark brown yarn, make two or
three stitches on either side of snout as
nostrils. Use long straight stitches for a
mouth.

Colour Variations

Saddleback pig or piglet, follow pig
or piglet instructions, using the
following colours: make front legs in
pink; make back legs, snout, ears and
tail in black. Make Saddleback pig's
body and head as follows: work first 28
rows of the body and head piece in
black, the next 10 rows in pink; rem.
rows in black. Make Saddleback piglet's
body and head as follows: work first 18
rows of body and head piece in black,
next 7 rows in pink, rem. rows in black.

Gloucester Old Spot pig or piglet,
follow the pig or piglet instructions.
Make all pieces in pink. Using dark
brown yarn, make spots on pig's back
with Swiss darning.

Tamworth pig or piglet, follow pig
or piglet instructions. Make all pieces in
ginger.

Readers can order World of
Knitted Toys at the special price
of £12.99 (RRP £14.99). Postage
and packing is free in the UK
mainland. To order, call the David
& Charles Credit Card Hotline on
(01626) 334555
and quote code
C095. Or send
your order with
a cheque to,
David &
Charles
Direct, PO
Box 6,
Newton
Abbot,
Devon TQ12
2DW.

The Long Winding Road

It doesn't matter how far I roam,
The winding road will call me home,
And home is where I want to be,
When the world feels much too big for me.

There in the kitchen, Mum mixes a cake,
And out in the garden, Dad leans on his rake,
While young Billy sails his boats in the bath,
The old collie, Mac, is asleep by the hearth.

But as I grow older, the road seems longer,
The urge to roam within me grows stronger,
The long winding road which has carried me
home,
Calls me away to places unknown.

And so I'm away on my travels once more,
I say my goodbyes and I close the door,
And travel the road, so winding and long,
The need to be home, no longer so strong.

The long winding road that takes me away,
Will bring me back home again one fine day,
To my heart I must be true,
And my heart belongs at home with you.

By
Teresa Ashby

"LET YOUR HAIR DOWN, MISS POLLITT!"

By Brenda Redfern

**It came as such a surprise to everyone when she did
— especially to Miss Pollitt herself!**

MISS GWENDOLINE GRACE AMELIA POLLITT stood on the pavement outside Hazel's Boutique and fell madly in love.

It was the most beautiful dress she'd ever seen. She had to buy it — she must — and there was no-one to stop her.

Or was there? Out of the corner of her eye Gwen suddenly spotted the little imp on her left shoulder. He was sheathed in red satin from horn to tail, and was whispering in her ear.

"Go on. Buy it," he encouraged with a wicked little grin. "You love the colour, the style, the material . . ."

She couldn't deny it and the more she looked, the more he went on.

"You can almost feel the swirling hem round your ankles as you dance. Imagine it . . ."

"Imagine the price," interrupted the angel's voice drily.

She was sitting prim and proper on Gwen's other shoulder, pricking her conscience with a smile of disdain and sensible words.

Gwen knew without a shadow of doubt that this was her mother's influence still at work — even though it was two years since the old lady had passed peacefully away.

The angel sniffed, folding her silvery white wings firmly behind her back.

"I'd like half an hour in that shop with a steam iron. Look at all those creased dresses not fit to wear."

"She's a bit out of fashion, isn't she?" The imp grinned playfully, digging Gwendoline with a sharp elbow. "Anyway, your dress is far superior . . ."

"Exactly — if she buys it she'll never wear it," the angel snorted.

"Oh, but I would!" argued Miss Gwendoline Grace Amelia Pollitt, annoyed at the angel's insinuation.

But because she was a sensible, cautious person and because the imp was a mite too pushy, she added, "If I decide to buy it, that is. I'll have to think about it."

And think about it she did, all morning in her office marked 'Private Secretary' at Brimington's Mail Orders.

Size ten and not terribly expensive — not really. Suitable for someone like her? Of course it was.

"It's captured your wayward soul," crooned the imp from his perch on the intercom.

"Mark my words," preached the angel, hovering above the door, "you'd regret wasting all that money."

"Oh, shut up!" Gwendoline snapped, taking her coffee to the typing pool and banging the door behind her.

She loved listening to the typing pool gossip. This morning the girls were excitedly discussing the farewell party to be given by Major Carrington Bligh, presently retiring from the Board of Directors.

"You *are* coming, Miss Pollitt . . . you've got to come, being J.D.'s right-hand man?"

THEY were looking at her expectantly. Candy, Sally, Jane, all watching, waiting for her answer. She hesitated, feeling a tiny pulse beating beneath the collar of her neat office blouse.

Sue had asked and it was Sue who sensed her hesitation.

"Come on, we're all going. She'll love it, won't she, girls?"

Miss Pollitt looked at them, with their bright and cheerful faces, their oh, so fashionable clothes. What could she say?

"I'll be expected to put in an appearance . . . but . . . I'm afraid I can't dance," she explained.

Sally North gurgled with laughter. "So what! You just do your own thing." She slipped from her stool swaying denim hips to the rhythm of clicking fingers. "Come on, Miss Pollitt, just loosen up!"

Gwendoline felt a familiar dig in her left rib, heard an impish chuckle, and her stomach gave a flip of excitement.

"I . . . may . . . just do that," she said.

Suddenly the girls were all talking at once. They'd help her with make-up — and wasn't she lucky having dark-coloured hair! Why didn't she wear it down?

"Can't say you've let your hair down much — now can you?" the imp persisted.

Gwendoline ignored him completely. "We'll see how it goes," she promised the girls.

Morning sped by in a bustle of preparation for the last visit of VIP Major Carrington Bligh, a favourite of Gwendoline's who'd complimented her on her dedication to Brimington's and who would certainly not appreciate her present giddy state of mind.

She'd have to be alert with pad and pencil in the inner sanctum after lunch.

Tuesday lunch break usually found Miss Pollitt in the supermarket having a few quiet words with the check-out girl if her calculator and the till didn't agree. But today . . . What the heck!

She whipped smartly round the shelves with a wire basket, tossing in meals-for-one, convenience foods, reaching on tiptoe . . . Oh, why were the cereal packages so out of reach?

It was then she wavered, toppled and felt herself falling, grabbing for something to hold. Once finding that something, she held on.

It was a shoulder, she realised, a broad shoulder clothed in blue waterproof, and as the world stopped spinning she looked along the shoulder and up the lean jawline into concerned brown eyes.

"Are you all right? You nearly came a cropper there."

She thought, quite illogically, that he looked like the sort of person who might smile quite a lot. His was a kind face, topped by unruly brown hair. It was only then that she realised she was still in this stranger's arms with a stupid carton of Cornflakes between them.

She heard a squeak of a voice which must have been hers.

"I — I'm sorry." She hugged the carton to her chest so that her eyes peeped over the top.

"I like a small packet, you see. The jumbo size go soft . . . Too much, you see."

"I know," he said gravely, helping her to her feet and retrieving the wire basket, apparently oblivious to her incomprehensible muttering.

THANKING him, she bundled away through the check-out without a backward glance, pausing outside the supermarket and drawing a deep breath.

A familiar male voice interrupted her reverie.

"I'm not in the habit of being pushy, but you seem a little shaken. May I offer you a lift?"

Somehow she managed to find her voice.

"Actually, it's very good of you, but I'm depositing my groceries, having a quick snack and then it's back to the office."

But he was already swinging her purchases in one capable hand, pacing his stride to the quick tip-tap of her sensible heels.

Gwendoline's eyes slid sideways as they passed the boutique . . . she'd ring and have the dress put aside.

She felt a quick thrill run down her spine, a shiver of anticipation.

"Cold?" he asked, watching her carefully. "Yes, you are."

He was taking her arm and within minutes they were in a nearby bistro.

"It's been an odd sort of morning," she commented across the checked tablecloth and found her glance captured by soft brown eyes.

"My name's Pollitt, Gwendoline Pollitt," she said hurriedly, her heart beating suddenly, "and I can only thank you again and apologise."

"No apologies needed and it's been a pleasure." They shook hands solemnly over the cruet. "Nicholas Owen, known I understand as 'Old Nick' in some circles."

Gwendoline's heart sank.

"Oh, I'm sure they don't intend . . . I mean nicknames usually denote a degree of affection . . ."

She felt herself blushing.

"The girls in my office are like that. Yet they're really caring in their own way. That's what had me rushing so."

She took a deep breath.

"You see, they want me to attend a sort of party given by the firm — Brimington Mail Orders, you know. I've never been able to before . . ."

He was listening attentively, nodding his head in such an encouraging way that she found herself telling him about the dress and about how she'd had to combine business with caring for Mother, who had been a darling, of course . . . But socialising had been impossible.

". . . And sometimes sickness and enforced immobility makes people a little trying," she told him and he nodded with understanding.

"So that eventually one would appreciate a plate-glass window to throw things at," he finished for her.

"Oh yes, I really have felt like throwing things many a time.

"*Time!* Oh, Mr Owen. I'll have to go. Thanks for everything, but you see we have this VIP . . ."

She was late, of course. Her day so far had been spent in a whirl, she mused, as she tidied her hair, picking up her notebook and arranging mid-afternoon tea for three.

"Four," Sally corrected. "The major's . . ."

"Never mind, Sally, I'll check."

Gwendoline opened the door to the inner sanctum and stopped, feeling colour flooding from the tip of her toes in an almighty upward sweep till she felt her face must be aflame.

It was "Old Nick' himself. No blue waterproof, of course, and the unruly hair was well under control . . . which couldn't be said for her state of mind.

Her boss, the Managing Director of Brimington's, sat behind his desk and as she moved automatically to her chair she realised Major Carrington Bligh was speaking.

"Let me introduce my nephew, Nicholas Owen. He's to take my seat on the Board, Miss Pollitt."

GWENDOLINE dropped her pencil and whilst retrieving it she noted well-cut slacks and leather shoes, obviously hand-made. Why hadn't she noticed? What must he have thought of her chattering on like some junior typist?

Blast it! He might have mentioned his connection with the firm when she told him where she worked. But, come to think of it, she hadn't given him time to get a word in edge ways . . .

"We've met already," Nicholas Owen was saying.

She nodded, hoping her smile wasn't as tight-lipped as it felt.

"And where may I ask did you happen upon my favourite Girl Friday, young man?

"Well, never mind." The major smiled. "The lad comes with my blessing, J.D. Been all over the world, knows mail order from pillar box to head office."

A gleam lit the major's eye. "Not that we haven't had our skirmishes, mind. There have been times when I'd have thrown him and his idea through the nearest window, what!"

With a start Gwendoline looked up, catching Nicholas Owen's eye twinkling a silent message, and she felt her mouth twitching as laughter bubbled up inside.

What had he said? ". . . sometimes one would appreciate a plate-glass window . . ."?

She felt warmth stealing through her, the joy of humour shared with a kindred spirit.

Then business absorbed them all, details were finalised and as she rose to leave the men to more private discussion, Nicholas Owen was there opening the door.

"Goodbye for the present, Miss Pollitt. I'm flying to Germany in the morning but I'm sure we'll meet again," he said formally, and as she passed, he whispered, "Buy that dress. Enjoy yourself." Then she was safely on the other side of the door.

She flung her notepad on the desk. What had she expected? Prince Charming taking Cinders to the ball?

Yes, admit it, for one fleeting moment the idea had floated dreamily across her mind; one shared bubble of humour and she'd been on cloud nine. He'd soon brought her down to earth and left her feeling deflated and yes, blast it, patronised!

But then she felt the imp poke her and whisper devilishly in her ear. "Show him a clean pair of heels, buy the dress, and have a ball!"

SHE would!

She did! Sweeping into Hazel's Boutique and out again, she left the bored assistant choking on her chewing gum.

She made an appointment to have her hair cut and styled and for good measure she'd have a manicure and a facial.

"*Great!*" the imp crowed.

"I'm speechless!" the angel gasped.

"Why don't you both mind your own business?" Miss Gwendoline Grace Amelia Pollitt suggested.

In an instant they were both gone.

Huh, she thought, they can't stand a bit of criticism, can they?

IF she felt a lump in her throat, if her knees shook and her pulse raced as she joined staff and guests for her pre-dinner sherry, she was darned if she'd let it show.

"You look radiant, my dear," the major's wife said in the powder room after the dinner speeches were over.

"Shall we join the young folk?"

"*Wow!* Miss P. You look ace!" It was Sally, her face incredulous through the powder room mirror.

"Come and let the others see that dress. It's brill!"

Gwendoline was swept away by their enthusiasm into a ring of merrymakers on the dance floor.

They did something called 'The Apple Tree' and gentle hands pushed her forward so that she took her turn whirling into the centre and weaving in and out of the other dancers.

She was floating, circling, with the dress swirling round her ankles as she'd dreamed it would. She was thistledown spinning until her heart leapt to the laughter and music.

The girls taught her to relax and "do her own thing," until, breathless, she subsided with a cooling drink.

At first she sat happily sipping and watching, her foot tapping to the music. The major fox-trotted past, dipping into an intricate step and winking at her over his wife's lace-covered shoulder.

Her glass was empty now and she'd love to be up with the crowd, but the floor was full of couples, she realised. Her foot stilled and she looked down into her glass.

They mustn't know she minded being alone. She must smile, smile until her lips were aching. In any case, if anyone asked her to dance she would stumble, wouldn't she?

The lights were dimming now, the couples were drawing closer, moving in a world that set her longing, aching inside with all the bubbling happiness draining away.

If only . . . She squeezed her eyes tightly trying to blot out the memory of unruly hair and broad shoulders, and then opened them wide, searching for escape.

"Chicken!" teased the imp, glad to be back. "Do your own thing. Go on — what are you waiting for?"

The angel pursed her lips disapprovingly.

No, the angel was right. She hadn't the heart.

She put the glass under her chair and started to move between the couples, slipping towards the door. Like this no-one would notice she was leaving.

She was almost there when a swirling couple knocked her sideways and she felt herself falling as if in slow motion. Then she was caught and held against a broad shoulder . . . the dancers moved on.

"Are you all right?" he asked.

"What are you doing here?" she asked, ignoring the tutting angel.

In answer he took her in his arms and eased her into the crowd of dancers. It was as if they were one; as if she was melting against him, following him easily with a tingling in her heart.

"I was actually on the tarmac at the airport, not very happy and asking myself why I didn't want to go."

She looked up at him, watching his eyes crinkle teasingly.

"And the answer came like a flash," he said. "I just had to see . . . that dress."

He nestled closer, his mouth against her hair.

"Say you're pleased to see me here, Gwen."

"She'll think about it," said the imp and angel in unison, but Gwendoline Grace Amelia Pollitt hadn't heard a word. ■

THE CANINE CONNECTION

By AUDREY GROOM

Ask anyone with a pet and they'll tell you — you can't stay aloof for long with an animal around!

"**Y**OUR Aphelandra shouldn't look like that," Emily remarked, eyeing the wilting Zebra plant with disapproval. "You've obviously not fed it."

"Would it prefer gold-top milk or soup?" I teased, and watched her face darken.

"Don't be flippant, Dinah," she said wearily, and I sighed.

Sometimes, it's hard to believe that Emily, with her neat, efficient ways, is indeed my sister. By comparison, I am hopeless. I am untidy, disorganised and – by her reckoning – I give my friendship and affection to all the wrong sort of people.

Now, I don't mean that Emily is a snob. She doesn't judge people by what they do for a living – but how they do it. She has, for example, the highest regard for a roadsweeper who makes a nice, neat job of sweeping the road.

But for a schoolmaster who forgets to send home notices of the next PTA meeting, or a vicar who loses his next sermon, Emily has nothing but scorn.

Of my late husband, Matthew, Emily had been, happily, tolerant. He was a "border-line case," she told me once. He was casual in his dress, but not scruffy. He worked hard and he never lost his temper.

Besides — and I think this was what really swayed Emily in his favour — he was absolutely, overwhelmingly polite to her, always.

I was distraught when he died, and Emily had genuinely mourned him, too. However, thinking children should be seen and not heard, she'd always found my two, Ros and Tom, a bit of a strain when she came to stay.

I didn't. I thought they were rather smashing, and had missed them terribly ever since they'd settled abroad — in California and Australia respectively.

One day, I'd go out and see them both, I promised myself. But, in the meantime, something had happened which had eased my loneliness, and made my longing for my family at least bearable.

I had met Sam.

Sam was wonderful, warm, loving, kind and almost as disorganised as I was. Although we'd only known each other for a matter of months, already I loved him very much – more than I had ever loved anybody, except Matthew. But of course he understood that, just as I understood about his Doris.

And that brought us closer together still. When he'd asked me to marry him, a few weeks earlier, I had said "yes" with all my heart.

I was sure it was this news, conveyed in a letter to my sister, which had brought her hot-foot to 'spend a holiday' with me.

That, and discovering what Sam did for a living. Something I was going to help him do, once we were married. And that was running a small boarding kennels.

Emily, retired now and living quietly, with her half of Mother's small legacy neatly tucked away in a building society, thought I should be doing the same.

She had come to stay with me for a few weeks, wanting, as she put it, "to have a serious talk about the future.

Had Sam been the sort to impress her on first sight, things might have been different. But of course he wasn't. Dressed to work out-of-doors, with animals, he wasn't exactly a candidate for Emily's approval.

"You must be mad, Dinah," she said, after meeting him. "Are you seriously considering marrying a man like that? He doesn't look as though he could manage one dog, let alone a kennelful.

"Besides," she went on. "You won't be much help. You can't even see to your plants properly."

And that's when the conversation about the Aphelandra took place.

"You're hopeless." She shook her head with familiar regret. This was the conclusion she usually ended up with. "Thank goodness Mother didn't live to see the mistake you're making.

"And I hope you're not thinking of handing her little nest-egg over to this Sam character."

"This 'Sam character' is going to be your brother-in-law soon, Emily, so you might as well come to terms with it," I told her.

"As for Mother and her nest-egg — yes, I shall offer it to Sam, if he needs it. And no-one could understand that better than she would have done."

Emily tossed her head and went to bed. And, as usual, I felt mean and guilty for insisting on doing things my own way. So, when Sam called in for a night-cap a bit later, I poured it all out to him.

"It's not all your fault, Di," he said. "The trouble with your sister, as I see it, is that she's never really been close to anyone. She's never been married, probably never even nursed a baby. Did she ever cuddle yours, Di?"

I shook my head, remembering Ros and Tom's awe of her as toddlers.

"No — that's it, you see. It's rather sad," he said.

I TRIED to be extra-specially nice to Emily next morning, to make up for my rudeness of the night before.

It was a lovely sunny day, so I was pleased when Sam came round in the afternoon, and suggested taking us both for a drive.

"Can't be too long though," he apologised. "Young Peter's gone home to his mum's with a bad dose of flu, so Harry's up at the kennels on his own."

By the time he had taken us to Downlands, by the river, and then up Silver Birch Hill to see the view, time was getting on.

"How about dropping in at the kennels just to see that all's well?" he asked hopefully. "We could have a cup of tea and show you round, Emily, before driving back."

He was using all his charm on her, and that's quite a lot! But sometimes Emily seems to almost freeze when you try to be nice to her, and all she gave was a polite nod.

Anyway, we got out of the car, and I ushered her into Sam's little cottage. He bustled about, putting the kettle on, while I hunted in the cupboard for biscuits and some cake I had made for him.

We had just started on it, in fact, when the front-door bell shrilled. When Sam had answered it, we heard him talking to someone in the hall.

"Off you go, then, Harry," he eventually called out as his visitor left. "Hope everything's OK."

He came back into the kitchen looking a bit worried.

"Someone from the village has just come up and asked Harry to go straight home. His wife thinks it's the baby coming. It's nearly a month early, so he'll have to get her to the hospital at once."

"I hope she's all right then." I frowned.

"Hmm. Me too." Sam also looked concerned. "And we've got another mother-in-trouble as well — Judy, the Westie. Harry thinks there's something wrong, so I'll go and take a look."

Sam looked even more anxious when he returned.

"I think the pups are coming, Dinah, but I'm just as bothered about Judy herself. Perhaps we should get her straight down to Bill's." (He's our local vet.)

"OK, Sam," I said. "Shall I come with you?"

"Well — I'll need someone, yes." He paused. "But there's the rest of the dogs to feed. Harry put their meals ready before he left, but if we both go . . ."

Suddenly it seemed as though Emily really took in what he was saying, and a look of absolute horror passed over her face. But this was an emergency, and I saw very clearly what I must do.

"Well, that's no problem. We've got Emily here. She's jolly capable," I told him, crossing fingers behind my back for luck. "She could either stay here and feed the dogs — or go in the van with you, Sam, and sit with Judy.

"I know that she'll want to help in one way or another," I added, watching my sister's face get pinker and pinker.

Emily clenched and unclenched her hands. I had never seen her look quite this way before. Yet I was sure, somehow, that it wasn't that she didn't want to help, but that she felt inadequate in some way.

Sam settled the question.

"Come on, Emily — you come with me," he said. "It's probably only a matter of sitting in the van and keeping an eye on Judy. I think we'll get her

to Bill's before anything happens. And Di knows all about feeding the dogs."

I'd never seen my sister look so apprehensive or out of her depth as when she followed Sam down the drive. In spite of the crisis at hand, my heart went out to her. Behind that mask of efficiency and disapproval, she was quite vulnerable. Why had I never seen it before?

I COULDN'T stand there thinking about Emily's problems all evening. There were about 20 hungry dogs to feed.

About an hour after I'd gone back indoors and cleaned myself up again, the phone rang.

"It's me — Sam. Judy *was* in trouble. She had a couple of pups OK in the van, but something was wrong — the others got stuck.

103

"Bill delivered the rest safely, but he wants to keep them at his place for the night, as they're rather weak at the moment. Anyway — I'll be home soon."

"That's great, Sam! And all's well here. But how's Emily?"

"Fine, actually," he replied. "Took it all in her stride. She was wonderful."

I replaced the phone with a bemused smile, and was waiting, impatient for their return, when it rang again.

It was Harry. They'd kept his wife in and he was still at the hospital.

"I can't promise to be back for a few days, at least," he said anxiously. "It depends on how things go."

I told him not to worry — he had more important things to think about, I understood.

"She's in good hands, Harry," I reassured him. "They'll be fine."

When Emily and Sam returned, my sister looked very subdued. She washed her hands carefully and I noticed that her dress was soiled from the van, but she didn't say anything. She just sat down and drank the tea I had made.

"I'll run you home now, Emily, shall I?" I suggested when she'd finished. "Then, if it's OK with you, I'll come back to help Sam."

"You needn't do that," Emily answered quietly. "I'll stay the night, too, if there's room. There might be something . . ." Her voice tailed away.

"It'll be terribly noisy, Emily," I warned her. "The dogs bark at the slightest noise. You won't sleep well."

"That's all right." She gave a small, wry smile.

Sam's eyes were bright. I could see he was pleased with her offer.

"Marvellous!" He grinned with relief. "Emily, I — well, I can't thank you enough.

"And don't worry about night-clothes," he added. "I bought two spanking new pairs of pyjamas last week. You two can borrow those."

Well, to see my formal sister padding round the kitchen in a pair of boldly-striped pyjamas and Sam's old dressing-gown, had to be seen to be believed.

And the next day was even stranger. I woke up early and went downstairs as I knew the kennels had to be cleaned out before breakfast. Sam was already working with a mop and pail.

"What happened to Emily yesterday?" I demanded.

He paused for a moment, leaning on his broom.

"I don't know, Di," he said. "I had to stop the van, of course, while those first pups were born. And I happened to glance at Emily's face.

"You know how tiny and helpless puppies are, and with Judy washing them and everything . . . Well, I don't think your sister could take it all in. She looked as if she was going to cry."

Even as we spoke, Emily was coming towards us. The grime had been sponged from her dress but her expression was softer than I'd ever seen it.

"Harry's just phoned," she told us. "They've got a little girl."

"Oh! That's splendid! Thanks Em."

She didn't even blanch at the abbreviation I so seldom used, but just asked, "Can I help?"

I thought quickly and went along to little Carly's kennel. She's a Yorkshire terrier who pines terribly for her mistress, and needs a bit of pampering.

"You could take this one into the house, if you like. Perhaps we can persuade her to eat," I said.

Emily lifted the small dog from my arms awkwardly, but held her quite firmly and gently as she walked away. Then, suddenly, she turned back to us.

"Sam, you will ring to see how the puppies are this morning, won't you?"

"Yes, Emily." He smiled. "Yes, I certainly will."

T was just over a week before Harry came back. In the meantime, Peter was still sick, so Emily and I were Sam's assistants.

During that time, we did manage to pop down to see the new baby, but it was easier to drool over Judy and her pups. They were soon back at the kennels and progressing nicely.

So when, at last, we returned to my quiet house, it seemed like a different world. And I thought I had better make the rest of my sister's stay more civilised.

"Emily," I began, while we were drinking a sherry that evening, "you've had an odd sort of holiday. I'm sorry things worked out the way they did."

"Don't be, Dinah," she said.

She was quiet and very subdued for Emily, for the rest of her stay. I didn't know quite how to treat her, really. And it wasn't until her last morning, when she had packed and her case was standing in the hall, that I saw just how much she'd changed.

"Dinah, you'll probably think me very foolish . . ." She hesitated. "But do you think — would there be any chance of me having one of Judy's pups?"

"Oh! Emily — I'm sure there would. But you — I didn't think . . ."

"That I liked dogs? No, I know, I didn't. Didn't like people much, either. Never sure how they'd behave, what they'd do next . . .

"I've always thought life was a rather hard, lonely struggle, Dinah. And, I suppose, I've always been a little jealous of you, and that made me bossy.

"I didn't know why, until now." Pausing, her eyes became wistful. "It's because people — and animals — love you, and you love them. It makes a sort of warmth all round you. Something I've never had."

"But, Emily, I'm dis—"

"No — let me finish, Dinah. You see, you care, really care — whatever the sacrifice or inconvenience.

"Sitting in the van, watching those pups being born, I was just amazed. Sort of humbled, I suppose, at Judy's instincts to look after them, to wash them and love them.

"And then your Sam — your wonderful Sam. Dinah, he was so gentle with them.

"I've never come close to all that before," she finished.

"No," I whispered softly. "No, I suppose not, Em."

"So." Her tone was a bit brisker now, more like her old voice. "I'll buy one of those pups, if I may. Perhaps I could fetch it when I come down for your wedding. You were going to invite me, weren't you?"

"Of course we were, Em!" And I did something I hadn't done since I was about ten. I kissed her. Then, for some reason, we both made a big thing of looking for our hankies.

Sam drew up at the gate in the car, ready to take her to the station. We walked up the path together, and she suddenly remembered something.

"I've got an indoor-gardening book at home, Dinah. I'll lend it to you. You'd better read the bit on Aphelandra. Cultured plants like things to be done a certain way, you know."

"Yes, Emily," I said meekly, and smiled. ∎

By S. Burkhill

"I Love Daddy Best . . ."

It hurt so much to hear those words — when he knew his stepdaughter meant someone else . . .

AILIE was wearing a strawberry-pink pinafore and frilly white blouse when they went off this afternoon. Usually she wears jeans and sweatshirts, but today June insisted she dress in a more ladylike fashion, and for once Ailie didn't argue.

She looked so grown up for six, like a miniature version of her mother, as the two of them walked down the path. June turned and waved before they got into the car, but Ailie didn't, and I felt a stab of hurt.

Silly, really. She had so many other things on her mind today, I couldn't expect the little gesture of farewell she always makes on parting.

It reminded me of the first time I saw her, four years ago.

My father's elder sister had died two months previously and left me the small flat. The property market was bad at the time, so I decided to rent it out for a year rather than try to sell. June and Ailie were the first response to the advertisement in the paper.

"Do you mind children?" June had asked. "Some people do, I know, but we'll be very careful with everything.

"It's nice," she added, looking round. "Nice furniture and décor."

"Nice!" the child in her arms echoed, and I smiled.

"No, I don't mind children," I told her. "You can move in whenever you like, if you want it."

"Beginning of July, then?" She raised an eyebrow. "We've got to give four weeks' notice on our present place. Will that suit?"

I said it would, and told her she could see the lawyer about the lease and everything, glad to have the business settled so quickly.

"Bye-bye!" Ailie lifted her hand and waved to me as they got to the door.

"Bye-bye!" I answered, and returned the wave.

There should have been no need for me to see them again, really. The solicitors were taking care of everything, but the rôle of landlord was a novel one for me and I wanted to make sure my tenants were settled.

"Just thought I'd check that everything's all right," I said, when I called round at the end of their first month. "No problems?"

"No, everything's fine," June answered as she invited me in. "Would you like some coffee, Mr Grant?"

"Tony," I said. "Thanks, that would be nice, if it's not any trouble. I'm just on my way back from my office.

"We don't usually work on a Saturday, but we're doing a stock check."

"What do you do?" she called from the kitchen.

"I'm with a publishing company, Production Manager."

The child was playing on the floor with some books, and I glanced down at them.

"That's right, you keep buying those ones," I told her. "Then you'll keep me in a job!"

"Cat!" Ailie announced, holding one up to me. "Pussy cat!"

"So it is," I agreed.

"Dog!" She turned a page and beamed at me.

"Don't get involved," June warned, coming back in with a tray. "She'll have you there all day, going through her repertoire."

"Still, dogs and cats are a change from flowers." She handed me a mug, and smiled.

"My parents look after her during the day, while I'm at work, and my mother's a fanatical gardener. She gives her seed catalogues to play with.

"I don't know any other two-year-olds who can differentiate between marigolds and pansies and roses."

"Magold!" Ailie said, and June shrugged eloquently.

I wondered about her. She looked about 23 or 24, around 10 years younger than I was. Was she a widow? A divorcée, more likely. Or possibly even a single parent, in spite of the ring on her finger and the "Mrs" Cunningham.

"I'm divorced," June said, as if reading my thoughts. "Well, almost divorced," she added.

What could I say? "I'm sorry" made it seem too much like a death, but I didn't know what the proper response for a situation like that should be.

Copping out, I nodded and said nothing at all.

"It's funny," she went on, reading my mind again, "divorce is so common now, yet people never really know how to deal with it."

"I suppose it's because they don't know the circumstances," I said. "They don't know whether commiserations or congratulations are in order."

She laughed.

"That's true. I'm not even too sure myself! Graham and I were married for just over a year, then, just at the same time Ailie arrived, he was made redundant."

She took a sip of coffee and said lightly, "I don't know which was the bigger strain on him.

"We sold the house, moved into a rented flat, and then he got the chance of a contract job in Germany for six months. It was supposed to get us on our feet again."

She paused and moved the tray which Ailie had decided to investigate.

"Maybe that was the mistake." She shrugged. "Anyway, having had another taste of the single life, he came to the conclusion it was preferable to crying babies and nappies hanging about the place.

"When the contract ended he came home for a couple of days and then took off for the Middle East. That's where he is now."

"It must have been tough on you," I said after a moment.

"It could have been worse," she said, philosophically. "I've got a part-time job, and he does send some money when he remembers. So we get by.

"At least we do now that we've got this place." She grinned. "It's a lot cheaper than the last flat."

Once more I was stuck for a response, but Ailie saved me the trouble of finding a trite comment by saying "Cow!" insistently.

"It's not a cow, it's a duck," her mother corrected.

"Cow!" Ailie repeated.

"No, it's not, it's a duck," I chipped in. "Look, there's a cow over there." I pointed. "*That's* a cow."

Ailie looked at it and her lips set in a firm line.

"Duck," she said, daring me to contradict her.

Grinning, I shook my head, wondering how any man could walk out on a little thing like that.

"All right, clever clogs," I said. "It's a duck."

* * * *

I didn't mean to get involved. I'd been involved before, but the girl hadn't felt the same way. Now I was definitely wary.

But taking some books round for the child wasn't getting involved. Not really.

Neither was suggesting a drive to the coast one Sunday afternoon at the end of August when I found myself at a loose end. It was just — just a friendly gesture.

It was a nice day. We went paddling in the water with Ailie and dried our feet with paper hankies afterwards. I could still feel the sand between my toes as I drew up outside the flat.

"That was lovely," June said. "Thanks for taking us. We've had a great time."

"I had a great time, too," I admitted. "We could maybe do it again one day — and take swimming costumes and towels next time."

Ailie started to wave bye-bye, but June stopped me.

"Er — would you like to stay and have something to eat?" she said, diffidently. "It'll only be cottage pie, but if you'd like . . ."

"I'd love to." I smiled.

We did lots of things together after that day. We went to the park to feed the "Cows". We had a day at the zoo. We went back to the coast as well.

Always it was the three of us who went out. The first time I saw June alone was in November, the week her *decree nisi* came through. She was quiet and sad-looking.

"Let's go out for dinner," I said. "Get your mother to babysit and I'll book a table somewhere nice for tomorrow night."

"It's not that I'm still in love with him," she said over the roast duckling. "Because I'm *not*.

"It's just — oh, I don't know. I feel so many different things. I feel angry that he doesn't seem to give a hoot for his own daughter. And I feel sad because I know there *were* good times in the early days.

"He could be so charming and such good fun — as long as he hadn't any problems to worry about and keep irritating him."

She pushed some Brussels sprouts around her plate.

"I feel relieved, too, in a way. Relieved that it's all over and Ailie and I can get on with making a life for ourselves.

"And I also feel confused," she added with a wry smile, "because I'm not used to feeling so many different things all at once!"

"Forget it," I told her, "just for tonight. Forget all about it. Have another glass of wine and eat your cow."

"Sorry!" She smiled at me across the table. "My cow's delicious. How's yours?"

I SPENT Christmas Day at June's parents; a happy, silly day, full of cracker-pulling and funny hats and all the daft things I hadn't done in years.

I watched Ailie open her presents, bubbling over with excitement as she tore at the wrapping papers. And I felt a hard lump in my throat when she settled on to my knee after dinner and fell asleep clutching my tie.

On New Year's Day I went to visit them in their own little flat.

"Happy New Year," I said, kissing June.

"Happy New Year, darling."

June looked thoughtful.

"I always get a bit depressed at this time," she told me. "You know — thinking about the old year and wondering what the next one will be like."

"It'll be a terrific year. I promise it will," I told her.

It *was* a terrific year. June and I got married on a cold bright Wednesday in October at a little registry office. It was a quiet ceremony, and Ailie stayed with June's parents while we had a brief honeymoon in Edinburgh.

"Ailie should've been here. She'd've loved this," I said as we went through the Museum of Childhood, looking at all the old-fashioned toys.

June laughed and punched me playfully. "I love my daughter, but even *I* don't want her on my honeymoon," she said.

"No, I suppose not," I laughed too, and took her hand.

Then her words suddenly struck me.

"*Our* daughter," I corrected. "You said 'my'. She's ours now."

"So she is," June said softly, and squeezed my arm.

We'd sold both flats and bought a house out on the edge of town. June's mother and Ailie were waiting there for us when we got back.

"Did you miss me, Tony?" Ailie demanded.

"Of course I missed you, chicken," I told her, lifting her into my arms. "We won't leave you behind again, I promise."

"D'you love Mummy better than me?" she asked later, when I went up to say goodnight to her.

"Mmm." I decided to tell the truth. "No. I love you both equally, but in different ways."

"How much?"

"Oh, 'bout that much." I held my hands wide apart.

"I love you, too." She lay down and poked her hand out from the covers to give me a little wave.

"Good night, Tony."

"Good night, sweetheart."

Life was good. People say there are bound to be problems with a ready-made family, but then there are problems with any family at all, aren't there? Ours were no different from any other couple with a child.

"You're always spoiling her, Tony," June would complain, though sometimes it was the other way round, and I would accuse June of being too soft with her.

Ailie was such a stubborn little madam at times and being defied by a child irritated me no end. But Ailie and I would both refuse to give in and make peace.

"Honestly, you're so like each other it's just not true!" June said dozens of times.

She said it just two months ago, in fact, but that time she tilted her head to one side and added thoughtfully, "I wonder if your own child will take after you as much as *she* does. I don't think I'll be able to stand having three mules in · the house!"

"Three?"

I stared at her for confirmation, and she beamed like a magician who's just brought off a successful trick. "Well, I think so. But don't go handing out cigars until we're sure."

We were sure a week later.

"What would you like best?" I asked Ailie. "A little boy or a little girl?" She was delighted with the news.

"I think I'd like a girl best," she said thoughtfully. "Boys aren't nice. I could play with a little sister.

"What'll we call her?"

"Oh, we'll have to think about that. We'll look up some names, you and Mum and me."

"What would you really like?" June said later. "Boy or girl?"

"Doesn't really matter," I told her. "I suppose a boy would be nice. Then we'd have one of each. A gentleman's family, isn't that what they call it?"

June smiled softly. "I love you so much, Tony," she said. "I wish . . . I wish Ailie *was* yours. Really yours, I mean."

"She *is*," I told her. "Just as much as this other child will be. I couldn't love this baby any more than I love her. You know that."

"Yes, I know it," she said. It was true. I had never thought of Ailie as anything other than mine from the night that June and I got back from our honeymoon. Or at least I hadn't, until last week . . . Until the phone call came.

"Graham rang today," June said slowly that night, after Ailie had gone up to bed. "He's in London. He wants to come up and see her."

"Well, he can't!" I answered a moment later, when the first shock had worn off. "I hope you told him that."

What right did he have to see her now? What right had he to come around upsetting our lives?

In the four years since the divorce, he had made no effort to contact his daughter.

There had been no Christmas or birthday cards, no presents — nothing. He hadn't even acknowledged the few letters June had written, like when she told him we were getting married and he needn't continue with his intermittent maintenance cheques.

What right did he have to Ailie now?

"He's got every right," June said wearily. "He's still her father, whether we like it or not. We can't forbid him to see her.

"And anyway, it wouldn't be fair to Ailie. We can't make a decision like that for her."

Of course we couldn't. I knew that, but it didn't help any.

"What did he say — exactly?"

"Not a lot. He asked how I was. And how she was. Then he said he'd arrived back in the country last weekend, and asked if he could come up and see us.

"Maybe — maybe he'll be going away soon," she finished.

"And maybe he won't," I said flatly. "Maybe he's going to settle here now."

"What if he does? What if he wants access to her?"

"If he'd been around right from the start it would have been different. But not now. Not now she's . . ."

Not now she's mine, I wanted to say, and couldn't.

June told Ailie about the visit the next day. She understood the situation, of course — well, as much as a child of six *could* understand.

It had been easier before, though, easier for all of us, when "Daddy" was just a shadowy figure who lived a long, long way away and whose name never cropped up in conversation.

She didn't say very much about it — just looked from her mother to me and nodded solemnly, then went off to play in the garden.

I didn't say very much either, feeling for the first time like an outsider in this little family drama.

Even today when June took her to meet him, I could do no more than tell her to be a good girl and give her a brief pat on the head.

And then I went and sat in the living-room, staring at the clock and reliving all the little incidents of her growing, all the hurts and happiness that I had shared and this other man, this stranger, had missed.

Would she think about that, I wondered. Would a child's mind be able to grasp the fact that I was the one who had been a real father to her?

Or would the pull of the blood tie be there, making her love this charming, attractive rogue and see old Tony for what he really was, just her mother's husband?

I T was after seven when they came in.

"Hello, chicken. How did you get on?" I asked, trying to sound casual.

"Fine."

June caught my eye before she went to dish up the casserole I had put in the oven, and smiled.

"It's all right," she said quietly.

What did "all right" mean, I wondered. Ailie didn't look all right. She was flushed and over-excited, and she pulled away from me when I tried to touch her.

"Did you have a nice time?" I asked.

"Yes, it was lovely. We went to a hotel for tea, and I had two doughnuts, and then we went to the park."

"Did you? That was nice."

"My daddy's got a big car," she went on, and I felt a thud in my stomach at her easy use of the name.

"He's got a big house, too — an apartment, and it's got a swimming pool, and he's all lovely and brown, 'cause it's summer nearly all the time where he lives.

"And he's got servants," she threw in, as June called us to eat.

For once Ailie didn't make a fuss about going to bed. She got washed and cleaned her teeth without even being told. I didn't bother to call her back for her goodnight kiss.

"What happened?" I asked June. "Is he staying over here? Does he —"

She shook her head and took a deep breath.

"I don't know where to start. I feel so relieved, and yet I feel angry, too.

"He's just back here for a couple of weeks' holiday. He says . . ." She paused. "He says he doesn't like loose ends, if you please, and it would be better if we could get them all tied up!"

"Loose ends? Ailie?" I squeezed the arm of the settee, wishing it were Graham Cunningham's neck.

"Anyway, the good news is that if you want to adopt her legally, he's agreeable."

"Does she know?" I asked after a moment.

"No. He sent her to get an ice-cream while we talked," she said. "At least he had that much sense. We can talk to her about it tomorrow."

At one time it would have been marvellous news. June had written to Graham Cunningham twice over the years to suggest it, but there had never been any response.

I should have been delighted, but I wasn't.

"Why did he have to see her?" I asked, harshly. "Why come into her life again, if he's just going to go out of it for good?

"How will she feel when she never sees him again? She seems — she seems to care for him," I added, and even the words hurt — terribly.

June squeezed my hand. "Of course she doesn't care about him. She doesn't know him.

"She's just impressed by his silly talk, that's all. She'll be back to normal tomorrow, and it'll all be forgotten about, you'll see."

* * * *

Ailie was lying on her back, looking up at the ceiling and clutching Rebecca, her rag doll, when I went in.

"You forgot your goodnight kiss, pet," I said awkwardly, brushing my lips to her forehead.

"Did you . . . did you like your dad very much?" I asked, knowing I should leave well alone, but unable to resist the question.

"Yes," she said.

I swallowed, thinking of that first night we spent in this house, and Ailie's childish demand for reassurance. June was right. We were so alike . . .

"Better . . . better than me?" I asked foolishly.

"Yes!"

Ailie sat up suddenly and glared at me.

"And better than Mummy, too! I like him best in the whole wide world, so I don't care if you send me away with him! I want to go, so there!"

I stared at her flushed, angry little face.

"Send you away with him?" I repeated. "Who's going to send you away with him?"

"You are!" she shouted. Her eyes grew bright, but Ailie would never give anyone the satisfaction of tears.

"You don't want me any more now you're going to have your own little girl, and that's why you brought him to take me away!

"And I'm glad! I am!" She stared defiantly at me and struggled as I tried to take her in my arms.

"Ailie, nobody sent for him!" I told her. "We didn't want him to come."

"You did."

"All right, then. We did send for him," I agreed. Sometimes you've just got to agree with Ailie, even if it means admitting that cows are ducks.

"But not for the reason you think," I went on. "We sent for him because — because you've been *almost* my daughter for a long time now, but the only person who can make you *properly* mine is your dad. He's got to sign a little bit of paper and then you'll be mine completely."

I took her hand, and she didn't pull away from me this time.

"And we had to send for him *now* because I wanted it all settled before the other baby came along. I wanted you to be first, Ailie, because you'll always be first with me.

"Can you understand that?"

She looked confused and uncertain, and I didn't blame her.

"And when he's signed that bit of paper, you'll be my dad — my proper dad?"

"That's right. Will you have me, Ailie? Will you let me be your dad?

"I haven't got a big car and a swimming pool and servants, but I do love you, chicken. You know that."

She bit her lip.

"I didn't really like him better than you and Mummy," she said slowly. "I only pretended I did. I didn't really like him at all. I didn't know what to say to him."

She looked up.

"And will I call you 'Daddy,' like the new baby will? Not Tony?"

"Uh-huh. Can you do that, chicken?"

"Daddy." She giggled. "It sounds funny."

"It won't sound funny for long," I said, tucking her in. "You'll get used to it."

I was at the door when she called me back.

"Daddy?"

The tears came, spilling out all the fears and frustrations that had built up over the week. Mine came, too, and I held her in my arms until the little body grew limp and she fell asleep. ■

I'LL SEE YOU IN MY DREAMS

By AUDREY GROOM

He'd worked so hard to make his dream come true, he'd never noticed that perhaps the dream itself had changed . . .

BEN carefully poured coffee into two mugs and pushed one across the kitchen table to his next-door neighbour.

"So, I've convinced you to join us at last, have I, Ben, you old hermit?" Ernest's genial face wore a satisfied grin.

Ben shook his head and offered the biscuit tin.

"I wouldn't put it that way, Ernest," he said. "It's just the idea of the contest which appeals to me."

"Yes, I thought it might." Ernest's friendly eyes twinkled. "So I'm glad I mentioned it. I'll call for you at two then, shall I?"

"All right." Ben's face expressed caution. "But don't feel too pleased with yourself. I'm not coming to fraternise, you know, or get all matey.

"Or," he added, with a meaningful glance, "to find myself another wife. We're not all young Romeos like you!"

Ernest laughed.

He was a good friend, Ben reflected later. They understood each other well enough. In fact, their friendship stretched 'way back, to before either of them had become widowers.

But although Ernest had been just as distraught at Mary's death as Ben had been at Rose's, he seemed to have made a better recovery.

As he washed and dried the coffee cups, Ben tried to remember whether Ernest had always been such a social chap. Certainly, he had taken on a new lease of life since he'd joined the local senior citizens' club.

Ernest had been seeing quite a lot of a pretty little widow, Sophie Bains, in the last few months, too. And when Ben had chaffed him about wedding bells, he hadn't altogether scorned the idea.

"Well, don't try to get me along to your 'lonely hearts club'," Ben had always said — until today. "I don't want to know."

I suppose there isn't much I want to know now, either, Ben thought, putting the mugs back on their hooks, where Rose had always kept them.

He liked pottering in his garden well enough, and he did a bit of shopping and cooking, read the odd library book and watched TV. One day was very like another, but there wasn't much that he especially wished for.

Well, apart from one thing. And that was a sort of daydream, really. One that he'd had since boyhood. He wanted to visit Paris.

"One day, I'll go there," Ben had whispered to himself, as he gazed at the picture of the Eiffel Tower in his school text-book. "One day."

He had told Rose about his ambition, pleased when she became enthusiastic, too.

"We'll go together, Ben," she had promised.

They might have made it across the Channel after he retired but, by then, her health wasn't so good. And, somehow, the dreams had faded when she had gone . . .

Yet, this morning, Ernest's bit of news had stirred Ben's heart.

Every year, it seemed, his friend's social club held a talent contest. Members were invited to do their 'party pieces' — to sing, dance, recite a poem or play an instrument in front of a panel of judges from the local theatre company.

Everyone had a good evening's entertainment and there was always a nice prize. But Ernest's trump card in his bid to lure Ben along to the club was that, this year, a local travel firm had offered a trip to Paris for the winner.

Of course, the bait would have been no use at all if Ben hadn't possessed what had always been described as a very good tenor voice.

Not having sung for some time, he tried out a scale or two in the bathroom, before Ernest called for him that afternoon.

Thankfully, his vocal chords seemed to be in better working order than his creaking back!

When they finally reached the hall, it seemed to Ben that the introductions and hand-shaking were endless.

"Come and meet Henry. And this is Ellen, and, of course, you probably know Bill Gafferty. And here's . . ."

It was all a bit much, really, for a widower like himself, who hadn't been out and about much recently.

The speaker's subject for the afternoon was, 'Planting Indoor Bulbs' and Ben, sure he knew all there was to know about that, snoozed a little.

But he woke up with a start when the Secretary made her announcement.

"Will all those who want to enter our talent contest please collect a form from me, and complete it by next week."

"I'd like one, please." Ben, smiling at Mrs Winsom, stuck out his hand.

"Oh, good," she said. "It is nice when new people get involved right away."

Ben didn't know about being involved. The people, the chat and the socialising were just part of the background as far as he was concerned.

They were all good people, he was sure. But this contest — now, that was the important thing.

He filled in the form as soon as he got home, and had it ready to hand over the following week.

"YOU'RE looking better already, Ben," Ernest announced with approval as he sat drinking another coffee in Ben's kitchen.

"We'll even have you enjoying company again before long and looking as if you think life's worth living."

"Don't count on it," Ben remarked, searching in the cupboard for more biscuits to fill the tin. But he supposed the idea of singing again did appeal to him. Especially if there was even the faintest possibility of him winning the prize.

And perhaps, although he wouldn't admit it to Ernest yet, the thought of meeting all those new faces didn't seem quite so daunting this week.

At the end of the meeting, later that afternoon, Ben joined the queue to hand in his form.

"Hello again, Ben. So you're going to sing for us in the contest," noted the Secretary, scanning the piece of paper. "That's fine. And who's going to accompany you?"

Ben gulped. That was a good question — who indeed? He had assumed that he would just go up on the platform, hand over some music, clear his throat and begin. But his own accompanist! He hadn't thought about that.

"I don't know," he confessed, feeling a little foolish.

Mrs Winsom drummed her ringed fingers on the table while she pondered the situation. Ben watched her anxiously, dreams of Paris fading fast.

"Well, you'll certainly need someone," she murmured thoughtfully. "Oh! I think I know who. Just wait a minute." And she went charging across the hall calling, "Elsie! Elsie!"

When she came back, there was a little slip of a woman beside her. She had pale, silky hair and a rather nervous smile.

"Now Elsie's a new member, the same as you." Mrs Winsom beamed at them both like some benevolent school teacher.

"But I know she plays the piano because a little bird told me," she went on. "Now, Elsie — would you mind accompanying Ben here, at the contest? He wants to sing."

"No, I don't mind at all," Elsie said quietly, her deep, pleasant voice hardly fitting her size.

"Good, good." Mrs Winsom scribbled on Ben's form. And then — just as though she were sending two children out to play — she said, "Well, now you can start rehearsing together, can't you?"

Rehearsing together! Oh dear, Ben hadn't bargained for that. He and Elsie eyed each other shyly.

"Er — I have a piano — if you've got some songs. We could try them out . . . Perhaps, next Monday?" she suggested.

"Fine," Ben agreed hastily, taking her address but feeling that things were anything but fine.

Ernest seemed to have left, probably with Sophie, so Ben walked home alone. Hands in pockets, he kicked loose stones as he went — a sure sign, since he was a small boy, that he was worried about something.

The fact was that after Rose's death, he hadn't drunk a single cup of tea or coffee in anyone else's home. Except Ernest's. And he didn't count.

Of course, Elsie might not offer him refreshment. Perhaps it would be a purely business-like association, with no chatting and socialising . . . ? Somehow Ben didn't see how it could be, and he was nervous.

Monday came all too quickly. Should he phone Elsie to say he couldn't make it, because he had a sore throat, he wondered, his hand hovering over the receiver. Then one of his glossy French travel books caught his eye, and he decided to brave it out.

ELSIE'S flat was tiny but neat. Just like her, in fact, Ben thought, as he put his music down on the coffee table.

For a long time, they just sat and looked at each other. Ben couldn't think of a thing to say. And neither could Elsie, apparently, because she suddenly reached for the music and began skimming through it.

"Shall we begin with this one?" she suggested with relief, picking out a song almost at random.

Ben agreed. It seemed quite a straightforward piece and he felt relieved to make a start.

It was difficult to say which one of them was the more nervous. Ben, repeatedly clearing his throat before starting to sing, completely off-key; Elsie, hitting all the wrong notes . . .

But sensing her shyness made Ben forget his, to a certain extent. He found that he wanted to put her at her ease.

"You play extremely well, Elsie," he said admiringly, once they had found enough confidence to get through the first song without too many breaks.

"And you've got a lovely voice, Ben," she answered, managing to smile. "Have you done a lot of singing?"

"Used to do amateur theatricals years ago," he admitted.

"Did you?" Elsie's face lit up with interest, and Ben could see a flash of the vitality that must have made her attractive in her younger days — still did, in fact.

"Joe, my husband, used to have the same hobby."

"Did he?"

"Yes," she said, with pride. "He was such a fine-looking man."

She crossed to a shelf in the corner, took down a photograph and brought it to Ben. He took one look and gasped.

"Good grief," he said, "Joe Stevenson!"

"That's right."

"I knew him," Ben said, his mind drifting back 40 years. "We sang together," he said, "in the 'Maid Of The Mountains'."

"Really! That must have been before I met him," Elsie said. "What a coincidence! But then this is rather a small town, I suppose."

She sat for a moment or two gazing down at the picture which Ben had put back into her hands. At last she looked up.

"Ben," she said, "I know we mustn't neglect your singing, but I would love to hear about that show you saw Joe in. Shall I make a cup of tea, to have while we talk?"

"Can't think of anything nicer." Ben smiled, realising that it was true. Somehow the awkwardness between him and Elsie was almost gone.

"Joe was a superb actor," he told her later. "And a good baritone. Almost inspired me to turn professional. I think I've even got the programme. somewhere . . . I'll bring it around to show you next time I come, shall I?"

"Oh! Please, Ben," she said.

So he went home, full of enthusiasm, and hunted through the old trunks and boxes in the attic. Pictures, Press cuttings, a bundle of programmes . . . What memories they all brought back!

And how Ben and Elsie pored over his souvenirs of a bygone age — photos from his own triumphs, and the treasure that she unearthed, too.

"Oh! I remember that chap."

"It was in this show that the door got stuck!"

"Who was that girl with the long black hair? I think I know her! Oh! Isn't that a lovely photo of Joe!"

And so on . . .

They didn't neglect Ben's rehearsing, but the time passed very quickly. Sometimes, the afternoon was over before they knew it.

"Good gracious, Ben — it's nearly tea-time," Elsie would say. "Would you like to stay for tea?"

After that had happened once or twice, Ben felt he really must return her hospitality, and invited her out for dinner.

"Thank you so much, Ben," Elsie murmured at the end of the evening, putting her hand across the table and touching his. "For this evening and for everything.

"I was very doubtful about joining the social club, but now I'm glad I did — and that —"

She blushed.

"That we met each other," he finished for her, covering her hand.

"Yes." She smiled. "It's been smashing, hasn't it?"

"Don't put it in the past tense, Elsie." Ben's voice was low, like hers. "It doesn't have to stop."

"No," she answered slowly. "No, I suppose not. But once you've won your trip to Paris . . ."

Ben laughed softly.

"You are sure I'm going to win, aren't you?"

"Of course," she replied. "And there's not long to go, now."

Her confidence inspired him. He would try his best for her.

STANDING at the side of the stage on the day of the contest, Ben felt awful. He had put on his best suit and shirt, but somehow the collar felt too tight. He must have straightened his tie a dozen times.

He had decided to sing 'We'll Gather Lilacs', with another real oldie, 'Little Grey Home In The West', if he was called for an encore.

"Of course you'll need an encore." Elsie, standing beside him, squeezed his arm.

Her faith in him put back some of his confidence, which had begun to ooze away with the waiting. But they were close to the bottom of the list and, as several popular acts trooped on and off the stage, Ben felt the tension rising.

Then, at last, they were on!

Elsie walked over to the piano, and smiled reassuringly at him as she sat down.

As she broke into the introduction, Ben stepped forward and let the song simply pour out of him. Even to him, the notes sounded rich and true, and the words clear and full of feeling.

As the last note died away, only the hammering of Ben's heart seemed to ease the silence. Then the audience cheered and cheered, and there was certainly no doubt about whether he should sing his encore.

But the waiting wasn't over yet. There were another two turns after theirs, so he and Elsie stood, hand-in-hand, watching them from the wings. When the comedian, in particular, was exceptionally good, Ben's heart began to sink quietly into his boots again.

Why should he ever have thought he would win, with all this talent to compete with? He'd just let himself get carried away.

When the show was over, refreshments were served while the judges made up their minds.

Those 20 minutes were the longest that Ben could remember.

"Would you like a cup of tea, Ben?" Elsie offered.

He shook his head.

"You have one," he said. "I couldn't manage anything at present."

She didn't leave him, though. She just stood with him, smiling in sympathy as he clutched her hand tighter and the perspiration stood out on his forehead.

Please, he thought, please let this waiting be over.

The clatter of tea-cups slowly died down, as Mrs Winsom rose to make an announcement. Six finalists were to be selected first of all, she told them; just to prolong the excitement.

Ben took a deep breath, grinning weakly, wryly, towards Elsie. He heard one name called out . . . two, three — and then another, more familiar: Benjamin Stanton. But that was him! And, gently nudged by Elsie, he walked on to the stage.

"Now." The judge held up his hands for silence. "I want you, the audience, to clap each of these contestants in turn — to add your vote to ours."

Ben felt curiously distant now. The applause sounded like one continuous thunder-roll, and if one lot was louder than the next, he was too keyed-up to notice it.

But at last it was all over, Mrs Winsom was speaking again, and the six were to be told their places in reverse order.

He held is breath.

Sixth, fifth, fourth . . . the suspense was killing him! Third, second . . .

Wonder of wonders — first! He'd done it! Someone was shaking his hand and everyone was shouting and clapping.

The judge held up his hands again.

"All right, ladies and gentlemen," he laughed. "Undoubtedly, Ben here is the winner. Congratulations, sir!" He shook him by the hand and Ben swallowed hard, trying to believe this was really happening.

"Now," the judge went on, silencing the audience, who had started to cheer again. "You all know that the prize for this contest is a trip to Paris for one, as presented by Terry's Travel.

"Well, they have been so impressed with the talent here tonight that they have decided to award an additional prize — a weekend for two at a hotel of the winner's choice, in Eastbourne.

"So, Ben, you can take your pick of the two prizes, and the runner-up can have the other. Where would you like to go?"

Ben's eyes were bright with excitement. This was it — he'd done it, really done it! He'd won the trip to Paris, the city of his dreams.

Like life flashing past a drowning man, pictures ran through his mind, pictures from his travel books: the Champs-Elysées, the Arc de Triomphe and, of course, the Eiffel Tower.

And then he looked sideways into the wings, where Elsie was nodding and smiling and mouthing, "well done."

"I'll take . . ." he murmured, almost to himself. "I'll take . . ."

There was a hush for a moment, with everyone waiting for Ben's decision.

Why did he hesitate? Everyone in the club knew he was a widower, and who'd turn down the chance to go to Paris?

Ben's answer, when it came, was slow and clear.

"I'll take the weekend for two at Eastbourne," he said.

Elsie stumbled towards him from the wings, disbelief written all over her face.

"Why, Ben, why?" she asked him. "You wanted —"

"I wanted to ask you to marry me, Elsie," he said. "And Eastbourne would be great for a honeymoon!"

No-one heard what Elsie answered. But when Ben kissed her, there, up on the stage, everybody cheered. Someone even began singing, 'For He's a Jolly Good Fellow', and soon the whole audience were joining in.

"Huh!" Ernest whispered to Sophie, watching the happy but slightly sheepish-looking couple on the platform. "For someone who wasn't going to act like a young Romeo, Ben's made a pretty good job of it!"

"I know," Sophie replied, slipping her arm through his. "Wonderful, isn't it?" ■

CAT BURGLAR

**She wasn't really breaking in ... She'd only come in
through the window to look for something that
didn't belong to her ...**

By Miranda Lawrence

HAD not expected to see Lisa again after saying goodbye to her at her wedding reception, so I was very surprised when she appeared at the shop door as I changed the notice from OPEN to CLOSED.

"Goodness!" I exclaimed. "I thought you'd be in Australia by now."

She swept past me in a swirl of honey silk and clattering sandals, and deposited a large wicker basket on the floor. She was panting, and even the blonde fringe flopping over her forehead seemed agitated.

"I was just about to go home," I said, indicating the racks of dresses, shrouded in their nightcovers. "It's after five."

I was tired. The unexpected cold spell had brought a surge of customers to buy raincoats and woolly jumpers. I regarded Lisa with apprehension.

"Whatever is the matter?" I asked, wondering if she was being chased by somebody, or something.

Her pink mouth trembled as she finally found her voice.

"Alex — it's Kelly," she answered miserably.

"Kelly?" Whoever could that be? Some Irishman, perhaps, whom she had jilted to marry her Australian?

I looked anxiously at the door, half-expecting to see an enraged suitor gibbering at the glass panel.

"My cat," she explained, pointing at the basket. "Oh, Alex, dearest girl, could you do me a terrific favour?"

I backed away. From experience I've learned that when a favour is described as terrific, it is usually something unpleasant.

"I've been trying to find him a home — ever since I've known I was going to marry Rob — and live in Australia." The words spurted out in little gasps.

"Nobody wants a grown cat — they all want little kittens — but I persuaded the woman who bought my house to let him stay there — so I thought everything was going to be all right.

"But when she moved in this morning, she found she's allergic to fur. Her face swelled up and she came out in a rash and got hysterical — so I couldn't leave him with her. And Rob and I are flying out to Australia in a few hours . . ."

She paused for breath and I quickly intervened: "But I can't take him, Lisa. I've told you, I live in an 'animals not allowed' flat."

"Yes, yes, I know, I know." She rushed on. "I'm not asking you to have him. I'm going to have to take him to the Cat Sanctuary. What else can I do? I can't leave him to roam the streets, homeless and hungry and frightened.

"The cat pound is right across town and I'm late already. So if you'll agree to take him . . .?

"It won't take you a minute, honestly." She kissed me on the cheek. "Oh, thank you, Alex. You're a wonderful friend."

She bent over the basket, murmured something unintelligible to the occupant, sobbed, and ran out of the shop.

I was stunned.

"With friends like that, who needs enemies?" I wondered out loud, amazed.

It wasn't as if we had been cradle companions or school chums. We had only known each other a few weeks.

We met when I came to take her place as manageress of the boutique. We got to know each other while she handed the job over to me. We lunched together and I went to her wedding.

Hardly a friendship that warrants a terrific favour.

More importantly, I was no cat-lover. I knew very little about them. My childhood companion was a Jack Russell terrier, and he disapproved strongly of socialising with them. And when I came to live in London, the 'no animals' clause in my lease ensured that no starving moggie attached itself to me.

But whether you like cats or not, it's no fun having to take one of to a home for unwanted strays.

Gloomily, I averted my eyes from the basket containing the abandoned animal, and went through to my office.

How I wished I lived above the shop, like the other shopkeepers in the terraced row. It would be wonderful to stagger up the stairs to home.

My office was small and stuffy. I opened the window a little and slumped on to my chair, kicking off my shoes.

A cup of tea would be soothing, I decided, swivelling the seat around to switch on the kettle. But as I was about to pop a teabag into a cup, a loud, heartrending wail came from the other room.

I froze.

Tensely gripping the teabag, I waited for further sounds. But there were none. The silence unnerved me more than the cry.

It was as though the poor creature had summoned its strength for one despairing call, and then given up hope.

I ran into the shop and kneeled beside the basket.

"It's all right, kitty," I murmured, feeling a hypocrite because no way was it 'all right' for that cat.

How awful to be cooped up in a tiny space. Surely I could do something to make its last hour of 'belonging' more pleasant?

I took the basket into the office and shut the door. I would let the animal stretch its paws and give it something to drink.

Undoing the thongs that kept the basket closed, I flipped back the lid. Pouring some milk into a saucer, I placed it on the floor.

"Nice kitty," I said feebly.

For a few moments, there was no reaction. Then two white paws appeared on the edge of the basket and a feline face rose slowly above them.

My first thought was that it wasn't surprising that Lisa had not been able to find a home for such an odd-looking creature. His face was splodged with patches of black and orange, with a blob of white across his nose.

He eased himself out of the basket, revealing a back patched with similar colours, and a black tail with one splash of orange. I couldn't see what colour he was underneath, because he kept his belly very close to the floor as he crawled slowly towards the saucer.

PLEASED with myself at having thought of giving him the milk, I sat down to watch him enjoy it. But he didn't reach the saucer.

Suddenly, he became a multi-coloured streak, hurtling through the air and landing on the windowsill.

I didn't jump up to intercept him, because the window opening was so slight, I didn't imagine it would prove an exit. So it was with astonishment that I watched a large, furry body flatten, and wriggle through the narrow space.

Leaping to my feet, I flung open the window, just in time to see a tail disappearing into the window of the antique shop next door.

Had I had any sense, I would have locked up the boutique and gone home, shrugging off the unwanted responsibility that Lisa had thrust upon me. But, fool that I was, I went in pursuit of the fugitive.

The shops had a common balcony, divided by a wrought-iron grill. It seemed easy enough to clamber over. I grabbed a canvas bag, thinking I would slip the cat into this to return him to his basket. Then I followed him through the window.

I found myself in a beautifully furnished office. Normally, I would have looked appreciatively at the walnut desk, the Chinese carpet, the handsome bookcase and the pictures. But at that moment, all I wanted to see was a cat.

"Kelly, Kelly," I called hopefully, remembering his name. Of course, he didn't reply. I couldn't blame him, really. After all, I wasn't offering him much of a future.

He had to be somewhere in the room, as there was only one door and it was tightly closed. So, pushing the window down to cut off that escape route, I searched for possible hiding places.

One of the desk drawers was open, just enough for a flexible cat to squeeze into.

Putting the canvas bag down beside the desk, I pulled open the drawer with one hand, while the other remained poised to grab a squirming bundle of fur and quickly deposit it in the bag.

The drawer contained papers and a few small boxes. But no cat.

Hearing the sound of movement behind me, I whirled around, ready to pounce. The door had opened and a man had entered the room.

"Who are you? What are you doing here?" I demanded. The words had tumbled out before I realised it, leaving me feeling a little foolish. After all, it as I was the intruder.

"I'm Oliver Holt," he answered very politely. "I'm an antique dealer and I live on these premises.

"And now, may I ask who *you* are? And how did you get in? I'm very interested, as I personally locked both the shop door and the house door."

"I'm Alex Morrison, the new manageress of the boutique next door," I told him. "And I came in through the window."

He was younger than I had expected the antique-dealer-next-door to be, though why I should imagine such a dealer should be antique himself, I don't know. This one didn't look as though he'd passed 35.

"Do you always call on people by climbing in through the window?" he inquired.

He looked cool and vaguely amused. In comparison, I felt hot and scruffy and flustered.

"Of course not," I protested. "I only came in that way because I was looking for a cat . . ."

"But I haven't got a cat," he said mildly.

I hastened to clarify.

"No, I don't mean *your* cat . . ."

"Your own, then?"

"No, *I* haven't got one, either. In fact, I've never had much to do with them. This one was left with me, but I let it out of the basket and it ran in here."

He regarded me quizzically.

"Interesting. What does it look like?"

"Well . . ." Kelly was not easy to describe. "It's sort of yellowish and black. Sort of spotted."

"Are you sure it's not a cougar?" he asked solemnly.

"I'll admit I don't know much about felines," I said acidly, getting a little exasperated. "But I do know a yellowish-black cat from a reddish-brown cougar."

"I'm relieved to hear it."

To put an end to this ridiculous conversation, I told him the whole story. He listened with grave attention but, as I finished speaking, I realised that he didn't believe me. I was quite shaken. Nothing is worse than to tell the exact truth and not be believed.

"A very inventive story," he commented admiringly. "Full of imaginative touches. Most people would have thought of a black cat called Sooty or a striped one called Tiger.

"But a multi-coloured Kelly! Surely that must be inspired by the old music-hall song: '*Has anybody here seen Kelly . . . Kelly from the Isle of Man*'." He stopped and considered for a moment. "Maybe it's a Manx cat. Did you notice if it had a tail?"

"Oh, don't be absurd!" I retorted. "It's not a story. Why on earth should I want to invent a cat?"

He raised an eyebrow and looked pointedly at the open drawer and open bag, and at my unshod feet.

I gasped.

"You think I'm a burglar?"

"Evidence points that way," he remarked. Then the corners of his mouth twitched.

"On the other hand, you could be a 'lady cop', thinking I'm a 'fence' and searching for stolen goods."

"Very amusing." I sighed wearily. "There's one way we can put an end to speculation and that is by finding the cat. He must be somewhere in this room. Would you kindly help me find his hiding place?"

We searched the room very thoroughly. I looked behind, under and on top of the furniture. He opened every drawer and cabinet. And he infuriated me by lifting up the corners of the carpet and peering underneath.

At length, he straightened up and folded his arms.

"Vanished!" he pronounced. "Perhaps it was the Cheshire Cat. You did say your name is Alice?"

"It's Alex," I snapped, near to tears. Wherever could that wretched cat have gone?

The only explanation I could think of, was that he had somehow slipped back out of the window before I closed it.

Then it occurred to me that he might have gone back into his basket. After all, he didn't know that he had been abandoned. In all probability, he would expect Lisa to return for him.

"I must get back to my office," I said urgently, suddenly sure that I would find Kelly back there.

"That is, unless you want to have me arrested for trespass, of course," I added sarcastically.

"You're free to go." He inclined his head graciously. "Would you like to exit through the front door, or would you rather go back over the catwalk?"

I DIDN'T bother to reply but flung open the window and scrambled across the balcony.

To my disappointment, the wicker basket next door was empty, and the saucer of milk untouched.

Feeling defeated, I sank down on to my chair again. What now? Where else could I look for Kelly?

Then I remembered reading that a cat has the ability to find its way home. Perhaps the buyer of Lisa's house would have kept her telephone number.

I rang and, obviously, the woman who answered the phone was the one I was hoping to talk to.

"Oh, I never want to see that cat again," she moaned. "The swelling hasn't gone down yet and I'm scratching and scratching. Oh, that horrible animal . . ."

Patiently, I sympathised. But I couldn't help feeling indignant on Kelly's behalf. It was hardly his fault if the woman was allergic to him.

"Ring me if you see him," I appealed. "I'll come straight over and get him out of your way."

I gave her my home number and sat up till midnight, waiting for a call that didn't come. Eventually, exhausted, I fell asleep as soon as I climbed into bed.

In the early hours of the morning, I was awakened by the rumble of thunder. The bedroom was momentarily lit up by a flash of lightning.

Storms held no terrors for me and, normally, I would have drifted back into sleep. But now I lay rigid with horror. That poor cat! He would be crouched in some strange place, petrified with fear.

The rain beat savagely against the window. Just imagine being used to a safe, warm home and suddenly finding yourself lost in an unfamiliar street, with lightning rending the sky and rain soaking your fur.

Poor Kelly. He must have thought the good life would last forever. That there would always be a warm bed, a full saucer, and someone to care for him. How bewildered he must be, out there in the storm.

I pulled the duvet over my head to shut out the noise of the thunder, but I couldn't sleep. As soon as it was light, I got up and put on my tracksuit. It was still raining a little, but I felt less conspicuous, disguised as a jogger.

I parked the car at the back of the shop and started on my search, peering over fences and around corners.

"Kelly," I called softly. "Kelly, please come to me. I promise I won't take you to the Sanctuary."

"Alex!"

For a moment, I suffered the delusion that Kelly was answering me. Then I realised that it as a man's voice. Oliver Holt was standing behind me.

"You are a keen jogger," he commented. "I suppose you have to keep fit for climbing drainpipes."

"Go away," I snarled. "I'm not in the mood for your warped sense of humour."

But as I turned away from him sharply, my foot slid on a patch of soggy leaves and I fell face downwards into a puddle of mud.

"Are you all right?" His voice was no longer mocking, but full of concern. He lifted me up carefully. "Have you broken anything?"

"Only my spirit," I snivelled. The mud was caking on my face.

He put his arm around me and leaned me against him, regardless of the muddy stain spreading on his shirt.

"Come along," he said. "A shower is what you need.

"There's the bathroom," he indicated, once we were in his house. "There's a dressing-gown behind the door and a towel in the airing cupboard. Perhaps I could get a dress for you from your shop."

"I've got a change of clothes in the car. In a bag on the back seat." I reached into my sopping pocket and found the car keys.

"Right," he said. "I'll be back in a minute."

The warm shower was a delight. The bathroom was lovely, with blue tiles, lots of green leaves dripping from baskets, and shelf a of African violets.

A bathroom to linger in, I thought. But Oliver yelled: "Bag outside door," so I dried myself quickly and reached an arm out to pull in the bag.

I dressed and made up my face carefully, thankful I'd brought everything I needed for work. I wanted Oliver to see that I cleaned up quite nicely.

W HEN I emerged from the bathroom, the aroma of coffee led me to the kitchen. Oliver greeted me with a steaming mug and we sat at the kitchen table.

"So, tell me – what were you doing, lurking around the back there at this ridiculously early hour?" he asked.

"Would you believe me if I said I was looking for Kelly?" I queried. "Or do you prefer to think I was 'casing the joint', to see what house to break into next?"

He laughed.

"I do believe that you were looking for the cat. But I can't understand why you should go to so much trouble, as you intend to take him to the pound, anyway."

"But I'm not," I protested. "I couldn't. Not now.

"Maybe I could keep him in the shop while I found someone to give him a home. I could tell the owner that mice were attacking the stock and Kelly got rid of them. Or something.

"But I can't bear the thought of him starving and frightened and out in the rain . . ." To my horror, I felt tears streaming down my cheeks.

"I'm sorry." I gulped. "It's just that I haven't had any sleep. I haven't had a minute's peace since that cat was thrust upon me. People have no *right* to inflict cats on other people."

Oliver handed me a large handkerchief and I mopped up my face, thinking, ruefully, that after all that careful making-up in the bathroom, I now looked a thorough mess.

A strong warm hand enveloped mine and I was pulled to my feet.

"Come with me to the bedroom," Oliver said.

I snatched my hand away, startled.

"Don't get me wrong." He grinned. "It's just that there is something there I think will interest you."

I let him propel me to the bedroom. The prominent feature was a magnificent antique brass bed. In the middle of it was a mound of multi-coloured fur. It was Kelly, looking very comfortable indeed.

Relief was followed by indignation.

"You mean he was here all the time?" I squeaked. "While I was worrying my head off and running around in the rain . . .?"

Oliver nodded.

"He must have slipped past me when I opened the office door. I was so taken aback at finding a pretty girl rifling my desk, I didn't notice. He appeared as I took my chicken casserole out of the oven last night. He likes my cooking."

Kelly raised his head, and a loud purring vibrated his body.

"You should apologise for practically calling me a liar," I muttered, rather childishly.

"Of course I do." He smiled. "If you'd known a bit more about cats and described him properly, I might have taken you more seriously.

"Yellowish and black, indeed! He's a tortoiseshell cat and a very fine specimen. And tortoiseshell cats are usually female, so he's a very distinguished gentleman."

Responding to flattery, Kelly stretched gracefully and leaped off the bed. Standing on his hind legs, he did a few pirouettes to reach Oliver's knee, where he firmly rubbed his head.

"He's a dancer!" Oliver cried delightedly. "That explains the name. He's called after Gene Kelly."

He scooped the cat up into his arms, and a furry head nuzzled under his chin.

"Would you like to join us for supper tonight, Alex?" Oliver invited. "After all, Kelly does owe you something. You have found him a home."

I didn't know it at the time, but Kelly had done the same for me. The three of us are very happy with the arrangement.

Kelly wouldn't have been happy in the pound. He was cross enough when he had to go to a cattery, while Oliver and I had a honeymoon. But I think he's forgiven us now. ■

Grandma's Garden

It's my first time in Grandma's room,
Since she went away,
I can't face all the relatives,
I'd just get in the way.

But as I stand here all alone,
I look at Grandma's chair,
Where she'd look at her garden,
And spend all day sat there.

I remember all the times I've had,
With Grandma on this seat,
And watering her flowers,
In the summer's lovely heat.

Her garden is a picture,
Full of love and plants and flowers,
With all her favourite little birds,
She'd talk to them for hours.

And as I think of Grandma,
Watching birds up in the trees,
I cannot help but feeling,
That she is here with me.

In her garden full of love,
She's walking on the lawn,
Playing with the singing birds,
And drifting with the dawn.

I know I can always find her now,
In her garden's where she is,
Touching me upon the breeze,
The sun's warmth is her kiss.

Night, night, Grandma,
God bless.

By
A. Johnson

The Surprise

She could just about cope with that. What shattered her composure was the unexpected guest!

By ELIZABETH ASHCROFT

GILLIAN turned into the High Street and joined the mainstream of traffic. She pressed her foot down hurriedly on the brake pedal as a teenager on a motorbike shot past her and tucked himself between her and the green double-decker in front.

Those little motorbikes just weren't safe, she thought crossly. They buzzed along like angry wasps with their drivers in oversized helmets and shiny leather gear, quite oblivious to the fact that many motorists could hardly see them.

She sighed, feeling the beginnings of a headache, after a tense, tiring day at the office. A bath would be heaven, she thought longingly. A bath, with lots of lemony-scented foam, to take away the cricks and aches of a not very successful week.

I just need to unwind, she thought desperately. I can't take the pressure much longer. The office, after 17 years away from work, had become almost alien to her; now it was all computers and faxes, handled by young girls in bright clothes with bright, modern hair. Gillian felt old and out of date.

In front of her, the bus droned slowly down the street, which was still jammed with workers returning home, Friday pay packets safe in pockets and purses.

They reached a bus stop and came to yet another grinding halt.

She bit her lip, fighting impatience and a ridiculous impulse to leave the car where it was and walk. A girl in her teens took her chance to cross then and darted past, all long, flying dark hair, slim, be-jeaned legs and baggy jacket.

For an instant, Gillian thought it was Carol, and she was about to call out. Then she remembered, and her heart sank in dismay.

The party, Carol would be at home just now, getting ready for the party. Gillian had completely forgotten it.

Oh, how could they, she mourned, pushing the car yet again into first gear and creeping past a long, doleful queue at the bus stop.

It was too much. They had no right to do it. Her thoughts flew back to breakfast that morning and the subdued air of expectancy and excitement.

She'd thought it was just their usual birthday morning secrecy which had caused Carol's eyes, so like Alan's, to flicker from her to Jason.

At 16 her son was so like Alan that sometimes she could cry. But it was three years now since Alan's death, and she'd cried all her tears . . .

But then they'd dropped their bombshell.

"A *party*?"

She'd stared, aghast, over the pretty wrapping paper and birthday cards

Party

scattered across the pine breakfast table.

Carol bounced excitedly in her chair, avariciously eyeing the perfume she'd just presented to Gillian.

At 15 she borrowed everything she could fit into, and much she couldn't. She stole Gillian's bath oils and perfume, was defiant one moment and the next overflowing with love.

Today, the love was uppermost.

"It's special, Mum! A special birthday for you, so we thought we'd do something special! It's all arranged, there's nothing for you to do except enjoy it."

Gillian took a deep breath. "But we haven't had a party since Dad died," she said weakly.

Even then, parties had been mainly for the children, with a few older neighbours and friends along to help out.

"That's why we're having one now," Jason put in quietly. His owlish spectacles slipped down his nose so that for one moment his serious brown eyes met hers without the distortion of glass.

"We thought it's time you — uh — had a bit of fun. Honest, Mum, you never go anywhere except the office, and you never do anything except potter round the house. You're not *old*!"

"I'm forty."

Forty. It had seemed, in her teens, an almost unattainable age. But since Alan's accident she'd almost forgotten the years drifting past. At first she was in a haze of pain, then came the effort of finding and holding down a job.

She'd found a few grey hairs lately, she remembered with a strange ache. She was getting old, and hadn't even realised it.

To Carol and Jason, she must seem like Methuselah.

Carol took charge with her usual impetuosity.

"All you have to do is come home from the office as usual, make yourself beautiful, and greet your guests.

"I told you, it's all arranged. Food, drinks, the lot."

"Here?"

Visions of tomorrow began to haunt Gillian. Saturday spent cleaning up after her home had been open house. Rings on the tables, grey-green olives squashed into the carpet.

It was all right for the children, she thought with a flash of something approaching anger. She would have to clean it all up, while they went gallivanting off on their usual Saturday pursuits.

Then she felt guilty, looking at their eager, troubled faces. They only wanted to make her happy, after all. So she smiled and hugged them.

"Darlings, it's a lovely idea. I can look forward to it, now."

It was the right thing to say, though far from the truth, and they rushed happily off to school.

But all she wanted, she reflected mournfully, joining the queue to take the turn out of the High Street, was a quiet life. To put her feet up, read a book. She was an old lady now.

And she looked a mess, she reflected ruefully. She glanced in the mirror. There were purple smudges under her eyes, lines of strain round her mouth, which used to turn up and now had a decided droop to it most of the time.

Oh, Alan, she thought despairingly. Why did you have to be in the car at *that* time, at *that* junction, at *that* moment? It was an old refrain.

As she turned right a car honked, and roared alongside her for a moment. Crossly she glanced across, knowing before she saw him that it was Chris Lord.

He was the new man at the office, at executive level, and full of confidence.

He waved and grinned. She nodded acknowledgement, smiling tightly, remembering the way he had walked roughshod over her plans for reorganising the office the very first week he was there.

"Sorry, Gillian," he'd said briefly, smiling at her across the desk, swept clear of all except necessities. He was so unlike old Mr Smith, who'd been surrounded by unused diaries, batteries of pens and pencils, and photographs of his wife and several grandchildren.

Gillian saw he was older than she'd first thought, a tinge of grey over his forehead where she'd thought it was sunbleached hair.

"It won't work, you know."

Offended, she bit back. "Oh, but it will. I've been here for a year, and working on this for the last two months."

And unspoken, there was the inference that he, the newcomer, had no right to turn down her plans so flatly.

His lips tightened, the smile leaving his eyes. "No, the chain of command must be more flexible. Not too many chiefs. Understand?"

Flushed with anger, she'd retreated. Only to have him stop her in the corridor a few days later.

"Going to lunch? Shall we join forces? I'm just off, too."

Taken aback, she'd stared at him, momentarily tempted. Then remembered his harsh judgment of her work.

"Chiefs playing with the Indians, Mr Lord?" she'd enquired tartly, and was startled at the look in his eyes. Fleeting surprise, a touch of sorrow? Surely not!

"Touché." Unexpectedly, he'd laughed. "Well, what's the verdict?"

No, she had shopping. She'd eat a sandwich in the park. Besides, she didn't think she liked him. "Sorry, I have some odd jobs to do."

But in fact she'd shared her bench in the park with just the grey squirrel and the stalking, pompous pigeons. She'd remembered the invitation and felt an odd regret.

It would have been nice, sitting across the table from a man again, eating a proper meal instead of snatched, hastily-made sandwiches.

Then she'd thought of Alan, his ready smile, his hand on hers. And the squirrel had become blurred, and the pigeons had whirred into the air as she threw the empty sandwich bag into the waste-bin.

Oddly, though, Chris Lord had asked her again, yet she'd still not accepted his offer.

Since then he'd often passed her on the way home in his dark green car, which whoomped noisily as he changed gears. Show-off, she'd often thought crossly, wondering where he lived.

Now, she put her foot down, an imp of mischief catching her. She chased him, then he slowed, allowing her to pass, smiling amiably at her.

She flung a triumphant glance at him, turned into her road, and hit the kerb clumsily, bumping horribly, knowing he would have seen. Momentarily she hated him for it, then had to smile at her own stupidity.

S O, she was home. And before she was in the house, she knew she was going to loathe every minute of this special party.

Carol and Jason had pulled out all the old party decorations, the ones she and Alan had bought over the years.

Golden cones swung in a huge, glittering circle in the hall. Jason had even rigged up the fairy lights in the conservatory.

They were pretty, she conceded fleetingly. The leafy, drooping ferns, the full blooms of the chrysanthemums looked surrealistic, almost fairy-like in the glow.

Jason looked at her hopefully, waiting for praise.

"It's lovely." That wasn't enough, she could see. "Absolutely beautiful, Jase. I love it."

The wide grin was ample reward. "And Carol says you're to keep out of the kitchen and the dining-room.

"She's upstairs, waiting for you. Go on!" He gave her a little shove, and she stumbled upstairs, thinking wistfully of a cup of tea.

Carol was in her bedroom, shortie housecoat flying out behind her.

"Mum! You're late! I've laid out your dress, and the bath's running, and you've got time to make yourself beautiful."

She could, unbelievably, smell the lemon bath foam. And there was a neatly-set tray of tea on the stool in the bathroom.

"Carol. Oh, love, that's perfect. I've been dreaming about that all the way home."

What good kids they were, she thought, going into her bedroom.

And then stared at the bed.

Oh, no! She couldn't! She couldn't wear that. It was the dress she'd worn to the Italian restaurant.

At 37 she'd felt young, and untouched by pain.

She went slowly towards the bed and touched the pale blue jersey gently. She'd bought it specially for her birthday dinner.

Alan had looked into her eyes across the crystal glasses and the champagne bottle and told her she looked wonderful, and she was always to wear that dress on her birthday.

"In a few years it won't even fit! I'll be fat, with all this Italian food!"

Now, she thought, she'd lost so much weight it would probably just hang from her shoulders. She couldn't wear it. Not to a party where no-one matters.

It was *Alan's* dress, not for the rag-tag of neighbours and old friends the children would have asked.

Resolutely she crossed to the wardrobe, rifled through it. But there was nothing else she could wear. She hadn't bought anything new for years; there had been nowhere to go, no-one to go with.

I can't, she thought wretchedly, sitting in the bath, foam drifting round her knees.

Why, oh why, couldn't the children have left her alone, let her celebrate this birthday quietly? She almost wished she could be taken ill, come out in infectious spots, sprain an ankle . . .

Then she stopped, mentally shook herself. There was no sense in feeling sorry for herself.

She was standing, indecisively, in her slip when Carol whirled into the room. A whiff of something delectably savoury came in with her, and Gillian felt the faint stirrings of hunger. Carol halted.

"Aren't you dressed yet? Come on, Mum, we're all ready. Jason, come and show Mum."

Jason, her inelegant, other worldly, clever son was actually wearing a suit — with a shirt, and tie.

Gillian blinked. Where were the grubby jeans, the too-tight T-shirts, the scuffed trainers?

"Jason. Jason." She fumbled for words, touched by his embarrassed pride. "You look marvellous. Really. Wonderful."

My handsome son, she wanted to say, but didn't dare.

He would be a very handsome young man, she realised with surprise. In a few years, heads would turn when Jason entered a room, as they did now for Carol.

Her daughter came in then, glowing in a cerise tunic, her hair piled loosely on top of her head.

My lovely children, she thought. But she knew better than to say so. They'd gone to such pains to look good for this party so, she knew, with resignation, that she would have to wear the jersey dress.

She pulled it on, then gazed at her reflection with mild surprise.

She actually looked rather pretty; the bath had made her hair curl, and her eyes were sparkling. She took a deep breath, dabbed on Carol's perfume recklessly, and went downstairs.

"Wow!" Jason's eyes widened at sight of her. "Hey, Mum. You look gorgeous!"

"Thank you, love."

Gillian, light-headed from hunger, felt a strange anticipation vaguely remembered from long ago. She recognised it as excitement. She dropped a light kiss on his cheek.

Then they heard footsteps on the path, bright, lively voices, a car pulling up. The party had begun.

T was an absolute disaster. Oh, not for anyone else, just Gillian.

She just couldn't stop herself remembering other birthdays — she and Alan, together.

She handed round delectable titbits concocted by Carol, and remembered Alan laughing across a candlelit table.

She drank white wine, and remembered the delicious taste of Chianti, that last birthday.

The noise eddied round her, cigarette smoke caught in her throat, and she smiled and though she felt like crying.

She watched Carol dancing with a new boyfriend — Colin somebody. Already he was holding her hand possessively, leading her to the table laden with carefully laid-out food.

Oh, don't be silly, Gillian told herself. You can't be jealous. Not of your own daughter! She saw Carol glance at her, and wave. She waved back, facing a wide smile and nodding approval from Colin.

For the moment everyone was engrossed in each other, or helping themselves at the buffet. Gillian put down her half-empty glass. She suddenly felt a stranger in her own home — a lonely outcast.

No-one was looking, so she slipped out on to the terrace. It was cold in the brisk night air, but Gillian was glad of the quiet, and this small time to draw breath and be alone. Then, at least, she didn't have to pretend.

Suddenly a shadow moved, and she jumped.

"Gillian?"

An oddly familiar yet not familiar voice. She peered into the dim light and stared, amazed, as she recognised him.

"Enjoying your party?" he asked quietly.

"Chris!" What on earth, she wondered, astonished, was he doing here?

"Are you — I mean. Oh, dear." She floundered to a stop. "Are you a guest? I didn't have anything to do with the invitations, I didn't know —"

His voice, usually forceful, was hesitant.

"I know. I know your children arranged it as a surprise and you didn't know anything about it. Incidentally, you look — rather lovely."

There was an awkward pause and she felt herself flush hotly.

He ploughed on with a touch of desperation, unnerved by her silence. "That's why I was — rather unsure about coming in. Because — you hadn't invited me."

Had she made it so clear that she disliked him, then, she wondered with dismay. And then she suddenly realised, seeing him there, that she didn't *dislike* him. She just hadn't allowed herself to like him.

"That's — that's just silly." She faltered. "You're very welcome. But — I don't understand." She stared at him. "How do you know Carol and Jason?"

He grinned, more like the man she was used to in the office.

"Colin," he said succinctly, "has fallen hook, line and sinker for your Carol. She invited him, and, knowing I'm on my own, asked me to come along as well.

"Kind-hearted, that girl," he added with humour. Then, at her blank look, he laughed.

"My son, Colin. The one who can't take his eyes off her. Apparently they met at our office, while waiting for us."

"Your *son*." Stupid, she hadn't even thought of him as married. "But you said — you're on your own?"

"Divorced. Six years ago. It's all in the past now, but it can still hurt, seeing family life again." He hesitated then. "I can't say — you don't seem very happy at your party, Gillian."

She sighed and leaned against the creaking old garden seat.

"I'm not." Now she was admitting it, it somehow didn't seem so terrible.

"I keep thinking of Alan — my husband. The kids have been marvellous, and it was a lovely thing for them to do. I never had a birthday party before. We always went out to dinner on my birthdays, Alan and I. Just the two of us."

They were silent for a moment, music drifting out to them through the open windows, mingled with the chatter and laughter of the other party guests.

Then Gillian smiled. "I'm sorry — I'm boring you."

He spoke abruptly. "It may be presumptuous of me. But — will you come to dinner with me? Now?"

"*Now?*" She stared at him blankly, unable to believe the small flicker of excitement in her heart.

"Yes, now. Leave the party, they're all enjoying themselves, and come and have a — oh, a Chinese meal, with me."

Not Italian. He hadn't suggested that. She couldn't have gone to that same restaurant tonight.

But could she possibly leave her party and go off with this man, one minute laughing, one minute serious but with a clear, sincere gaze in eyes that begged her to take a chance with him?

Gillian hesitated, unsure what to do, trying to come to terms with the situation.

Through the window, she saw Jason dancing with a girl from their street and Carol laughing with Colin. They didn't need her here.

She could tell Carol where she was going, then enjoy her birthday the way she always had done, privately.

But with a stranger. Not Alan, who'd been dead three years. Maybe it was time, perhaps, to break away from the memories. Oh, she couldn't forget them. But she could not let them rule her life, her future.

"I'd like to come. Very much." Gillian spoke quickly, knowing she was finally committed. "I'll tell Carol, then meet you out here."

Chris's hand touched hers fleetingly, and she knew with joy he would not be a stranger for long. They smiled briefly at one another.

She pushed her way through the crowded room to tell Carol. And wondered, momentarily, at the cat-that-had-the-cream smile on her daughter's face as she hugged her.

"You go on, Mum, enjoy yourself. All the older ones are leaving now, anyway. It's mostly only us young ones left."

It was true. Her 40th birthday party had somehow turned into a teenage rave-up. A good job, Gillian thought with warmth, that her mother had been invited. She would stay watchful till the last stragglers had gone home.

She caught up a warm coat and slipped out of the front door to where Chris was waiting. He took her arm and, fellow conspirators, they made their way down the path Alan had laid all those years ago. A path laid down with love — and now perhaps, the way to future happiness. ■

I PROTEST!

OK, so she was interested in conserving wildlife, but he was more concerned with preserving their relationship!

By Sarah Burkhill

SUPPOSE they'll look all right when they're finished," Rachel said with a noticeable lack of enthusiasm.

That's the trouble with women. They look at a muddy building site with four half-completed blocks of flats and see — well — a muddy building site with four half-completed blocks of flats.

137

No vision, that's what's wrong. Now, a man could look at the same thing and imagine the finished article — a first-class luxury development of five-storey executive apartments, set on the edge of town in beautifully-landscaped gardens.

At least that's how the builders' publicity agent had described it, and as yours truly *is* the builders' publicity agent, I have enormous faith in his judgement.

"Which one will be ours?" Rachel asked.

"The one on the left, third floor."

They hadn't got to that bit yet, so I pointed out another block which already had its third floor and told her it would be just like that.

"Try to imagine it with all its furniture and fittings and you'll get a better idea," I said.

"Picture yourself stepping into a spacious, thick-carpeted lounge with velvet curtains framing the large bay window, or going through to the well-planned, roomy —"

"We can't afford carpets and curtains," Rachel interrupted with her usual dreary practicality. "We'll be lucky if we can afford to *eat* for the first ten years."

Some people can't resist looking on the black side, can they?

OK, I knew the flat would stretch our budget a bit. Even with the discount Barrons had given me, it had been hard going to raise enough cash for the deposit.

In fact we'd only managed it by deciding on a much quieter wedding than we had originally planned, and agreeing to skip the honeymoon and move in straightaway.

But it would be worth it, of course. It really was a terrific investment.

"It's not supposed to be an investment. It's supposed to be a home — our first home," Rachel said when I reminded her of this.

"Well, there's nothing to stop it being both, is there?"

We walked round to the front again, Rachel complaining about getting mud on her new red wellies.

"How are we supposed to get *in*?" she said suddenly. "I don't fancy having to go up and down that bumpy old lane every time I want shopping."

I raised my eyes to the heavens.

"Don't be silly. They're building a proper road," I told her. "Look, it'll go down there through the trees, and join up with the main road to town."

"Mmm. And when will it all be finished?"

"In about three months," I said confidently, omitting to tell her that this was providing the weather didn't do anything nasty.

"They'll be ready for occupation by the end of August," I went on. "That'll be a month before the wedding, so we'll have plenty of time to get ourselves organised."

"You're sure?" she said.

"Positive," I replied.

Ever noticed that when you make statements like that, something always goes wrong?

Not that it seemed like anything was going wrong. When I visited the site again the following month, work was progressing nicely and the builders were beginning the perfectly ordinary task of draining a pond to make way for the access road.

It was the next morning, Friday, when the problems started. I was cocooned in bed wondering whether to get up and have a proper breakfast or snooze for another 15 minutes, when the phone rang.

"Andy?" Jack Frame of Barrons barked into my ear. "We're having a bit of trouble at the site. It looks like ending up as a publicity matter so you'd better get over here and have a look."

Deprived of both doze and breakfast, I pulled on some clothes, had a quick cup of coffee and went over.

Whatever the trouble was, it wasn't immediately obvious. The weather was OK, the crews had turned up, the machinery looked to be in reasonable order.

"What's the problem?" I asked.

"Them!" Jack pointed.

"Them" was a group of eight people, positioned round the pond and wearing unfriendly expressions.

"They're from a local wildlife group," Jack said irritably. "They say we're upsetting their toads or something. They don't want the pond drained."

Toads? I remembered hearing something about toads when we were back at the planning stages. I tried to think back.

The Millthorpe Conservancy Group, that was it. They'd been worried in case our building plans were going to disturb the toads, who apparently had established prior rights in these parts.

We had assured them that in an area that size there would be plenty of room for both toads and luxury flats, and there was no reason why the two couldn't exist in perfect harmony.

They'd grumbled a bit, as these people usually do, but that had been the end of the matter.

"Look, we've been through all this before," I said to one of them, who had introduced himself as Robin Greaves. "There's acres and acres of space for you —"

"But you didn't say you were going to drain the pond," he jumped in. "Although toads are mainly terrestrial, they breed in water.

"If you drain that pond you're depriving them of their breeding habitat, and . . ."

". . . and that's tantamount to wiping them out!" one of the women finished.

"Toads, not roads!" she shouted at me.

"Toads, not roads!" The rest of the group took up the chant.

Honestly, it would have been laughable if it hadn't been so annoying. Jack Frame and I backed off.

"There're only eight of them," I said. "Can't you just shift them?"

"But there're two old ladies and a young girl," Jack pointed out.

"Well, we could shift them *gently*," the foreman volunteered. "Two old ladies and a girl aren't going to put up much of a fight.

"As for that Greaves chap . . ." He smiled. "I'll get Big Davie to take care of him."

"It's not as simple as that." Jack looked round edgily and whispered into my ear. "See that guy over by the trees? He's a reporter from the local rag. *And* he's got a camera!"

I could see it now. "Old Ladies Manhandled By Building Magnates!" the headline would read, together with a carefully contrived photograph.

"Mmm. *Not* good publicity," I agreed.

I took a walk round the pond, to the accompaniment of the "Toads, not roads" chant, and came back to him again.

"I think the best thing you can do is forget it for today," I said. "Let them make their protest. One day isn't going to spoil the schedule, is it?

"These things blow over quickly. Not many people'll get worked up about toads — it's not like seals or something cuddly, I mean."

Yes, that was definitely the best idea. By tomorrow they would be back to saving shellfish, or protecting earthworms or whatever the latest thing was. Best to leave them be for just now.

T**HAT** was my second mistake of the day.

The next day there was a full page spread about toads in the paper, and when work began again after the weekend another 20 or so people had joined the protest.

We decided to be as conciliatory as possible, and called a meeting in the Town Hall to explain to everyone that Barrons the Builders were also very concerned about toads and things, but in all fairness it was their land and there wasn't a lot they could do about it, was there?

Rachel was very upset over the business.

"Don't worry," I assured her. "Even with this delay, they'll still have the flats finished for the wedding. I promise."

She frowned at me.

"That's not what I meant. I was thinking about all those poor toads!"

This from a girl who screams the place down if anything creepy or crawly ventures near her!

"I didn't know you'd suddenly developed a passion for amphibians," I told her.

"I haven't," she said. "But it does seem a shame. I mean, the toads were there first, weren't they? How would you like it if someone came along and snatched away your breeding grounds?"

Four months before my wedding, it was a subject I didn't really feel like pursuing.

Anyway, there was no point in having an argument about it. Rachel had already decided she was going to the meeting, and if she was concerned before that, she was even more concerned afterwards.

It was that blond creep Greaves, of course, that convinced her, babbling on about toads being deprived of parenthood and Barrons being responsible for mass toadicide or whatever he called it.

It was just as well I went with her — not that I could do anything to stop her getting involved, but at least it gave me an idea of what I was up against. Just watching her getting all dewy-eyed about generations of baby toads who would never see the light of day made my heart sink.

"Toads, not roads!" she cried, leaping to her feet. "Ponds before profits!"

Oh, I ask you.

Things got worse, of course. When people tell you that it can't get any worse, don't believe them. It can *always* get worse.

When Rachel joined the protest group, it got much, much worse.

I mean, how do you convince the public that Barrons are honest, decent, toad-loving people when your fiancée is standing on the site of her new home shrieking that they're murdering usurpers?

"Right! That's it!" I said authoritatively at the end of the week. "You're going home, madam. You've become an embarrassment to me, and I'm not having it, d'you hear?"

I tried to yank her back to the car, which wasn't easy, for her other hand was wrapped round a tree and she had no intention of letting go.

"Rachel, come away!" I hissed.

'No!" she declared. "*I'm* an embarrassment to *you*! Of all the cheek! How do you feel explaining to Robin and the others that I'm actually *engaged* to one of Barrons' people?"

It was *Robin* now, I noticed. I hauled on her arm.

"It's a question of loyalty," I wheezed, pulling. "A woman's got a duty to stand by her fiancé. This job is our future, can't you see —?"

"In that case . . ." She suddenly let go her hold on the tree trunk and I catapulted backwards on to the ground.

"In that case . . ." she continued, looking down at me, "we'd better get *dis*engaged before I put your precious job at risk."

She took off her ring and dropped it on to my chest.

"Maybe you can get your money back, then you can put down an even bigger deposit on your investment."

So saying, she stamped off to join Robin and his band of merry men.

T**HIS** is getting beyond a joke, Andy," Jack Frame complained. "Can't you do something to stop it?"

I grunted. "Well, I tried phoning and telling her what an idiotic little fool she is, but she wouldn't see reason.

"Six years now we've been together, and she goes and does this to me! And us almost at the altar!"

Jack ground his teeth.

"I'm not talking about your personal affairs, Andy. I mean about this protest nonsense.

"We're over a week behind schedule already. *And* Barrons is getting a very bad Press."

He paced about his office, looking like a barracuda with toothache.

"I want them shifted, Andy. And I want them shifted *soon*."

It was a combination of his last words and my drive home through Marley Wood that gave me the idea. He wanted them shifted. Then that's exactly what we'd do. Shift them!

Jack wasn't too enthusiastic at first, seeing as how it

was going to cost Barrons money. However, when I pointed out what excellent publicity it would be, he agreed to go along with it.

So did the reporter from the Chronicle, and he did a very nice job on the story, I must admit.

"Find a Toad a New Abode!" the headline ran. It was followed by the news that conservation-conscious Barrons, ever ready to help our amphibious friends, had selected a site with pond at Marley Wood and were willing to relocate every single toad that could be captured.

That was where the public came in. For every toad brought in the following Saturday, one pound would be donated to a wildlife charity.

The captured toads would then be carefully boxed and transported to their new home in the evening.

It was quite a day. Can you imagine about 150 people, grannies and kiddies, housewives and students, all roaming around an area of 15 acres, chasing toads?

Yes, well . . . It was pandemonium , of course, but everybody had great fun. Except possibly the toads, but their turn would come later.

Rachel was there, naturally, but it was late afternoon before I got a moment alone with her.

"It was a very good idea," she said in a chastened tone. "Was it yours?"

"Well, it certainly wasn't Grotty Greaves'," I replied. "That's the trouble with these people. They come in shouting the odds, but they never bother to think of a solution acceptable to both sides.

"Give and take, that's what you need in life. A bit of compromise."

"Yes," she agreed soberly.

Jack Frame came up then to report on how the toad hunt was going, and he looked dubiously from Rachel to me.

"Andy, are you sure you want to cancel your contract for the flat?" he said. "I mean, it's all right by me — we'll get it resold easily enough.

"But if you want to change your mind, you'll have to tell me right away."

"No, I'm quite sure," I said, noting with some satisfaction that Rachel was looking even sicker now.

"Um — did you manage to get your money back on the ring?" she said softly after Jack had taken off again.

I didn't say anything, just herded her into the car and drove over to the other side of town. I'd just had a brilliant idea. And when I have a brainwave I have to act on the spur of the moment.

"There. What do you think of that?" I asked when I eventually stopped the car.

That was a decidedly overgrown, run down, apparently undesirable property which I'd actually had my eye on before Barrons had offered me discount on a flat.

It had ivy undermining the stonework, umpteen slates missing from the roof, rusted guttering and an old wooden plaque informing the world that it was called Toad's Hall Cottage.

It also had a second plaque, informing the world that it was for sale. I didn't think it would have been sold since I saw it last.

"It's going for a song, but we'll still have to spend a lot of time and money renovating it," I said. "What do you think?"

Rachel looked a little dazed. I suppose it had something to do with the fact that she had just been driven at top speed half-way across town to a destination unknown.

"Well," I repeated my question, "what *do* you think?"

At that moment she came to. She looked at me and at the house and then at me again. Then she gave a little gasp and her eyes opened wide with delight. "I think it's gorgeous!" she declared. "Absolutely out of this world." She seemed delighted.

My plan had worked.

I looked at her lovingly. "I'll make an offer for it on Monday then," I said. "It has lots of potential," I added.

"Oh, yes," she agreed, "lots. I can just see it now; roses round the door, coal fire in the grate . . ."

This wasn't quite the kind of potential I meant — but I didn't think it would be wise to tell her that I thought it would be an even better investment than the flat.

I knew she'd never have been particularly happy about the flat — but the house she definitely loved. And I loved her, too, and proved it by slipping her ring back on to her finger.

"It's more *you*," I said a little later as we investigated the interior. "You're more roses and ivy growing up the wall than waste disposals and entry by voice box only.

"And I actually think it's more *me*, too. I think I could get really into gardening — maybe even have a vegetable plot."

Rachel smiled at me indulgently.

"Oh, Andy, I think we're going to be very happy here," she said in that soft voice which would have had me convinced even if I hadn't been already.

Then she frowned slightly. "Why was it called Toad's Hall, do you think?"

"I don't know. But it's quite appropriate, isn't it?" I grinned. She didn't!

"It — hasn't got any toads, has it?" she asked hesitantly.

"What if it has?" I retorted.

'I'm scared of them," she answered sheepishly, lowering her head.

There was silence then. I was too stunned to speak. Then I opened my mouth to protest.

"After all that fuss —" I started.

"Well, my girl," I turned away, so she couldn't see my smile, "if there are any toads here, then you'll just have to compromise and live in harmony with them."

"But, Andy . . ." Her voice wobbled a little. And I couldn't tease her any longer. I started to giggle and after a while she joined in, till we were both laughing heartily.

We never did find any toads, but we had at least learned how to live in harmony. ■

ON THE RUN

While the future of the Croft Douglas swallows is in question, it's a matter of life and death when Gideon stumbles across a fugitive who may just have pulled off an artful dodge . . .

I HAVE a letter that reads, "Dear Gideon, I'm lying in bed with a bad cold, waiting for my visitors of the last twenty years. How come your swallows have come back, yet ours haven't?"

These popular little birds have had a hard time this year because of the sometimes atrocious early summer weather conditions.

At Croft Douglas we usually have at least six pairs of swallows who come to claim the choicest nesting beams in the roofs of the barn, bull pen, byre, stables and turnip shed.

This year, only four swallows eventually arrived, so there are just two nests, one in the eaves of the barn and the other on the beams above Prince's loose box in the stables.

Today the sky is full of young swallows on solo flights, whilst their parents are busy feeding a second brood of fledglings. So nature seems to be busy resolving this year's problem of the swallow population.

But there's yet another problem to be solved here in the Highlands.

SINCE afforestation plans were first put into action, there are now dense jungles of fir-trees choking up the hillsides.

There is no birdsong in these forests that give so much sanctuary to hooded crows and foxes, who can breed and multiply safely here.

Although we have frequent confrontations, the foxes are animals to be admired because of their cunning and determination to survive at all costs. This will be tested to the full today because of previous lamb and poultry losses.

The farmers have complained and a pack of foxhounds has been called in to try to scare the predators off.

This is the only pack of hounds in this part of the Highlands, led, I am positive, by one of the fittest men in Perthshire.

I call him Hector the Hound, because he knows all his dogs by name and treats them as individuals.

And Hector follows his hounds the hard way — on foot.

The hounds are friendly animals, but are dedicated to the task in hand, and they do succeed in frightening the foxes back into their "fox holes" in the forest.

There they'll find their traditional food like lizards, beetles, mice and rabbits.

Hector phoned to say the hounds would probably be crossing our land before noon and an hour later I

144

heard their distant, mournful baying.

It's the sort of sound that turns the blood into ice water and clutches the heart with a handful of fear.

I decided in that haunting moment I never, ever, wanted to be hunted.

It was then I saw the ripple working towards me through a bed of bracken.

A big foxhound surfaced with its long, pink tongue lolling out, and surveyed me suspiciously.

I put on what I hoped was my most formidable look and growled, "Go away!"

The hound stared at me, sniffing the air suspiciously, then gave me a last "have you something to hide?" look before turning to lope effortlessly up the hill to catch up with the rest of the pack, whose excited cries had reached a crescendo.

Gradually the noise faded and disappeared into the distance.

THAT'S when I spotted the well-grown fox cub lying almost at my

feet, in a bed of wild flowers. Now I knew why the foxhound had been so puzzled.

Cleverly, the cub had sought the protection of this big bouquet of flowers to disguise its own scent with summertime smells.

The cub was watching my every move with anxious eyes, so I slowly retreated to demonstrate that I had no wish to disturb him or declare his hiding place to the hounds, whose baying was by now just a faint, distant sound from somewhere on the edge of the forest.

I could also just hear Hector blowing on his hunting horn to gather the hounds together again and make for home.

I headed for home, too, knowing that the young fox cub wouldn't move for a while. And when I returned later there was only the circular mark of its body in the bed of wild flowers.

I can only hope that this fox cub will remember the favour I've done him and reward us by never, ever being a bother to our speckled hens! ■

J.T.

ADOPT-A-GRAN

What a super idea, she thought. Grandad will be delighted . . .

By JOYCE BEGG

I AM in the unusual position of having two grandfathers and no grandmothers so, when the school organised an Adopt-A-Granny scheme, I was quite keen.

My mother wasn't so sure. "What about your grandads, Judy?" she asked. "You could help them more than you do. They can always use a bit of assistance. Don't they come first?"

"In terms of my own affection, of course they come first," I answered loftily. "In terms of their need for an Adopt-A-Granny scheme, they seem to me to be perfectly self-sufficient."

Mother stared at me and said something faintly sarcastic about me and my 'O' level English. But we both knew I was right.

Grandad Deane is a retired navy man, who calls his kitchen "the galley" and talks about "the plumbing in the head." I don't think he has actually ever referred to "the bulkhead" in his tiny self-contained flat, but no-one would be surprised if he did.

When I go to Grandad Deane's, I'm always reminded of those ships of old, where even the captain's state-room only seemed to measure three feet by four, but still contained a bed, table, chest, chair, wardrobe, *and* washing facilities — all balanced on gimbals.

Grandad Deane's house isn't quite small, but everything is so neat and tidy it gives the appearance of being miniaturised. I'm sure he'd be happy in a single-berth caravan, with doors that turn into tables, and a bathroom you have to enter backwards.

He himself is a thin, straight sort of man who wears white shirts and striped ties, or sometimes a white polo-neck sweater, a navy blazer, and dark trousers with a crease that could slice bread.

He talks in short brisk sentences, as though he doesn't want to waste time talking at length, especially if all you're discussing is the weather or the state of the pound.

Grandad Fletcher, my other grandfather, is a much more relaxed sort of person. He lives in a council house with a garden, a toolshed, and a greenhouse where he potters by the hour.

The inside of his house is usually clean, but not exactly a model of tidiness. My mother says it is chaotic, but then she's a Deane.

It's a homely sort of place, with lots of soft fat chairs, usually adorned with pipe ash or cat hairs. He has photographs of his grandchildren on the mantelpiece, and a painting of Lake Windermere (a bit amateurish, but easy on the eye) on the wall above the telly.

His cat is a rather beautiful creature called Lucy, who has a black, white and orange coat, and is the laziest cat on the planet. She reminds me of those lions that lounge around sleeping under trees for four days at a stretch, before getting up to kill something to eat.

But although Lucy certainly spends a great deal of her life unconscious, she is regularly presented dainties without ever having to go out and knock over a wildebeest.

So in their different ways, my grandfathers manage very well. Grandfather Deane is a fair baker, and makes a brilliant curry. Grandad Fletcher is fond of stew and potatoes, and likes those tinned puddings that you boil for 30 minutes and come out totally saturated in jam or syrup.

Neither of them look in the least undernourished or neglected, so I thought the Adopt-A-Granny scheme could better profit from my time and energy.

And besides, Mr Powell, my Modern Studies teacher, would be pleased with me. Mr Powell is very keen on awakening his class's 'social awareness'.

He is also five foot eleven, with dark grey eyes and fair hair that curls at the back of his neck.

The council had given Mr Powell a list of people in the area who lived on their own and were, to a greater or lesser degree, housebound. A few of them were men, but the title of the scheme was not changed to accommodate them.

Mr Powell rather tentatively suggested it might be, but then Alicia Haldane, whose mother is into feminism to a slightly embarrassing degree, said that women had been living with male titles for generations and only now were referred to as chairpersons, and things like that. Men could be grannies for a change, and just see how much they like it.

Mr Powell, while not necessarily in agreement, couldn't think of a logical argument against it, so the Adopt-A-Granny title stayed.

ANYWAY, I was allotted to Mrs Gibb. This was actually extremely convenient, because Mrs Gibb lived in Brookfield Road, which is halfway between school and home. I could call in on my way from school in the afternoon, or even pop in early in the morning, if necessary.

Mrs Gibb is everyone's idea of a granny. She has a round face which smiles a lot, although there are quite a few lines on it as well, tight white curls all over her head, and bright blue eyes.

The trouble is that she is greatly troubled by arthritis, and walks with two sticks. She has a home-help who comes two mornings a week, but she can't get to the shops herself. And some things she finds very difficult, like peeling potatoes.

I don't know whether or not my social awareness has been heightened by our acquaintance, but I do now realise how many things one takes absolutely for granted — like running upstairs or unscrewing the lid of a jar of beetroot.

It was Mrs Gibb who mentioned the Old Timers' Annual Fancy Dress party.

"I hope I'll be able to go," she said, as I peeled carrots and onions for her soup. She loves to have a pot of soup on the go.

"Why shouldn't you?" I asked.

"It'll be difficult now that Mrs Arnold has broken her wrist. She came for me every week."

"Won't the O.T.s organise a substitute driver?"

"They might do. But they might forget. I don't like to mention it."

It was right then, while washing a leek, that I had my first brilliant idea. It was so brilliant that I stood there for ages staring out of Mrs Gibb's window, dripping water into my rubber gloves and on to my sleeves without even noticing.

"Judy?" Mrs Gibb said.

"Mmmmmm?"

"Is something wrong?"

I came back to earth.

"No. Everything is fine. I've just had a flash of inspiration. My grandad could drive you. In fact, he might well go to the party. That's just the kind of thing he needs."

"I wouldn't dream of imposing —"

"But you wouldn't be," I put in. "He loves to be useful. And he'd enjoy the company. He's been a bit lonely since my grandmother died.

"He's got Lucy, of course, but it's not the same," I added. "She's moulting again, as well."

"Pardon?" Mrs Gibb asked, a little bewildered.

I laughed.

"The cat. Lucy's a cat. And she leaves fur everywhere."

The more I thought about Grandad Fletcher, the more I realised that he would benefit from the refining influences of female company.

He is a bit apt to drop pipe ash, accumulate piles of dirty coffee cups, and drape his laundry over the backs of chairs. Mrs Gibb, although inhibited in her movements, has high domestic standards.

"I'll ask him, shall I?"

Mrs Gibb's normally round, smiling face took on a worried frown.

"I don't want to ask any favours. I'm sure one of the regular drivers —"

"Believe me, you'd be doing *him* a favour," I reassured her, setting about the leek with renewed vigour.

"When's the party?" I enquired. "Wednesday afternoon? Right. I'll go and see him this evening after tea, and find out if he's going to be free. And then I'll check his wardrobe."

"What's wrong with it? Woodworm?"

"Not that kind of wardrobe, Mrs Gibb. The clothes kind. If I don't keep an eye on him he'll turn up in green wellies, gardening trousers and the oldest Aran sweater in the solar system.

"It's so old it sticks out all round like a bell," I groaned. "He looks like one of those dolls you can't knock down."

Mrs Gibb smiled.

"Maybe he should come like that. After all, it is a fancy dress party."

I stopped with the knife in mid-air.

"That's a thought. Won't he have to dress up?"

She shook her head with a laugh.

"Not this time. Mr Thomas did come as Rupert Bear last year, but he got so over-heated we all thought he was having a stroke.

"That was the same year that Mrs Mitchell came in a yashmak and a pair of net curtains. She said she was 'Turkish Delight', but I'm afraid there was a lot more Eastern promise in Mrs Beaumont."

"Who was she dressed as?"

"Widow Twanky."

I got a fit of the giggles at this point.

"So this year," Mrs Gibb went on, "we decided just to have masks."

"Have you got one yet?"

She shook her head.

"I was going to try to make one, but my fingers haven't been up to much this week."

"The toy shop has a great selection," I told her. "I'll get one for you, if you like. I'll get one for Grandad, too."

Mrs Gibb's worried look came back.

"Don't make him feel he *has* to do anything. I know he'll be welcome at the party, but if he'd rather go straight home, that's absolutely fine. Not everyone likes parties."

"Don't worry. I'll talk to him."

And, of course, Grandad Fletcher was dead pleased to help Mrs Gibb, although he had his doubts about the party.

"I don't know that I want to be thought of as an Old Timer," he protested.

"I don't see why not," I said, wondering why old people can't be honest about their age. "You're probably older than Mrs Gibb.

"And anyway, the O.T.s are a very with-it group," I said encouragingly. "They went to Yugoslavia last year on a coach trip."

So on Wednesday afternoon, as arranged, Grandad called for Mrs Gibb, took her to the party, and had a brilliant time.

I was at school, naturally, having seen Mrs Gibb briefly in the morning when I handed her the two masks (Boy George — my favourite pop star — and Minnie Ha Ha) but I heard all about it when I saw her again at tea-time.

"It was a lovely party." She smiled. "Everyone enjoyed it — even Mrs Mitchell, although she'd thought it was a bit tame, settling for masks."

"Who did she go as this year?"

"As far as I could gather, she was supposed to be a court jester. She looked more like Noddy, to be honest. But she'd gone to a lot of trouble over her mask, I'll say that for her." She sat down slowly in her chair and settled herself before carrying on.

"Your grandad's a real gentleman, Judy. We got along famously."

"Terrific!" I grinned. "I bet he enjoyed the party, too, didn't he?"

"He said he hadn't laughed so much since your dad fell off his bike outside the Co-op."

Grandad Fletcher confirmed her remarks when I phoned him later that evening. He also said he was mad at himself for not joining the O.T.s ages ago and described their party games at length.

But it was just as well Mrs Gibb had filled me in already, because I would never have made any sense of my grandfather's account. He was laughing so much it bordered on hysterics.

T was just incredibly bad luck about Grandad Fletcher's toe. I mean, it must *be* possible to drop a tin of cat food on to your toe without making the nail go black and half your foot swell up.

But that's what happened to Grandad Fletcher two weeks after the party — and just as he and Mrs Gibb were developing a real relationship, too.

I couldn't bear to see their friendship flounder, all because of a tin of cat food, so at half past eight on the Wednesday morning I phoned Grandad Deane. Naturally he'd been up for hours, cleaned the kitchen floor and polished all the taps in the bathroom.

"Are you free this afternoon, Grandad?" I started. "Only it's Mrs Gibb and Grandad Fletcher. They can't get to the O.T.s."

This was complete jargon to Grandad Deane, of course. So I had to explain the whole thing to him.

"They sound as if they need an ambulance."

"Not at all. Grandad Fletcher's perfectly mobile. He just can't drive. He says he can't get a shoe on and doesn't feel safe driving in his bedroom slippers. He's quite right, too. They look as if they're older than he is.

"Will you take them, Grandad?" I finished.

Grandad whuffed a bit, as though trying to think up an excuse not to go, but Grandad Deane has a stiff Senior Service bearing and a heart as soft as the strawberry cream in a chocolate box.

So that afternoon, Grandad Deane called for Grandad Fletcher, made several remarks on the state of 'the galley' (pointing out that it was no surprise he'd dropped the tin of cat food, when there wasn't an inch of free counter-space), and then helped him down the front steps and into the car.

Then he called for Mrs Gibb, helped _her_ down the steps and into the car, and set off for the O.T.s in his 1959 Wolsley, polished to a blinding radiance.

On Grandad Fletcher's insistence, he stayed for the O.T. meeting. And although the Morris dancers who were booked to perform for them were not really his idea of riveting entertainment, he said he did enjoy meeting the people in the club and might consider going back the following week.

So that became the established pattern. One or other of the grandads would drive and the three of them would set off for the O.T.s for an afternoon's fun and hilarity, followed by a cup of tea and a cake.

It didn't sound like riotous living to me, but I could tell by Mrs Gibb's face on Wednesday afternoons how much she had enjoyed it.

The other members used to tease her about her boyfriends, which I thought was slightly vulgar, until I had my next brilliant idea.

ROMANCE!

Why not? Mrs Gibb loved the company of the grandads. She spoke a great deal about Grandad Fletcher — and Grandad Fletcher in his turn was clearly in need of the love of a good woman (if only to tell him to put away the cornflakes packet, and not to leave his underwear draped over the sideboard to dry off).

They would be so good for each other, I decided. I was amazed I had been so slow to think of it.

That was when I began my campaign of subtle innuendo. I mentioned Grandad in every second sentence to Mrs Gibb, and pointed out his good features — such as his easy temper and his kindness to animals.

At the same time, I would praise Mrs Gibb to Grandad Fletcher, remarking on her sense of humour and her cheerfulness in the face of constant pain.

They both listened to me most attentively, and I would have sworn everything was moving along most satisfactorily.

Then Mrs Gibb got flu.

She phoned me in a dead croaky voice before I left for school one morning, to tell me not to call in. In the first place, she'd got the flu and didn't want to pass it on. And in the second place, she didn't feel like anything to eat, so she didn't need me to peel the potatoes or go to the shops.

I said I would come anyway, but Mrs Gibb got quite agitated at that, because she knew my exams were coming up.

So did I, of course. A good bout of flu seemed a splendid alternative to me, actually.

However, my mother agreed with Mrs Gibb and promised that she would call in herself, just to make sure Mrs Gibb had everything she needed and that the doctor had been called. So I had to be content with that.

Mrs Gibb's doctor did call, and said she was to stay in bed — undisturbed if possible — for a week, and that the health visitor would make sure she was OK.

I felt ridiculous. What is the point of an Adopt-A-Granny scheme if it collapses the minute somebody gets an infectious disease?

Mr Powell in school said he could see my point, but as long as Mrs Gibb was being properly cared for, my responsibility stopped there and I should concentrate on passing the exams.

"Think how Mrs Gibb would feel if she knew you failed because you were looking after her? She would fret herself into a decline."

He had a point there. Mrs Gibb is a lady of very high social awareness.

ON day three of the flu, I reckoned Mrs Gibb would be well enough to answer the phone, which I knew was right by her bedside.

"It's you, Judy! How lovely to hear from you," she said, in a voice so faint as to be distinctly alarming.

"How are you?" I bawled. Isn't it funny how if someone talks to you dead quite on the phone, you assume you've got to shout to be heard?

"I'm fine," she said, a shadow of her former cheery self. "I'm being very well looked after. Your grandad —"

"Grandad? Is he there?"

"He has been most helpful and attentive. I don't know how I'd have managed. He's been making cups of tea and barley water and plumping up my pillows."

"Has he?" I was delighted. "I hope the tea's OK, he tends to stew it a bit."

"Nonsense! It's perfect."

"That's wonderful. Well look, Mrs Gibb, Mum says I've not to tire you, so I'll ring off now and phone you tomorrow."

I hung up, and did a small dance down the hall. This was working even better than I could have foreseen. All my subtle innuendoes to Grandad Fletcher were paying off. Mind you, I wasn't sure that he'd be an absolute ideal nursemaid. But at least he cared enough to risk getting flu.

I phoned briefly every afternoon that week. Mrs Gibb always answered and I always got the same story. Grandad was next to sainthood, and could not be praised too highly.

The first indication I got that all was not well was when Grandad Fletcher appeared on our doorstep late one afternoon, looking for his tea.

He had on his green wellies and his oldest duffel coat, circa 1943, and he was wet and filthy.

"Grandad!" I exclaimed, too astonished to move from the doorway.

"Aren't you going to let me in? In case you hadn't noticed, it's raining and it's almost totally dark."

I moved aside, and he dripped quietly on to the hall carpet.

"You'd better go into the kitchen and take off your wellies. How's Mrs Gibb?"

I don't think he heard, because he still had his hood up.

In the kitchen my mother was cooking spaghetti bolognese. Grandad sniffed appreciatively and then asked if she'd put any garlic in.

"You haven't answered me, Grandad," I said, helping him off with his coat.

"Of course I've put garlic in," my mother said.

"I'm not keen on garlic."

"Is Mrs Gibb OK, Grandad? Is she fit to be left?"

"Eh?" Grandad said.

I got a bit impatient at that. So much for the great lovers.

"Mrs Gibb."

"Oh, she's fine, I think. I don't really know. I've spent all afternoon changing a tyre. The garage must have fixed it on with nails."

I blanched.

"You mean you haven't seen Mrs Gibb?"

"Of course I've seen her," he replied, wrestling with the green wellies. "I took her a bag of oranges on Thursday."

"What?"

I could feel the blood draining out of my face. Mrs Gibb had been lying! She had deliberately fibbed down the phone, so that I wouldn't go over to Brookfield Road and get the flu. No wonder it was always she who answered my calls. No-one else was there.

Especially not my fabulous, caring, socially-aware grandad.

"How could you!" I cried, and charged out of the kitchen.

I could hear a plaintive, "What have I done?" behind me. But I didn't wait to answer. I grabbed my anorak, flew out of the door, and ran all the way to Brookfield Road.

When I got there, I realised I'd forgotten the key. I stood muttering on the doorstep, not wanting to ring the bell but anxious to get in. I was pondering the problem, wondering if a neighbour might have a spare key, when the porch light came on and the door opened.

"Oh, hello. It's you. I thought I heard someone. She'll be delighted to see you."

I was transfixed. I know my mouth was open. I probably looked like a landed cod.

"Are you going to stand there all night? Only I've left the pasta boiling and it's all at a critical stage."

T was all so simple. I'd just got hold of the wrong grandad. And when I think of it, it's much better this way. Grandad Fletcher really is perfectly all right on his own — with Lucy, of course.

When he gets fed up with stew and steamed pudding, he comes round to us for a change. He doesn't need anyone to look after him. He says he's happy in his squalor after 43 years of having to be tidy for Grandma.

And now that he's joined the Old Timers and made all these new friends, he doesn't even feel lonely.

Grandad Deane, however, is quite another case. It is easy to assume, isn't it, that because someone is self-sufficient, they don't need anyone else? That's what I thought Grandad Deane was like. A bit brisk, and not exactly sociable.

In fact, he's shy, but he loves company and he especially needs someone to look after. He appears to have found the ideal recipient for his care and attention. Mrs Gibb thinks he's Mr Wonderful.

They're going to announce their engagement at the Old Timers' Christmas party, but they're not going to rush into marriage. They'll wait till Easter. I'm to be bridesmaid and Grandad Fletcher is to be best man.

Mr Powell is almost as pleased as I am, although he admits he did not foresee this as a result of the Adopt-A-Granny scheme.

I was all for setting up a matrimonial agency, to be run by me and Mr Powell. But Mr Powell said he did not think that the romance between Mrs Gibb and Grandad Deane was necessarily a trend-setter.

I'm not so sure. The O.T.s have booked a coach trip to Paris next year. How can anyone fail to feel romantic in Paris? ■

THE HOUSE WHERE OPPORTUNITY KNOCKS

It certainly did for the girl who inherited both it —
and its unexpected tenants . . .

By Louise Brindley

THE phone call that changed my life could not have come at a worse time — the office had never been busier.

"It's for you," Sally Smith called. "Personal.

"A Mr Felton. He says it's urgent."

"I don't know anyone called Felton!" Then, putting on my efficient telephone voice, "Hello . . ."

Tears were in my eyes when I hung up. "What's the matter?" Sally asked, her eyes as round as saucers.

"My Aunt Lizzie died yesterday." I stared at Sally, numbly.

"Shall I get you some coffee?"

"No thanks. I haven't time. I must see Mr Anderson at once. I'll need some time off to see to things in London."

"Rather you than me," Sally said fervently. "He's in a terrible mood."

It was pouring with rain when the Inter-City train left Sheffield for King's Cross.

Hunched in my seat I stared out at the rain-soaked scenery, remembering other times, other happier visits to Aunt Lizzie's.

How simple and uncomplicated my childhood had been. Full of fun and laughter and holidays with Aunt Lizzie. But that was before Dad died and Mother took ill.

I was just on the verge of leaving school when that happened, which meant giving up my art scholarship and finding a job near home so that I could look after Mum.

It hadn't been easy, but I'd tried to disguise that fact from her. Even so, I knew she worried about me.

"It doesn't seem right," she would say. "A girl of your age should be out meeting other young people. Time passes so quickly, you know, when you're young."

"Don't worry about me, Mum. I'm quite happy to stay just as I am now."

It was a safe, comfortable way of life that could not last for ever.

When Mother died, I carried on much as before and yet, somehow, it all seemed pointless without her.

As the train sped towards London, I knew Mother was right when she said, "Time passes quickly." I had meant to take time off to visit Aunt Lizzie.

Now it was too late.

I pushed to the back of my mind the real reason why I put off visiting her . . . We hadn't hit it off too well at our last meeting . . .

MR FELTON was at King's Cross to meet me — tall, cadaverous-looking, with strands of dark hair arranged painstakingly over his head.

"Miss Waring?" he asked cautiously, and gave a brief, wintry smile when I nodded.

"My car's parked outside," he said huskily, popping a cough-sweet into his mouth.

Mr Felton said dryly, as he steered the ancient car through a maze of streets, "Of course, Miss Waring, you realise that as your aunt's sole surviving relative, you have inherited everything, her house, moneys, and all her personal effects?"

"Oh, I never thought . . ." I stared out at the traffic lights.

"But . . . my job . . . I'll have to sell the house."

"I'm afraid that will not be possible," he said with a sneeze.

"Why not?"

"Because — atishoo — a codicil to your aunt's will states that her tenants must remain — atishoo — in situ for at least twelve months."

"Her — tenants?" I stared at him uncomprehendingly. "I don't understand."

My heart sank as I imagined the house filled with distressed gentlewomen.

"How many of them are there? You see, Mr Felton, I must get back to my job as quickly as possible . . ."

"Perhaps we could discuss this a little later . . ." he suggested irritably, so I let him concentrate on his driving.

I fell silent as the car made its slow way to Aunt Lizzie's house, where I had spent the happiest days of my childhood.

I remembered the little girl who had slept so soundly beneath a rose-sprigged eiderdown in a room overlooking a strangely exotic tree with red-gold leaves — the sumac tree.

If rain fell at all in those days, it came in the evening to freshen the earth.

At those times, the sumac tree would seem a-dazzle with raindrops, like a ballet dancer.

Then, my future had seemed as magical as the tree. Now here I was nearly 30 years old, afraid to step out of my safe little shell, and wondering what had happened to the magic . . .

When the car drew up outside the red brick, Victorian villa, I unlatched the gate and walked up the path to the front steps.

Glancing up at the bay windows, I half expected to see Aunt Lizzie's smiling face at one of them.

I could not stop myself remembering the last time I'd seen her — at Mother's funeral, two years ago.

"You are free now, Caroline; free to live your own life, to think about yourself for a change . . ." she told me.

"I'm fine as I am, thank you." Grief had made me tired and irritable. The thought of freedom scared me.

"You mustn't be afraid of life, my dear," Aunt Lizzie whispered, as if recognising that fear.

"Try not to live in the past too much."

Suddenly I was not only scared, but angry.

"Oh, I suppose you think I should just forget about Mother."

"You know I didn't mean that," my aunt had replied, and I knew I'd hurt her . . .

SHAKING my head clear of memories, I waited while Mr Felton unlocked the door, then I walked into the hall, puzzled by the silence. Perhaps the sitting tenants were lying down, having their afternoon naps. I smiled wryly at my unconscious humour.

With Mr Felton sneezing behind me, I made my way to the kitchen and brewed some tea.

In the sitting-room, sipping tea, I knew it was time to tackle Mr Felton.

"This codicil to my aunt's will places me in a difficult position." I said. "Who are these sitting ducks — I mean tenants?" I blushed at my slip-up.

"What am I supposed to do about them?"

"I see no reason for concern," Mr Felton said, business-like. "The property will be yours to dispose of twelve months from now. Meanwhile, you will draw the revenue from the rooms."

"Yes, I suppose that's true." But who will look after a houseful of old folk, I wondered.

There didn't seem much point in voicing my doubts to the solicitor. He looked decidedly peaky himself.

"Perhaps you should go home to bed," I suggested. "We can sort things out when you're feeling better."

When he had sneezed his way to the front door and departed, I peered cautiously into the rooms for a glimpse of the sitting tenants.

No-one! The house was empty. And yet, in a curious way, it was not empty at all. My aunt's presence was everywhere.

The top back attic with its old sloping skylight and wide dormer window had been turned into an artist's studio. There were easels and canvasses, paints and brushes.

The walls were hung with pictures and sketches — whoever had painted them had real talent.

I sighed, remembering the scholarship I'd given up.

The room next to it was obviously a man's room, by the row of pipes on the mantelpiece.

Under the jutting dormer window was a desk with a typewriter, piles of paper, reference books, and bottles of typewriter-correcting fluid.

I could not help glancing at the sheet of paper in the typewriter:

Inspector McGraw picked his way silently between the tombstones towards the flickering light of the torch . . .

So the occupant of Room Two was a writer, but — judging from the amount of correcting fluid he used — a rotten typist.

The room next to the bathroom, on the lower landing, had been turned into a photographer's studio.

I gasped in amazement at the jumbled mass of cables snaking across the floor, the intricate assortment of spotlights surrounding the room. But what really took my breath away were the photographs on the walls.

Closing the door behind me, I walked along the landing to the room which had once been mine.

Nothing in the room had changed. It was just as I remembered it.

I crossed to the window. Even in October the sumac tree was a magical sight.

Here in this room I could almost believe I was a child again, and Aunt Liz was calling me to breakfast, promising a trip to the zoo afterwards, or a picnic, or —

The front door slammed suddenly and I came back to the present with a jolt.

I hurried downstairs to meet the hostile gaze of a young woman with frizzed blonde hair.

"You must be Liz's niece," she said contemptuously. "You took your time getting here!"

She walked heavily upstairs, a camera case slung from her left shoulder.

So this was the photographer, one of my sitting tenants.

"Who are *you*?" Nettled by her words, her attitude, I was ready for a confrontation.

Leaning over the banister, the girl said insolently. "I'm Mandy Rogers, since you obviously require identification."

Well . . . So this was one of my 'sitting ducks', unable to look after herself. How wrong can you be, I wondered.

And what other shocks were in store for me?

Ten minutes later there was a bumping at the door, and a breathless girl, slim and dark, wearing round, red-framed glasses, clutching a canvas shopping bag in one hand, and a portfolio in the other, stumbled into the hall.

"Oh, hello," she said. "Sorry I can't shake hands. Oh, please don't close the door, Bill's coming with the fish."

She smiled disarmingly. "My name's Susie Bolder, by the way, and you must be Caroline Waring, Liz's niece."

"Yes, I am," I admitted, weakly.

"Oh, thank goodness! Here's darling Bill with the fish."

The man carrying a plastic bag and a briefcase must have been around 35.

"I could only get mackerel," he said apologetically. "That's all they had left."

Then, catching sight of me, "Oh, you must be Miss Waring. I'm Bill Drummond."

"Are there any more?" I asked foolishly.

"Any more — what?" Bill sounded cautious.

It was on the tip of my tongue to say, "Sitting ducks," but I managed to restrain myself.

"Residents," I said awkwardly.

"Oh no," Susie said. "There's just the three of us."

Before I'd met them I'd been worried they were too old, now I was worried they were too young.

"You had better give me the fish, Bill," Susie said, "and I'll start supper.

Miss Waring can have my mackerel."

She turned at the kitchen door, to explain, "I have to go out again soon."

Probably to some wild party or disco, I thought.

"Susie teaches art at the local technical college," Bill said quietly, as if he had read my thoughts.

"By the way, Miss Waring, we were so sorry about Liz. She was a wonderful person, but I guess I don't have to tell you that."

"It's such a pity you weren't there when she died," Susie said in her obviously forthright way.

"If you'll excuse me, I think I'll go upstairs." I knew Susie had not meant to be unkind, but it hurt just the same, the implication that I had neglected Aunt Lizzie, which, of course, I had.

Supper was a curious meal: thick, greenish-coloured lentil soup, strongly flavoured with garlic; granary bread and goats' milk cheese, followed by natural yoghurt.

I steadfastly refused the offer of Susie's mackerel.

Bill Drummond gave me a quizzical glance across the table. "It must seem a bit, well, embarrassing, that codicil to your aunt's will," he said.

"Well, yes," I stammered. "I must admit that it did come as a surprise. You see, I — I have to get back to my job as quickly as possible.

"My boss, Mr Anderson, wasn't very pleased when I asked him for time off. I had intended to clear the house within the fortnight, and put it up for sale —"

I didn't get a chance to explain that I hadn't known I was sole beneficiary, before Mandy Rogers gave a snort of disgust, jumped to her feet, and rushed out of the room.

"You must excuse Mandy," Bill said gently. "She was very fond of Liz."

The implication being that I was not?

"Just because I hadn't been to visit her for some time, does not give you the right to assume that I didn't — love her." My voice shook, and tears blurred my eyes.

"She was my aunt, remember, long before she became your — landlady!"

I, too, jumped to my feet and rushed out of the room, knowing I had made a fool of myself.

Sinking down in a chair in Aunt Lizzie's room, I covered my face with my hands.

Bill Drummond came in ten minutes later, bringing with him a tray of tea and biscuits.

"Please," he said, "drink this, and accept our deepest apologies."

"Oh, it wasn't your fault," I said wearily, "or Susie's." I sneezed suddenly.

"Bless you," Bill said. "I know what you mean. But *I* wasn't very tactful, was I? But please believe me when I say that Liz was much more than a mere — landlady.

"I, for one, owe her much more than I was ever able to repay. You see, she visited the library where I work and took the trouble to talk to me.

"That's how she discovered I wanted to be a writer: that I hadn't a hope of writing anything in the digs I was in at the time." He smiled reflectively. "So she invited me to move in here. I can't tell you what that meant to me:

the peace and quiet, her interest in my work.

"It was the same with Susie and Mandy. Liz kind of rescued them, too. Oh, I know that Mandy's looks belie it, but she's a tender, warm-hearted girl, deep down, with a real flair for photography."

"Now, thanks to Liz, she is beginning to break through into the big time."

"As for Susie, she has started to sell her paintings at last. We owe it all to your aunt."

"Thank you for explaining things to me," I said, "and thanks for the tea and biscuits." I shivered suddenly.

"The truth is, I don't feel very well. I think I had better go to bed."

"What you need is a good night's sleep," he suggested. "The shock of all this has been too much for you.

"And, the name's Bill," he said, before he left the room.

I COULD not believe that anyone could go down with influenza so quickly. Next morning, I dragged myself downstairs to the kitchen, to find Mandy Rogers, drinking coffee.

"What on earth . . .?" she asked, sounding very cross.

"I must have caught Mr Felton's cold," I explained, leaning weakly against the table.

"Cold, nothing!" she retorted. "Go back to bed immediately. I'll ring the doctor!"

"But I can't be ill now," I protested. "Not with the funeral and everything to arrange."

"We can do all that's necessary," Mandy said coolly.

Perhaps it was my weakness, but suddenly I had to ask, "Why do you dislike me?"

"Old people need love and attention — she didn't get that from you. I guess that's why she kind of adopted the three of us — to fill your place.

"And yet it was always Caroline this, Caroline that. Liz adored you." Mandy bit her lip.

This time I wasn't angry — this time I understood.

How strange, I thought, after the doctor had been and warned me to stay put until his next visit. I had imagined myself looking after my sitting tenants, now the shoe was on the other foot.

Not that I was a very good patient. "I'm not hungry," I said. "I don't want a boiled egg."

"Try a little soup, then," Bill said patiently.

"Soup!" I shuddered.

Bill laughed quietly. "Don't worry. I'll open a tin." His glance was warm and sympathetic. "Perhaps you would rather one of the girls brought it upstairs . . ."

"Oh no, it isn't that." Tears filled my eyes. "I just feel so — so useless — lying here. It's hard to explain, but I feel as if I have let Aunt Lizzie down again.

"I really did love her, but I was such a proud, stubborn little fool. You see, the last time we met she said I mustn't be afraid of life. It came as a shock to realise that she had guessed how frightened I was."

I blew my nose hard. "I — I'm sorry, Bill, I didn't mean to say all that. I — I'll try a little soup, if you like."

"Good." He touched my hair lightly with his fingertips. "And try not to worry so much. I'm sure Liz understood."

I wanted to believe that. Just as I wanted to believe he was being so kind because he liked me, and not just because I was Liz's niece.

But I couldn't convince myself of either of those facts.

Later that evening, he and Susie came to my room together, smiling and happy.

"What do you think," Bill said proudly, his arm round Susie's shoulders. "This clever little thing has just landed a commission for a portrait! Isn't that marvellous?"

"Yes, yes it is! Congratulations, Susie!" I answered, glad they'd included me in their news, and at the same time dismayed.

He's in love with her, I thought bleakly, and was stunned to realise how much it mattered.

One afternoon, Susie brought her easel, brushes, and a canvas to my room. I was over the worst of my influenza by that time.

"I hope you don't mind," she said, "but I started to paint the sumac tree, from your bedroom window, and I'd like to finish it before winter comes."

"No, of course I don't mind."

We chatted happily and before I knew it, I was telling her about the scholarship, and my mother.

"Oh, that must have been tough," she said sympathetically. "But it's never too late to begin again.

"Look! Why don't I bring you a pad and pencil — or charcoal, if you prefer, and you can sketch me painting the sumac tree."

And so we worked away in silence, till Susie ventured. "Why don't you wear your hair loose, Caro? I guess you'll think I have an awful cheek, but it suits you better that way."

I flushed. "Caro," she had called me.

"I suppose I put it up because it was less trouble that way," I said, "and made me appear more efficient than I really am."

"Hey," she said, "you can type, can't you?"

"Yes, I consider myself a pretty good typist." I wished she hadn't mentioned it, reminding me, as it did, of yesterday's phone call to my furious boss, telling him that I would not be fit to return to work for a while.

Now Susie was talking again. "He won't ask you, so I shall. The fact is, he's found a publisher for his novel but Bill can't type for toffee . . ."

"I'll do what I can to help," I promised.

"Thanks, Caro."

"Gosh, you draw really well. What a pity you're going home. You could have joined my art class. It's such fun."

"I'd have liked that," I said wistfully. Then I looked at her painting of the sumac tree, and caught my breath. No wonder Bill was so proud of her.

"It's lovely," I said. "I wonder, would you sell it to me, to remind me . . ."

"To remind you of — what?" she asked gently.

"Oh, so many things. Aunt Lizzie, you and Mandy, and Bill."

"Now, how could anyone forget any of us?" she laughed.

"Especially Bill."

"You're very fond of Bill, aren't you?" I asked.

"Of course. I adore him," Susie replied.

Later, Mandy came to my room. She smiled gently at me.

"I don't suppose you'd care to pose for me?" she said, off-handedly.

"Me? When?" I asked.

"Right now. Of course, you'll need make-up, and your hair looks terrible scraped back that way, but I can fix all that."

I sat dumbly in Mandy's studio as she went to work on me.

"Now," she said, "sit over there while I get the lighting right."

Catching sight of myself in a mirror, I gasped with pleasure. Mandy had made me look almost beautiful. "Pretty pleased with yourself, aren't you?" she enquired in that brittle way of hers.

"Makes me wonder how you get any pleasure out of hiding behind that plain spinster act."

"What?" Suddenly I was angry.

"Great," she said, "that's just the expression I need. Hold it!" She grinned suddenly.

"I know, I've been beastly to you. Put it down to jealousy that Liz was your aunt — if you like.

"But I'm pleased to see you have some spirit left. You know, you are quite an attractive woman when you stop being afraid all the time."

I should have been angry all over again. Yet it wouldn't have done any good — we both knew she was right.

T'S terribly good of you to help me out this way," Bill said. "But are you sure you feel up to it?"

"Yes, quite sure. In any case, I could do with the practice before going back to work."

"We'll miss you, Caroline," Bill said quietly. "By the way, you look terrific. You really are a very pretty girl."

"Because of this make-up?" I said coolly.

"It has nothing to do with make-up," Bill said softly. "Yours is the kind of beauty that comes from within." I gazed up at him, my heart hammering.

"And Susie says your drawing shows great talent." How could I have imagined Bill returned my feelings when it was Susie he loved?

"Really? Well, we'd better get on with Inspector McGraw." I knew my voice was icy, yet I just couldn't help it.

Bill turned away, a closed, puzzled expression on his face. "Of course," he answered.

I had this terrible feeling I'd hurt him and yet I could think of nothing to say that would help. And then, all too soon, there was only one day to go.

Bill had been very quiet, so I was very surprised when he said, "Is there anywhere special you'd like to go tomorrow, since it's your last day?"

"Well yes. I'd like to go to the zoo. Aunt Lizzie used to take me there when I was a little girl."

"Fine," Bill said. "We'll make an early start."

Bill was waiting for me in the hall. "Where's Susie?" I asked.

"She's not coming. She's going to wash her hair or something . . .

"Why? Did you specially want her to come with us?"

"No. I just thought . . . Oh never mind."

It was a fine, warm day, and it felt so good to be alone, really alone with Bill. But I couldn't let myself dwell on that.

My heart was already heavy at the thought of leaving him.

And so, even though we laughed together as we fed the monkeys, parrots, and polar bears, I kept him at arm's length.

Over tea in the refreshment room, I said brightly, "I do hope your book will be a great success."

"Thanks, I'll send you an autographed copy." There was an edge to his voice.

"You needn't worry about the twelve months' clause. I'm sure Susie, Mandy and I will be out of your hair long before that."

"There's really no hurry," I said, trying to hide the hurt in my voice.

"And I'm sorry about today," he said, his tone suddenly gentler. "You haven't enjoyed it very much, have you?"

I shook my head. "You can't go back, it seems."

"Perhaps not — perhaps not . . ." And there was a strange kind of sadness in his voice.

EY," Sally whispered frantically in my ear, "I saw this paperback in the window

162

H of the bookshop. It was part of a display.

"Look! The picture on the cover could be your double."

I gasped in amazement! It *was* me! The photograph Mandy had taken six months ago! The title of the book was, 'Inspector McGraw and the Jack-o-Lantern', by William Drummond.

With shaking fingers, I flipped over the pages. The dedication read: *For Liz and Caroline, with my love.* Tears stung my eyes.

It was raining when I arrived home for lunch about one o'clock.

The postman had left the package inside the porch — a big narrow oblong package.

Susie had enclosed a letter with her painting of the sumac tree.

Darling Caro, she had written, *I always meant you to have this, knowing how much the tree meant to you — and Liz.*

I always had the feeling that you and Bill were meant for each other, which was why I chose to absent myself from your zoo outing. But I guess things didn't work out. I'll never know why.

He's terribly in love with you. The poor darling has been impossible to live with since you went away.

Now for my news. I'm getting married! His name is Robert Fortescue-Williams, a student in my art class!

Bill is to be our best man, and Mandy has actually consented to be bridesmaid.

Oh, Caro, I'm so ecstatically happy! It would make everything perfect if you could come to the wedding. Please . . .?

`Love,
Susie.`

B **ACK** at the office, Sally greeted me, nervously. "The boss wants to see you in his office — immediately, he said."

"Yes, I thought he might."

"Well, after all, you are an hour late back from lunch."

"Yes, I know I am." I smiled.

"This is simply not good enough, Miss Waring." Mr Anderson glared as I entered.

"No, it isn't," I said quietly. "It never has been, has it — neither your attitude to your staff, nor your unsympathetic approach to our problems.

"The world does not begin and end in this dusty old office. You, my dear man, don't know *how* to live!"

"What?" Mr Anderson sank back in his swivel-chair, eyes popping. "Miss Waring, you are . . ."

"Fired! I know! Thank you so much, Mr Anderson. Thank you, and — goodbye!"

I swept out of the office.

"'Bye, Sally," I said.

"But — where are you going?" she stammered.

I glanced over my shoulder for the last time. "Would you believe a wedding?"

Who knows, I thought, there just might be time to make it a double celebration.

Oh, dear Aunt Liz, if only you could have known . . . I wonder, perhaps you planned it this way, all along . . . ■

ONE COOK TOO MANY

"I'm a breadwinner — not a breadmaker," her husband protested.
"Besides, I've retired . . ."
"So have I!" she replied.

by AUDREY E. GROOM

WITH brisk efficiency Doris Pinfold handed Harry the meagre plate of what she had proudly described as a beef and vegetable stew. Bert Pinfold, seated opposite him across the table, gave a quick little smile when his wife handed him his portion.

"Oh! Thank you, dear," he said, his head bobbing up and down. "Thank you very much."

Poor old Bert, Harry thought as he plunged the soup spoon Doris had provided into the watery, tasteless meal. Yes, poor old Bert, he thought again.

Fancy living on this sort of grub all your life. Fancy living with someone as cool as Doris all your life, come to that!

And with a sudden, unexpected, warm rush of feeling he thought of his own wife, Winnie. Oh, he did miss her. Indeed he did.

But at the same time, as he took another spoonful of the rather tasteless meal, he was angry with her for leaving him in this position.

It felt strange, he reflected sadly, to find yourself at 55 years old, without a wife for the first time in all the years of their married life — even if it was only for a week.

It had been so unexpected! I mean, Winnie had always been a proper wife.

She had cooked and cleaned and washed and cared for him, for every one of their 30 years together. Just like his mother had done before her, in fact.

Just as Doris Pinfold did for Bert, Harry supposed, looking around the clinically clean dining-room and weighing up the spotless tablecloth and Bert's white shirt.

Only Winnie seemed to keep house much more warmly and comfortably. And her stew was so much nicer, too!

That's why it had all been such a shock to him — Winnie's sudden 'declaration of independence' or whatever else she liked to call it.

It had happened about two weeks after he'd taken early retirement.

Those first two weeks had been glorious! He had gone to bed when he felt like it, risen late and dozed in front of the TV in the afternoon.

In fact, Winnie had even given him breakfast in bed some mornings. For, of course, she still had to get up early to take the dog out for a walk.

But then had come that never-to-be forgotten day when an unfamiliar expression had crossed Winnie's face and she had said she wanted to talk to him.

She had been vacuuming away happily enough, or so it seemed to him. He had even obligingly lifted his legs so that she could run the cleaner underneath them.

And then, quite out of the blue, she had taken the newspaper out of his hands, put a cup of coffee in front of him and said, "Harry — I want to talk to you."

Harry didn't like being without the paper. It made him feel naked, somehow. Nowhere to hide and nothing to concentrate on while she chattered.

He might really have to listen to what Winnie had to say. And somehow he didn't like the idea of that — not with that strange look on her face.

And he found he was right to have been apprehensive. Her words were quite enough to totally shatter his peace of mind.

"Harry," she began. "How long is it since you retired, dear?"

"Er — two weeks, Winnie — you must know that, love. Two weeks . . ."

But she cut him short.

"Yes, two weeks, Harry. I shouldn't have forgotten, should I? Because it seems to me I've made more than twice as many cups of coffee, baked at least twice as many cakes and taken twice as long to do everything in that time than I ever did before!"

Harry's mouth dropped open. What was she talking about? He thought she'd hardly noticed him about the place. She always seemed to be so busy!

He frowned — this was quite a disturbing turn of events.

And there was more.

"Well now, Harry," Winnie went on. "We're the same age, give or take a week or two, aren't we?"

He nodded slowly.

"So I thought . . ." She smiled. "I thought," she said again, "that it would be very nice if we could both retire at the same time."

Harry reached for his coffee cup. He definitely needed something to revive him. But it was empty. He looked at Winnie appealingly and was about to ask her to pour him another cup when she forestalled him.

"There's plenty more in the kitchen, love," she said. Weakly, Harry staggered to his feet.

"Perhaps you'd fill mine, too, Harry, will you?" She handed him her cup.

By the time he returned to the dining-room, he had recovered his composure a little.

After all, he had thought, while pouring the coffees, it was all very well to talk about retiring together. But just how could a *woman* retire? There would always be meals to cook and clear, clothes to wash and vacuuming and dusting to do.

Women's work didn't stop — it couldn't stop. And he was about to tell her so — only she got in first, as he placed the refilled cup in front of her.

"Thank you, Harry," she said. "Anyway, I thought that if we shared all the household chores that have to be done, I wouldn't get so tired. And that would give me more time to do the things *I* want to do."

Things *she* wanted to do! What was she talking about?

Surely all women liked cooking and polishing and sewing.

Apparently, Winnie had other ideas about that, too.

"You see, Harry," she said, "I've always wanted to paint. Well, now I've joined an art class, two days a week, and I'll need time to paint at home, too. So we'll give this sharing the chores a try, shall we, love?"

Before he even had time to answer, she got up and came over to him and kissed his bald patch.

"I'm just off to the hairdresser's now, dear, and I'd be pleased if you could peel the potatoes ready for dinner, while I'm gone."

WELL, that was just the beginning, for the days that followed had been strange ones for Harry. For instance, just as he'd been about to snuggle further down into the bed the following morning, Winnie had nudged him.

"Your turn to take the dog out this morning, Harry," she'd said. "And I think I'll just have some toast and tea up here, before you go out. It'll make a nice change."

And then she'd wanted help making the bed and suggested he washed up the breakfast things while she did the dusting.

Oh, it went on and on! There seemed to be more jobs to do as the weeks progressed.

Sometimes, he tried to reason with her about it but each time she'd simply turned the new 'Winnie look' on him and said, "But you don't want me to do it all by myself, do you, Harry?" And what could he say to that?

Really, it was almost worse than being at the office. After a while, he decided things had gone far enough. He'd have to make a definite stand if he was ever to call himself master in his own house again.

The opportunity presented itself when Winnie was preparing lunch one day and began to tell him how to make custard.

"No, Winnie," he said finally and with what he hoped was a stern look. "I do not intend to learn how to cook."

Winnie paused in her custard stirring for a few minutes and stared at him. Then she shrugged.

"Oh, well, never mind then, Harry," she said. "It's up to you."

In fact, she made so little fuss about it that he really couldn't be sure whether he'd won that round or lost it.

But at least he still had his meals provided for him in the good, old-fashioned way, and that pleased him.

Then, a few weeks later, Winnie dropped yet another bombshell.

"I still wish you'd tackled some simple cooking, Harry," she said to him one evening as they were enjoying their dinner together.

"Now, Winnie," he said. "We've been into all that. You've got as much time as you want for painting now, haven't you? And you quite enjoy cooking, don't you?"

"Oh, yes," she said. "I do, Harry. It's just that — well, I'm going away on a painting week at the end of the month and it would be so much easier for you if you could cook."

Harry frowned and cleared his plate crossly. That was the trouble with women. Give them an inch and look where it got you.

Well, it was no good! A man had to take a stand on some things or a woman would do just what she liked with him. Especially a woman of Winnie's calibre.

Perhaps when she came back and saw him pale and thin from having lived on bread and cheese for a week, she'd be sorry.

But he'd underestimated Winnie. She obviously didn't intend to give him

even the doubtful satisfaction of suffering in her absence.

"Don't worry," she told him, a few days later. "I've arranged all your meals for when I'm away. Doris next door will be happy for you to eat in there with them."

Harry gulped, speechless.

In the first place, he couldn't imagine Doris Pinfold being *happy* in the accepted sense about anything.

She always looked quite the reverse. So did poor old Bert, her long-suffering husband, when her stentorian voice called him in from the garden for tea.

And in the second place, Harry didn't know that he fancied eating his meals with them, anyway, even if *they* were happy about it.

However, what else was there

to do? Oh, he could always give in and say, "Well, just tell me how to make scrambled eggs then," or "How long do potatoes have to cook for?" But he jolly well wasn't going to do that!

So, here he was, eating Doris's meagre stew, facing Doris's husband across the table and feeling quite sorry for himself. It was the second night he had come next door for dinner. Last night's offering had been worse than this.

Released from the uncomfortable situation an hour later, he stomped off with muttered thanks to retreat to his own empty kitchen. There he crossly cut himself large hunks of bread and cheese to fill up the gaps that Doris's dinner had left and sat down. Dejectedly, he began to thumb idly through Winnie's weekly magazine, which lay on the table.

He just could not face Doris's cooking for a third night, he thought, chewing meditatively. He toyed with the idea of phoning Winnie at her painting week to say he had developed an ugly rash or was coming down with bronchitis.

But no! He couldn't stoop that low. A man had his pride. Besides, he had the uncomfortable feeling that Winnie might not react in an appropriate way.

"Oh! Harry, I am sorry," she would most likely say, in her new phase. "Take some lemon and honey and go to bed early, dear. You'll probably feel much better in the morning."

At that thought, Harry suddenly felt so poorly and neglected that he was quite convinced he *was* coming down with something.

Angrily, he flipped through a few more pages of the colourful magazine — and there was the cookery page.

ENJOYABLE MEALS FOR ONE was the title and my goodness, didn't that dinner look superb!

Almost against his will, Harry feasted his eyes on the beautiful browned meat, the succulent round peas and the golden baked potatoes. He read the recipe and his mouth watered.

Quickly, he turned the page, determined to forget the dangerous thoughts that were creeping, insidiously, into his brain.

BUT Harry couldn't forget. He was still thinking them the next morning. Guiltily, feeling he was betraying his own sex, he found the magazine again. Then he went to look in the freezer for a pork chop and peas. Mind you, explaining to Doris-next-door that he wouldn't be round that evening for dinner was a bit awkward.

He had the uncomfortable feeling that she was convinced he was entertaining a lady friend in Winnie's absence. But she could think what she wanted — it was a hazard he was prepared to face for the sake of his stomach.

Well, it took a lot of effort and dinner that night *wasn't* superb. The chop was overcooked, the potatoes almost splintered and the peas were mushy. But it was all his own work, and a great improvement on Doris's offering!

Agreeably full, Harry sat back afterwards, glowing with unexpected satisfaction.

"I reckon I could do better than that — with practice," he said and thumbed through one of Winnie's cookery books while he drank his coffee.

The pictures intrigued him and whetted his appetite still further, and were an uncomfortable reminder of his hasty declaration that he would *never* learn to cook.

But the memory of the tasteless, stringy meat Doris had served up still lingered and his empty stomach groaned. His appetite won. The glossy, colourful pictures of delicious and perfectly-prepared meals lured him on.

Of course at first he was slow and his efforts were not too successful. But he persevered.

By Saturday he had tried out liver and bacon, beef casserole, shepherd's pie and — quite a triumph — mixed grill.

He was beginning to think that steak and kidney pie and sausage toad wouldn't be *entirely* beyond him . . .

Winnie's return, though he looked forward to it, still posed a problem. He had declared he would never learn to cook. Was he now to relinquish this new-found pleasure simply to maintain his male dominance?

It was a serious problem and one to which he devoted much thought. But the answer came to him suddenly as he poured himself a second cup of coffee after washing up one evening. Harry smiled to himself.

On Saturday, when Winnie returned from her week's fling with culture, she found the kitchen filled with delectable smells. She paused on the threshold, an amazed look on her face.

"You're never — *cooking*, Harry?"

"Yes," he said, a note of satisfied pride creeping into his voice. "Yes, Winnie, my love, I am. I find I have quite a flair for it."

At first, he thought she was going to laugh, but looking at her again quickly, he saw that her face was quite straight.

"Anyway, Winnie," he went on. "I expect you're tired. Come and sit down. I'll pour you a glass of sherry while I finish off in the kitchen."

Later, over dinner, Harry surreptitiously watched her expression and smiled proudly when she sat back afterwards.

"Harry, dear," she said, smiling, "that was quite delicious.

"Er — didn't you like Doris's dinners, then?" she went on.

He frowned. "No. No, not really, Winnie."

"Oh, well," she said. "Don't worry, I'm back now, Harry. I'll do a nice piece of roast beef tomorrow and —"

But Harry interrupted.

"No, Winnie, no," he said and cleared his throat to make his important statement, so that she could see he was not to be trifled with.

"No?" she queried.

"No," he said, using his stern voice again for best effect.

"I've decided, my dear, that I'm going to do the cooking in future."

Well, if his wife felt disappointed at losing the most enjoyable of the household chores, she didn't show it, he'd say that for her. She accepted the situation quite philosophically.

In fact, she just kissed him and murmured, "Anything you say, Harry dear."

Wonderful little woman. She was, after all, still the same, loving wife she'd been for the last 30 years. She still accepted his decision with a good grace, when he really put his foot down about something.

It was good to know who was boss, he thought. He smiled, humming a little as he did the washing up and pondering just what to cook for Sunday lunch. Roast lamb, maybe? Or why not be more adventurous and try pheasant — or even . . .

In the sitting-room, Winnie relaxed with a cup of coffee. She smiled gently. Everything, she considered, had gone just according to plan. ■

E.T. AND THE MEDICINE MAN

She had found a novel way of introducing herself to the man next door. Now she had to make sure he didn't forget her!

By LYNDA FRENCH

OW many times had I wished ET was a dog? Or that I was a doggy person, rather than Lisa Brown, cat-lover?

I know for a fact that dog owners are *never* short of company. Take an Alsatian or Old English sheepdog out for a run in the park, and somebody is bound to stop and admire it, and ask its name. Good friendfinders, dogs . . . Unfortunately, however, I have a cat. And ET is not the most sociable of cats.

I couldn't really take ET for a walk (even if he'd allow such an indignity) because I wasn't the sort of person who could brazen out the odd looks I'd get. Somehow, I just couldn't see myself as a crank in avocado wellies with a cat on the end of a lead.

I have always been very conformist. I don't like outrageous clothes or wild parties, and I'm happy in my safe — but dull — job.

Still, there was one thing to be said in favour of a staid, well-paid job. By not going anywhere or buying anything for a couple of years, and ignoring the comments of my extravagant friends as they jetted off to far-flung shores for the summer, I'd managed to acquire my very own home. It was only a tiny, two-up-two-down in a terrace, but the important thing was that it was *mine*, all *mine*!

No more flat-sharing problems! No more trying to track down the phantom coffee-swiper, or arguing over whose turn it was to scrub the black ring of mourning from around the bath.

No grumbling landlady telling me I couldn't invite men round for supper.

Not that owning my own place seemed to have made much difference to my circle of menfriends, but that wasn't the point.

After a while on my own, though, I was beginning to realise that houses were meant for at least *two* people and their furniture. Number 89 Alderslake Road felt rather empty, especially as I couldn't afford a three-piece suite as well as a mortgage.

Well, maybe not exactly *empty*, but definitely *lonely*. Even though ET was a terrific conversationalist . . .

He mewed, he wheedled and he purred, running the whole gamut of the feline language at the top of his voice. He loved my ankles, tickled my knees with his tail, and in the evenings lay deadweight and somnolent on my lap.

On cold winter nights, he even allowed me to put my feet on him in bed — sheer bliss!

However, after a few months of admiring my wallpaper, I started to hanker after human company.

I'd had odd twinges about a husband and children in the past, notably when I watched my friends walk down the aisle. But the matrimonial state had never seemed as attractive as it did now, when I could contemplate it in solitude. In short, I was feeling rather broody!

He wasn't featured on the list of amenities, along with the central heating and blue bathroom suite, but I'd been informed by a reliable source that there was a bachelor living in the house next door to mine.

I'd never seen him, though, because he kept himself strictly to himself. I never heard any noises coming from my neighbour's house, so I wrote him off as a middle-aged fuzzy-slipper-wearer, who listened to Radio Three, and went to bed at ten with a mug of Horlicks.

Perhaps I shouldn't have laughed, as I drew this little picture in my mind's eye, for if I wasn't careful I would end up as the female equivalent. After all, I had just passed my 30th birthday, so now it was downhill all the way. In another 10 years time, I would be Crimplened and sensible . . .

But I didn't want to be "that funny Miss Brown". I wanted to be like the young woman on the *other* side, blonde and bubbly. I envied her earth-mother lifestyle with three tiny kids so close together I wondered if it was physically possible.

I envied Tessie her husband, handsome, chunky and also a blond (but a natural one). He must have been an avid DIY enthusiast, for he wandered around with a large hammer permanently clutched in his hand.

Was the house in a terrible state of disrepair? Did the kids keep on breaking things? Or was the hammer some sort of threat — after all, the poor man was outnumbered.

I even envied Tessie's fraught Saturdays, galloping out of the front door with her shopping trolley, while I was still dressing-gowned and sleepy. I'd see her sweep past with the three protesting kids rammed headfirst into their clothes and holding hands like those rows of paper dollies.

I tried to talk myself out of marriage when she came back, laden, with all three trailing wearily behind and at least one howling. I tried again as I heard bedtime refusals floating out of the window in triplicate.

I clutched my career-girl status to me like a comfortable old shawl, defying anybody to take it away and replace it with domestic insanity.

Who needs men, I asked myself?

I found out who, when winter crept into the pipes and flooded my floor, and the local cowboy came riding into town in his rusty van, leaving me with a load of dubious workmanship and a very large bill.

If it wasn't the plumbing, it was my telly on the blink, making me bitterly

regret the fact that I'd bought monochrome and elderly, rather than renting colour.

And the last straw was ET and his cold . . .

All of a sudden, ET stopped being a walking, fur-covered stomach, constantly yelling for food. He was hunched up in a sad little heap on the sofa, sneezing. His eyes were watery, and he developed a barking cough (if that was the right word for a cat?).

ET was all I had in the world! Worried silly about the cuddly little tom, I decided to take him to see yet another person whose expensive expertise I needed.

That sounds easier than it actually was. Deciding to take him to see the vet was one thing; the operation itself was to prove something of a major problem.

This is what I call living dangerously, I thought, as I tried to persuade ET into a pet carrier.

Suddenly he'd recovered most of his strength, and fought back so strenuously, I nearly lost half my fingers in the process.

At last, I managed to wedge the box firmly on the back seat of my car. But still, every time I looked in the rear-view mirror, I could see it jiggling frantically up and down. What ET was going to do to me, once he got out, was nobody's business!

Unlike me, however, the vet was a very capable woman who looked as if she wouldn't stand any nonsense, and ET knew it. For once he didn't utter a sound when she stuck a cold stethoscope on his tummy and peered down his ears.

"It's nothing to worry about, Miss Brown," she said cheerfully. "He's just caught a virus. Keep him warm, tempt him with some tasty food, and give him two of these tablets a day."

"How do you give a cat a tablet?" I asked stupidly. (Well, you couldn't exactly offer ET a glass of water, could you?)

"Crush it up and hide it in his supper," she said briskly, clearly thinking I was a complete idiot.

BY the time I reached home, the cardboard box was on its last legs. No sooner had I put it down in the sitting-room than ET erupted, snarling, and slunk off to watch television.

How convenient, I thought. Unwatched, I crushed a tablet between two teaspoons and mixed it up in a bowlful of his favourite cat food. I called ET, and he came weakly into the kitchen, sniffing the air.

He peered at his dish, and then instead of slurping it all down in one go, hissed rudely, then marched out again with his tail at a very ill-used angle.

The food was still there the next day, completely untouched. Cruelly hoping ET was starving, I tried to take advantage with another pill in some warm milk. But now, he was well and truly off eating.

I wasn't, though. I was having a dinner party that night for some friends at the office, to christen my new wok. I was just slicing some nice lean beef into strips ready for the spicy marinade, when two great big eyes appeared between my feet, and a sad little voice said, "Wrowl?"

Here was my chance. Instead of offering him the usual tough, gristly trimmings, I cut ET a lovely juicy cube of lean meat, embedded yet another pill in it, and let it fall to the floor. I gave a sharp intake of breath, of course, so he would think it was an accident. Cats get a kick out of stealing things.

But I was starving my guests to no avail. ET gave the piece of beef a dirty look with one eye, and me an even nastier one with the other.

Right now, he didn't like me very much. Still sneezing, he sloped off to sleep in the Ali Baba basket. He was going to keep his *flu* thanks, it was preferable to poisoned meat!

"Help, I've tried being subtle," I told the vet, when I phoned, "but your tablets seem to be flavoured with a powerful cat repellent."

The brisk, no-nonsense voice suggested I tried being unsubtle, and adopted an I'm-bigger-than-you approach.

"Try wrapping him up in a towel, with his paws tucked inside, then he won't be able to scratch you. Then open his mouth with one hand, and pop the pill on the back of his tongue with the other. Next time he swallows, the pill will go down . . . it's as simple as that."

As simple as that? For safety's sake I wrapped ET in my two biggest bath towels, as tightly as I dared.

I felt a bit cruel, because he looked rather sweet, with his big, round, innocent eyes peering over the top, his facial markings prettier than ever.

But when he opened his mouth, what came out was definitely NOT pretty, it was the ultimate feline insult. I stopped feeling sorry for him and stuffed the pill down his throat as far as it would go.

Out it came again, twice as quick!

I was getting rather fed up by now. I picked up the soggy pill and tried once more. The minute I got within an inch of ET's mouth, I suddenly found myself staring at the back of his head.

So, it would seem he had perfected another yoga position in addition to his favourite one of the left back paw behind the right ear. The head screwed on back-to-front . . .

The next thing I knew, first one, then the other three paws had worked loose. ET erupted from his Terry cocoon and went into frenzied orbit round the kitchen, leaving a trail of dirty pawmarks on the worktops, and his autograph in red on the back of my hands.

At the top of his voice he threatened to call in the cruelty people. *I* was the one who needed the cruelty people, I thought ruefully, as I sucked my poor old knuckles.

But I refused to be outwitted by a tiny tom cat who stood 12 inches high at the ears, and only weighed three quarters of a stone. Once more, I cornered him, bundled him up, and this time he was so taken aback that, when I stuffed the pill down his throat, he gulped in surprise. I rubbed my hands in satisfaction. At last, success!

However, my self-congratulation was somewhat premature.

And 15 minutes later, when I found a second-hand antibiotic tablet sticking to the hall carpet, I did the most sensible thing I'd done during the last 48 hours. I panicked, and ran straight round to my next-door neighbour, with ET under my arm, his tail flailing in protest. Not the fraught mum, for she had enough on her plate, but the unknown quantity on the other side.

What a way to introduce myself to my next-door neighbour, I thought.

He was going to get rather a shock when he opened the door to a dishevelled, red-faced female still in her carpet slippers, who wanted him to sit on a cat while she dosed it with medicine.

HE wasn't the only one who got a shock. I certainly had not expected him to be in his mid-30s. And certainly not tall, slim, and devastatingly handsome. He was definitely not the Radio Three type! I felt such a fool as he looked me up and down. But ET saved the day, jumping straight into his arms and purring ecstatically.

"Please, can you help me?" I began. "ET's ever so strong, and I need somebody to hold him while I give him some medicine . . ."

"ET? Is that from the film?"

This lovely man was smiling at me, but it wasn't in a puzzled or patronising manner, it was with genuine interest.

"No," I said. "It's short for English Tabby. You know, common old alley-cat, no pedigree."

"Well, come on in. I don't think we'll get much done on the front doorstep. I've got just the thing in the kitchen."

He popped ET into a stout, heavy-duty plastic shopping bag, and zipped it up so that only his head poked out.

Strangely, my bad-tempered cat wasn't protesting in the slightest. He purred like an engine as my neighbour stroked the top of his head. The purring didn't stop, either, when he gently prized his mouth open.

"Got the pill handy?" he asked me quietly.

For the third time I dropped it on to ET's tongue. This time he didn't get a chance to spit it out, for the minute the tablet was gone, my neighbour held his jaws shut, which I thought was really incredibly brave of him.

"I hope you don't work with your hands," I joked.

"No, my head. I'm an accountant." He smiled that devastating smile again. Never before had sums seemed quite so fascinating.

"Here, what are you doing?" I asked, suddenly alarmed as he stared unwinkingly at ET, his face only a few inches away from the cat's.

"I'm mesmerising him . . . look into my eyes, cat . . ."

After about 10 minutes, there was a huge gulp from ET, and my neighbour looked up. I saw for the first time that his eyes were dark blue, fringed with the sort of eyelashes you'd be jealous of on another woman.

They still stared unwinkingly. You can mesmerise *me* any time, I thought!

"I don't know how to thank you, Mr — er . . ." I stammered, knowing that my gratitude sounded out of all proportion, but that was due to the effect those eyes were having on my metabolism.

"Partington, Roger Partington. You're welcome, Miss — um . . ."

So he could stammer, too. But I was sure I wasn't having the same effect on him. In his case, it was probably nothing more interesting than nervousness.

174